Basic Law Office
Management
for Paralegals

Basic Law Office Management for Paralegals

Jeffrey A. Helewitz
Adjunct Professor of Paralegal Studies
Baruch College
Marymount Manhattan College
Queens College

ASPEN LAW & BUSINESS
A Division of Aspen Publishers, Inc.

Summary of Contents

Contents   vii
Preface   xv
Acknowledgments   xvii

Chapter 1. Organization and Structure of a Law Office   1
Chapter 2. People in a Law Office   25
Chapter 3. Law Office-Client Relationship   45
Chapter 4. Law Office Billing   63
Chapter 5. Law Office Accounting   103
Chapter 6. Marketing the Law Office   137
Chapter 7. Administrative Systems   165
Chapter 8. Management Concepts   195
Chapter 9. Document Preparation   225
Chapter 10. Law Office Technology   251

Glossary   283
Index   295

Contents

Preface   *xv*
Acknowledgments   *xvii*

CHAPTER 1:   ORGANIZATION AND STRUCTURE OF A LAW OFFICE

CHAPTER 1: ORGANIZATION AND STRUCTURE OF A LAW OFFICE	1
Chapter Overview	1
Organizational Structure of a Law Office	2
Sole Practitioner	2
Small Firm	3
Large Firm	3
Boutique	5
Corporation	5
Goverment	6
Legal Clinic	6
Legal Structure of a Law Office	7
Sole Proprietorship	7
Partnership	8
Professional Corporation	9
Limited Liability Company	10
Design Structure of a Law Office	11
Space Management	11
Physical Layout	11
Security	13
Ethical Considerations of an Office's Organization	13
Chapter Summary	14
Key Terms	14
Cases for Analysis	15

       Bane v. Ferguson   *16*
       Johnson v. Shaines & McEachern, PA   *18*
Exercises   22
Situational Analysis   23

CHAPTER 2: PEOPLE IN A LAW OFFICE   25

Chapter Overview   25
Attorneys   26
    Partners/Shareholders   27
    Staff Attorneys   28
       Associate   28
       Senior Associate   28
       Contract Attorney   28
    Other Attorneys   29
Law Clerks   30
Paralegals   30
Administrative and Secretarial Staff   31
    Office Manager   31
    Librarian   32
    Secretaries   32
    Receptionist   32
Other Staff   33
    Clerks   33
    Security Personnel   33
    Investigators   33
People and Ethics   34
Chapter Summary   34
Key Terms   35
Cases for Analysis   36
      Gautam v. De Luca   *36*
      The Florida Bar v. Furman   *40*
Exercises   44
Situational Analysis   44

CHAPTER 3: LAW OFFICE-CLIENT RELATIONSHIP   45

Chapter Overview   45
Concepts of Public Relations   46
Confidentiality   50
Personnel-Client Relationships   51
Client Relationships and Ethics   53

Chapter Summary   53
Key Terms   54
Cases for Analysis   54
      In re National Mortgage Equity Corp. Mortgage
         Pool Certificates   *54*
      People v. Mitchell   *58*
Exercises   61
Situational Analysis   61

CHAPTER 4:   LAW OFFICE
BILLING   63

Chapter Overview   63
Types of Fees   64
    Retainer   65
        Pure Retainer   65
        Case Retainer   66
        Retainer for General Representation   66
    Contingency Fee   67
    Flat or Fixed Fee   76
    Hourly Fee   76
        Attorney Hourly Rate   76
        Client Hourly Rate   77
        Blended Hourly Rate   77
    Court-Awarded Fee   79
    Prepaid Legal Services   79
Determining Fees   80
    Financial Needs   80
    Ethical Prohibitions   81
Costs and Overhead   82
Timekeeping   82
Billing Procedures   86
Fee Collection   87
Chapter Summary   87
Key Terms   88
Cases for Analysis   89
      Cluett, Peabody & Co. v. CPC Acquisition Co.   *89*
      In re Union Carbide Corp. Consumer Product
        Business Securities Litigation   *94*
Exercises   100
Situational Analysis   100

CHAPTER 5:   LAW OFFICE ACCOUNTING   103

Chapter Overview   103
Client Funds   104
Basic Bookkeeping Concepts   106
Basic Acounting Concepts   107
    The Balance Sheet   107
    The Income Statement   110
Creating a Budget   113
Cash Flow and Accounts Receivable/Payable   115
Inventory Control   117
Reading Financial Statements   119
    Liquidity Ratio   119
    Asset-Management Ratio   120
    Profitability Ratio   121
Accounting and Ethics   121
Chapter Summary   122
Key Terms   122
Cases for Analysis   124
    Kelly v. State Bar of California   124
    In re Disciplinary Action Against Lochow   130
Exercises   135
Situational Analysis   136

CHAPTER 6:   MARKETING THE LAW OFFICE   137

Chapter Overview   137
Basic Marketing Concepts   138
    Marketing Existing Clients   139
    Marketing New Clients   144
Strategic Planning   145
Advertising   146
Marketing and Ethics   147
Chapter Summary   148
Key Terms   148
Cases for Analysis   149
    In re R.M.J.   149
    Peel v. Attorney Disciplinary Commission of
      Illinois   154
Exercises   162
Situational Analysis   163

CHAPTER 7:   ADMINISTRATIVE SYSTEMS   165

Chapter Overview   165
Personnel Systems   166
    Hiring and Firing Issues   166
    Policies and Procedures   171
    Compensation   173
    The Staff Manual   174
Filing and Recordkeeping   175
    Basic Filing Systems   175
        Alphabetical   176
        Subject   176
        Geographic   176
        Chronological   177
        Numerical   177
    Preparing Documents   178
    Storage   178
        Nonelectronic   179
        Electronic   179
Library Management   180
Administrative Systems and Ethics   181
Chapter Summary   181
Key Terms   182
Cases for Analysis   183
        Brown v. Ford, Bacon & Davis, Utah, Inc.   *184*
        Elliott v. Montgomery Ward & Co.   *186*
Exercises   192
Situational Analysis   192

CHAPTER 8:   MANAGEMENT CONCEPTS   195

Chapter Overview   195
Basic Management Principles   196
    Management Concepts   196
    Recruitment and Hiring   196
        Application and Resume   197
        Interview   200
        Test   200
    Employment Contracts   201
    Time Management   202
    Personnel Management   204
    Motivation Techniques   207
Work Organization   208
    Creating an Effective Team   208
    Team Operation   209

Group Dynamics and the Office Team   210
Performance Evaluations   211
Problem Solving   214
Negotiations   215
Firing an Employee   217
Management and Ethics   217
Chapter Summary   218
Key Terms   218
Cases for Analysis   219
      State ex rel. Nebraska State Bar v. Kirshen   *219*
Exercises   222
Situational Analysis   223

CHAPTER 9:   DOCUMENT PREPARATION   225

Chapter Overview   225
Business Letters   226
   Format   226
   Good News/Bad News   230
   Courtesy Copies and Filing   231
Memoranda   232
   Interoffice Memos   232
   Opinion Memos   233
   Persuasive Memos   234
Legal Forms   235
Editing and Proofreading   240
Document Preparation and Ethics   240
Chapter Summary   242
Key Terms   242
Cases for Analysis   243
      Federal Intermediate Credit Bank of Louisville,
        Kentucky v. Kentucky Bar Association   *243*
      Latson v. Eaton   *245*
      In re Schroeter   *247*
Exercises   249
Situational Analysis   250

CHAPTER 10:   LAW OFFICE TECHNOLOGY   251

Chapter Overview   251
Information Systems   252
   Microcomputer   252
   Minicomputer   252
   Mainframe   253

Computer Hardware   253
    The System Unit   254
    Main Memory   254
    Secondary Memory   254
    Input Devices   255
    Output Devices   256
    Communication Devices   256
Computer Software   257
    Word Processors   258
    Database Management Software   260
    Legal Research Databases   262
        Lexis/Nexis   262
        Westlaw   263
        Databases Containing Nonlegal Information   263
        CD-ROM   263
        The Internet   263
    Electronic Spreadsheets   264
    Litigation Support   265
        Creation of Documents   265
        Manage the Calendar   265
        Case Management   266
        Perform Calculations   266
        Conduct Legal Research   266
        Managing Evidence   266
        Court Automation   266
Technology and Ethics   267
Chapter Summary   267
Key Terms   268
Cases for Analysis   270
        West Publishing Co. v. Mead Data Central, Inc.   270
        Smollen v. Dahlmann Apartments, Ltd.   280
Exercises   281
Situational Analysis   281

Glossary   *283*
Index   *295*

Preface

Basic Law Office Management for Paralegals is meant to be an easy-to-use, readable text for the paralegal student. It incorporates all of the topics recommended by the American Association for Paralegal Education for a course in law office management. The features of this book include edited judicial decisions that both highlight the subject matter and focus the material in a manner suitable for paralegal students or the practicing paralegal.

Acknowledgments

Permission to reprint copyrighted materials from the following is gratefully acknowledged:

Exhibits 2-5, 8, 14, 17, 18: Julius Blumberg, Inc., New York, N.Y. Forms may be purchased from Julius Blumberg, Inc., NYC 10013, or any of its dealers. Reproduction prohibited.

Exhibit 11: Julius Blumberg, Inc., New York, N.Y. Reprint from Blumberg-Excelsior, 1-800-Lawmart.

Exhibit 12: Reprinted with permission from Rosenberg, Mine & Armstrong, 122 East 42nd St., New York, N.Y. 10168.

Exhibit 13: Reprinted with permission from Martindale-Hubbell, New Providence, N.J. 07974.

Basic Law Office
Management
for Paralegals

1 Organization and Structure of a Law Office

In a small partnership when you're not the dominant partner you're sometimes forced to do things against your better judgment. When you're in solo practice you get to make your *own* mistakes.

Ansley J. Robin
Sole Practitioner
Pittsburgh, Pennsylvania

CHAPTER OVERVIEW

What is a "law office"? To most people the term "law office" conjures up visions of Victorian wood-paneled cubbyholes where elderly attorneys sit surrounded by dusty volumes, or the sleek and polished glamor of offices portrayed on television programs. In fact, the modern law office is neither. A law office is an attorney or a group of attorneys who practice the legal profession assisted by various support professionals. Most important, the modern law office is a business, and the first requirement to understand law office management is to appreciate the fact that a law office, to be successful, must be operated in a manner similar to all businesses.

All businesses are concerned with two broad areas of operation: practice management and administrative management. **Practice management** determines the type of work to be accepted and how to organize the workload to accomplish the tasks that must be performed most effectively. **Administrative management** is concerned with hiring and firing policies, financing the business, and seeing to it that all necessary supplies and materials are on hand to accomplish the work of the firm. How decisions affecting these two management areas are arrived at is dependent on how the law office is organized and structured.

All law offices can be categorized by the organizational or legal structure of the business. The organizational structure of the office has a direct impact on practice management: Is the office that of a sole practitioner, a large law firm, a "boutique" practice, or a legal clinic? Each of these types of law offices is designed to attract a specific type of client, which in turn determines the nature of the work of the attorneys. The legal structure of the office, on the other hand, determines the administrative management of the business. A partnership has different administrative needs than a professional corporation or a limited liability company. Additionally, the organizational and legal structure of the office directly affects administrative decisions with respect to the physical design of the facility.

This chapter will introduce and discuss all of the concepts concerned with structuring the modern law office; consider it the door that opens the way to understanding how law offices operate.

Organizational Structure of a Law Office

One of the most important practice management decisions affecting law office management is determining the structure of the practice. Generally, there are seven types of law offices:

1. sole practitioner
2. small firm
3. large firm
4. boutique
5. corporation
6. government
7. legal clinic

Sole Practitioner

A **sole practitioner** is an attorney who practices law on his own, perhaps with some support staff. The sole practitioner has the most flexibility in terms of his practice because all management decisions are exclusively his and may be made immediately as the need or occasion arises. The sole practitioner bears full responsibility for all decisions made by the office and does not have the luxury of sharing decisions or problems.

Many times a sole practitioner may work out of a room in his house or share office space with other attorneys whose practices are totally independent. The sole practitioner may or may not have a secretary or a support staff, such as a law clerk or legal assistant. The nature of the practice is dependent on the desires and qualifications of the sole practitioner. Statistically, approximately 10 percent of all attorneys work as sole practitioners.

 EXAMPLE:

Carol graduated from law school several years ago and decided to practice on her own. She created an office out of a spare room in her house and developed a small criminal litigation practice by going to court and getting cases of indigent criminal defendants assigned to her. Carol does all of her own typing and billing, and has no support staff. Carol is a sole practitioner.

Small Firm

A **small firm** law office is generally defined as a group of no more than 25 attorneys who practice law collectively for their mutual benefit. The actual size of a small firm is dependent on the location of the practice. "Small" means one thing in New York City and Los Angeles and another in a suburb of Madison, Wisconsin.

Two advantages of a small firm over a sole practitioner are that responsibility is shared among all of the attorneys in the office, and more varied work can be accepted because of the expertise and inclination of the different attorneys. On the negative side, decisions must be made jointly and therefore may take more time to implement than if left to the discretion of just one attorney.

Unlike sole practitioners, small law firms generally have a support staff of moderate size, usually supervised by the office manager. The **office manager** is responsible for all administrative decisions affecting the office, such as hiring support staff, ordering supplies, and managing the firm's finances. The office manager may be one of the attorneys or may be someone hired specifically to fulfill that function.

Because several lawyers are involved, small firms generally hire secretaries, law clerks, paralegals, and a bookkeeper to ensure that the office functions smoothly and efficiently. Thus, specific office space is required, with areas established for each member of the staff as well as for supplies and equipment.

EXAMPLE:

During law school Jean worked part-time as a law clerk for a sole practitioner who specialized in real estate law. After graduation, Jean wanted to expand the type of work she did and so joined with two other graduates to start their own office. Jean does real estate and litigation, Alice has a corporate practice, and Kay specializes in family law. They hire a secretary and rent office space, and Alice agrees to be in charge of the office management. Jean, Alice, and Kay have created a small law firm.

Large Firm

Generally, a **large law firm** is a firm with over 75 attorneys. A **medium-size firm** falls in the range between 25 and 75 attorneys. There is no upper limit on the number of lawyers who may be employed by a large firm, and sometimes the numbers can be quite staggering, with well over

300 attorneys in a single office. Note that the size of a law firm is determined by the number of attorneys in the practice; the number of support staff is not considered.

According to recent statistics of the American Bar Association, approximately 75 percent of all attorneys work in a medium- or small-size firm. Structurally, the medium- and large-size firm share many similarities and therefore should be considered together.

Because of the large number of attorneys involved in such practices, management takes on a whole new perspective when compared with that of a sole practitioner or small firm. Large-size law firms are likely to have **management committees** that make the practice management decisions for the office. The committee may be composed of several attorneys in the firm, plus a **director of administration** who is in charge of the office's administrative management, a **financial director** who is in charge of all monetary concerns of the office, and a **personnel director** who is responsible for hiring and firing staff. Occasionally, the management committee is overseen by a group of senior attorneys who are designated as the firm's **managing partners** and select the members of the management committee.

Large law firms have a correspondingly large number of support staff in order to operate the office. The large law firm may maintain its own law library requiring the services of a law librarian. The financial director will have a staff of bookkeepers and junior accountants to help manage the firm's money, and the office may also have a **director of marketing** who is responsible for finding new business for the office. There may also be a **paralegal coordinator** who is in charge of all of the office's legal assistants. All of this is in addition to the regular support staff of the office, such as secretaries, clerks, receptionists, and so forth.

A diagram of a large law office's structure may look as follows:

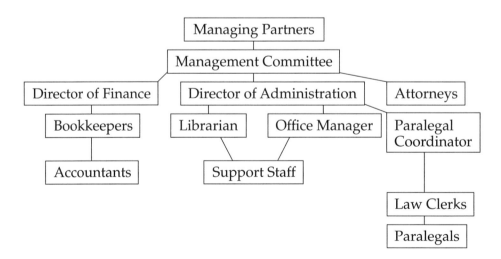

In a large firm responsibility is shared among a greater number of persons than in a small firm, and there tend to be areas of specialization within the decision-making process. The structure of the large law office is, of necessity, more formalized than that of a small firm, as is the type of work each person will be assigned. Most attorneys and legal support staff in a large firm have distinct areas of specialization with respect to the nature of the practice.

EXAMPLE:

Smith and Jones is a large law firm with over 125 attorneys. The office has five attorneys who only handle corporate matters. If a problem arises in the corporate area that requires litigation, a different group of attorneys in the firm handles the litigation.

Boutique

A **boutique** practice is a law office of any size that specializes in only one area of law. Although there are various ethical prohibitions against a lawyer holding herself out as a "specialist," many firms, as a result of their practice management policies, will only accept work in a specific area of law and consequently become known as specialists in that field. Many people with a legal problem seek out these boutique practices because of the work history of the attorneys.

EXAMPLE:

A woman is charged with murdering her abusive husband. In seeking out legal representation, she looks for an attorney who has a history of representing defendants in domestic violence cases; she is, in fact, looking for an attorney with a boutique practice because she believes that an attorney who practices exclusively in this area will be best able to defend her.

Corporation

Because of the increasing costs of legal representation, many large corporations have hired attorneys as full-time employees. They are considered **in-house counsel**. These attorneys work exclusively for the corporation and are salaried employees entitled to all employment benefits conferred on the company's employees. This corporate legal department will have its own support staff of law clerks, legal assistants, and secretaries, but all management decisions are made by the corporation. If special legal problems arise, the corporation may hire an outside law firm to represent it, and the in-house legal staff will work as legal liaisons between the corporation and the retained law office. Structurally, these law offices are considered a division of the overall corporation.

EXAMPLE:

In order to reduce the costs of its legal fees, Acme, Inc. has created a legal division in corporate headquarters consisting of five attorneys, two secretaries, two law clerks, and one paralegal. The office handles all corporate contracts and employment disputes. The head of the office is called the **general counsel.** When the corporation is sued for violations of environmental protection laws, it hires an outside law firm that specializes in environmental law to represent it.

Government

Federal, state, and local governments all hire attorneys to represent the governments' interests. Each agency has an in-house legal staff, similar to the corporation discussed above, headed by an attorney known as the **general counsel.** The nature of these law offices is similar to a corporate in-house legal division combined with a boutique practice because the attorneys specialize in the area of law administered by the agency that employs them. These government law offices are in addition to full-fledged law enforcement government agencies such as the U.S. Justice Department or a city's corporation counsel, which are comprised mainly of lawyers and act as outside counsel would to a corporation. Government law offices employ all of the same support staff as a corporate law division, and the attorneys are government employees. Management decisions are made by the government agency itself and the general counsel.

EXAMPLE:

After graduating from paralegal school, Hwa goes to work for the U.S. Department of Agriculture's district office in her city. She works for a government attorney who deals with farm subsidies. As a government employee Hwa receives all government employee and pension benefits.

Legal Clinic

The last category of law office can be subdivided into two main areas: nonprofit and for-profit **legal clinics.** Nonprofit clinics, such as Public Defenders, Legal Aid, and Public Interest Research Groups, are similar to boutique practices specializing in distinct areas of law, but the legal services are only available to a limited group of clients, typically indigents or persons who cannot afford other types of legal representation. Structurally, these nonprofit clinics are operated in a manner similar to a small law office, but, financially, the source of their funds is government and private grants and contributions rather than client fees.

For-profit legal clinics started in the early 1970s and are specifically designed to provide low-cost legal services to persons who cannot afford the typical cost of legal representation but do not qualify for assistance by nonprofit clinics. These clinics are also operated in a manner similar to a small- or medium-size law firm and offer a variety of low-cost services to the public. Paralegals often help to make these clinics profitable because many aspects of the practice can be handled by paralegals supervised by attorneys rather than by the attorneys themselves.

EXAMPLE:

A young couple, married for three years, are having problems and wish to divorce. Both are employed; they have no children. Rather than pay a large fee to a medium-size law firm, the couple goes to a legal clinic that can represent them in a no-fault divorce proceeding for a fairly modest fee.

As can be seen in the above examples, there really is no one form that a law office must take. Each provides legal services, but the nature of the work, the decision-making process, the responsibilities of the attorney, and the size of the staff depends on the structure of the office itself. The type of office determines the practice management of the business.

Legal Structure of a Law Office

Understanding its organizational structure is only the first step in understanding the law office. In order to fully appreciate the management problems of a law office one must understand the legal structure of the office as well. Generally law offices will fall into one of four legal classifications:

1. sole proprietorship
2. partnership
3. professional corporation
4. limited liability company

Sole Proprietorship

A **sole proprietorship** is a business that is owned and operated by just one person. The sole proprietor owns all of the business property and manages the business for himself.

There is no legal formality necessary to create a sole proprietorship. Once a lawyer is licensed, he can simply start engaging in the practice of law as a sole proprietor. Management of a sole proprietorship rests exclusively with the sole proprietor, who has total freedom and discretion to change the nature of the practice or administration of the office. A sole proprietor may employ other persons to assist in the operation of the business, but those persons are never considered owners of the enterprise.

There are two major disadvantages of operating a business as a sole proprietorship. First, the only method of financing the business is by contribution by the sole proprietor, either directly or in the form of bank loans to the owner or fees earned. And, second, the sole proprietor has unlimited personal liability for all obligations of the business. The sole proprietor is not only exclusively responsible for his own actions but may also be liable for the actions of persons engaged by the sole proprietor if those actions are done at his direction or on behalf of the business itself.

Most sole practitioners operate their law offices as sole proprietors. Until fairly recently, sole practitioners had no other choice with respect to the legal organization of the office. Because all of the risk of the business rests with the sole proprietor, many sole proprietors hire few, if any, support staff in order to reduce the financial risk of the office.

EXAMPLE:

In the previous example, when Carol began practicing law from her house she established a sole proprietorship. If a client is hurt on her premises, she has unlimited liability for any injuries the client sustains.

Partnership

A **partnership** is defined as an association of two or more persons engaged in business for profit as co-owners. Most law firms have historically been operated as a general partnership of the attorneys.

Unlike a sole proprietorship, management and decision-making responsibilities are shared among the partners equally, although the partners may agree to assign primary decision-making responsibilities to specific attorneys. Each partner is legally considered to be an **agent,** or legal representative, of the partnership, and all agreements he or she enters into on behalf of the partnership bind all of the partners.

As with sole proprietorships, there are no legal formalities necessary to create a general partnership; however, because more than just one person is involved, most partnerships are created by signing a **partnership agreement** that establishes all of the legal rights and obligations of the partners. The partnership agreement may also establish the organizational structure of the office, giving specified partners areas of control over management, finances, personnel, and so forth. Each partner, however, must be a licensed attorney.

A partnership may be considered more advantageous than a sole proprietorship because the office can be financed by contributions from all of the partners, and each partner can bring a special area of expertise that will increase the effectiveness and profitability of the office. However, one of the major drawbacks of a general partnership is that each partner still remains individually liable for all of the obligations of the office, just like the sole proprietor. The primary difference is that in a general partnership each partner must contribute his or her share to the total liability of the office.

Partnerships typically have more support staff than do sole proprietorships, especially for partnerships that are structurally organized as medium- or large-size firms. However, the partners still remain liable for all actions of their employees done at their request or on behalf of the partnership.

A partner remains liable for all obligations of the office that arose while he was a partner. If a partner withdraws from the partnership, she is not liable for obligations that arise after the date of departure, but may still be responsible for all liabilities that occurred while she was a partner until the **statute of limitations** on any potential lawsuit runs out. The statute of limitations is the time limit in which a person may bring a lawsuit from the date of the alleged injury. If a person joins an existing partnership, she is only liable for obligations that arise from the date of joining, unless she has specifically agreed to assume existing obligations.

 EXAMPLE:

When Jean, Alice, and Kay (recall the previous example) opened their law office, they created a general partnership. Each has decided on an area of legal responsibility, and Alice has assumed decision-making authority for the finances of the office.

Professional Corporation

Until the mid-1960s, the learned professions were prohibited from incorporating. At that time several states passed statutes known generically as **professional corporation acts** that permitted doctors, lawyers, and other learned professions to operate businesses as corporations. Today, every jurisdiction has a professional corporation statute.

There are several requirements necessary in order to create a professional corporation. First, a **certificate of incorporation** must be filed with the local secretary of state. The certificate of incorporation is the creating instrument of the business. Second, the business must attach to its name the term "Professional Corporation" (i.e., "P.C.") to alert the public that it is dealing with a professional corporation. And, third, all shareholders of the corporation must be licensed to perform the professional services for which the corporation was organized. For attorneys, this means that all shareholders of the corporation must be licensed attorneys, and no one else may own a share of stock in the corporation. Beyond these three general requirements there may be additional requirements specified by a particular state statute.

The corporation is financed by the attorneys purchasing the shares of the company. The corporation is managed by a **board of directors** elected by the shareholders. Organizationally, the professional corporation looks just like any other corporate entity and is operated in a similar manner. A single attorney may incorporate as a professional corporation, as can a large number of lawyers. The advantages of incorporating a law office as a professional corporation are primarily financial with respect to taxes and employee and pension benefits, issues that are beyond the scope of this text. Liability in certain circumstances may also be limited to the assets of the corporation, and the attorneys may not be individually liable for the obligations of the corporation that are not based on legal services rendered.

 EXAMPLE:

In order to take advantage of some employee benefits only available to corporate employees, Jean, Alice, and Kay decide to incorporate under their state's professional corporation statute. They file a certificate of incorporation with their secretary of state and name the new entity JAK Legal Services, P.C.

Limited Liability Company

Since the late 1980s a new form of business entity has been created. A **limited liability company** is an unincorporated association of persons engaged in business. The owners of the company are called members. They buy membership shares in the business, and the business is operated either collectively by the members or by managers hired or elected by the members. At the time of this writing approximately two-thirds of the states have enacted limited liability company statutes.

The advantage of operating a business as a limited liability company (LLC) is the limited personal liability of the members for obligations of the business. Many states permit professionals to become LLCs under special sections of the statutes, and several states permit one person to become an LLC.

In order to create an LLC a certificate must be filed with the local secretary of state, and the company name must indicate that it is a limited liability company. However, because not every jurisdiction permits LLCs, and the requirements vary from state to state, a law office operating as an LLC in one state may find itself a general partnership if it provides legal services in another jurisdiction, engendering unlimited liability for its members.

 EXAMPLE:

Carol the sole practitioner decides to limit her liability by becoming a limited liability company. Her state permits one person to become an LLC, and she creates her office as a limited liability professional company (a variation required in some states if a professional wishes to become an LLC). Carol still has unlimited liability for injuries to her clients due to her own malfeasance in practicing law, but liability for physical injuries sustained on her premises is now reduced.

The legal organization of the law office is one of the primary factors determining how administrative management decisions are reached. Because of the liabilities involved in each of the different types of legal entities, hiring and firing decisions, as well as the acquisition of property and equipment, are directly affected by the legal nature of the office. So too are financial decisions because of the way in which each business form may be capitalized and financed.

Design Structure of a Law Office

Once the organizational and legal structures of the office have been established, the final structural component of the office must be addressed — the physical design of the facility. The look and arrangement of the law office itself has a direct impact on the *image* of the office: How does the outside world view the firm? As stated at the opening of this chapter, most people have very distinct mental images of the look of a law firm, and a well-designed office will help to reinforce that mental picture while at the same time providing an effective work space in which to carry on the actual work of providing legal services.

Space Management

The design structure of a law office must take into consideration the two practical needs of the office: providing space for the professional and support staff and providing space for the support facilities such as copying, storage, library research, and so forth. Most offices hire professionals, typically architects, to help structure the area available to provide sufficiently for these two space needs. Only once the spatial requirements have been satisfied can the decoration of the office be considered.

Physical Layout

There are three typical design methods that are used to divide up space in a law office. The first method is the **traditional office design**, one that has a reception area, individual offices for all attorneys with a secretary's office immediately outside each lawyer's door, and specific room set aside for copying, storage, and the like. Although this method may be the most comforting because it is the most traditional, it does not necessarily make the best use of limited floor space and may create a network of cubbyhole-sized offices in which each person may have privacy but may also feel isolated from the rest of the office staff. Many law offices that wish to convey a conservative image use this physical approach to office design.

EXAMPLE:

Traditional Office Design

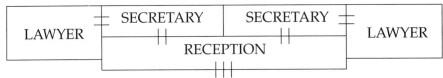

The second method of design is the **open space** concept in which areas are not closed off, and space is shared by groups of persons working in similar capacities. In this type of facility several attorneys may share one large room and all secretaries work in a common area. This design concept emphasizes light and space and community, but provides little, if any, privacy. Additionally, because several people are working in the same area, noise and conversation may become a harmful factor in work productivity. The open space concept is favored by law offices that wish to project a young and liberated image.

EXAMPLE:

Open Space Design

The third approach to spatial design is not really a design at all. In order to reduce the costs of operating an office, many attorneys share space with other attorneys who are not part of the same law firm. This type of arrangement can come about by an attorney simply renting an empty office in a larger organization, or by renting space in a "professional building" in which the rent includes certain support facilities such as reception, conference rooms, and copying. These arrangements arise out of practical monetary reasons and do not incorporate the concept of office design into their structures.

There are several new trends in the design structure of law offices that should be mentioned. If space itself is not limited, many larger law offices are providing dining room, day care, and gym facilities for their staffs, all of which help to foster a team spirit among the members of the firm and help improve work productivity. Some offices provide space known as **war rooms** that are used for special projects, bringing personnel from all other areas of the office to one space until the project is complete. Finally, many offices are now placing all conference and support facility rooms on one floor in order to maintain control over the use of these facilities.

All of these design concepts influence not only the image of the law office but also the attitude of the employees, which relates directly to work productivity. The more comfortable a person feels in a work environment, and the easier it is to have access to support facilities, the more productive the person will be. Therefore, the design structure of a law office should not be considered a poor relation to the organizational and legal structures of the office; instead, it should be regarded as equally weighty in creating an effective business organization.

Security

One element of office design that has an important impact on the effectiveness of the office in providing legal representation is the internal security system that is chosen. The law office must be fully conscious of securing all documents received and generated by the attorneys. An effective design structure must take into consideration the appropriate method of office security for the firm.

Filing and recordkeeping are related issues. See the discussion in Chapter 7 at pages 175-180.

Ethical Considerations of an Office's Organization

There are two main areas of ethical concern that may arise with respect to the organization and structure of a law office. The first involves deciding the work and type of client the office will accept. This goes beyond creating a boutique practice — it may, in fact, become a form of client discrimination.

Under the American system of law, all persons are entitled to legal representation, and it behooves attorneys to represent all persons, even those the attorney may personally dislike or whose causes the attorney disfavors. Attorneys are prohibited from accepting only "popular clients" and refusing to defend the unpopular ones, such as members of the Ku Klux Klan, terrorists, or persons whose ideas are generally nonconformist. A law office must be available to all persons regardless of race, creed, national origin, or any other nonlegal limiting factor.

The second ethical concern deals with the potential liability of the law office. Although many options exist for attorneys to structure their practice in a manner that can relieve them of liability, ethical problems may result if the attorney attempts to shield his or her own personal incompetence by the legal structure of the office itself. At some point all people must take responsibility for their own actions or for the actions performed on their behalf by someone else.

CHAPTER SUMMARY

There are three major structural components to every law office. The first is the organizational structure of the office, which indicates how the business is managed in terms of workload and responsibility. This is called practice management. There are several types of structures in which a law office may be organized: a sole practitioner; a small firm; a medium or large firm; a boutique practice; a corporation; government office; or a legal clinic. Each type of structure creates its own method of internal management.

The second major structural element of a law office is its legal organization. How a law office is legally created determines all of the rights and obligations of its members. Most law offices are created either as a sole proprietorship, a general partnership, a professional corporation, or a limited liability company.

The third, and final, major structural element of a law office is the design of its physical facility and its filing systems. An office's design has a direct impact on the image it projects as well as the productivity of its personnel. Typically, more thought, time, and expense are put into the design of the office than into its organization or legal structure.

Key Terms

Administrative management: The process of hiring and firing employees, financing the company, and ordering supplies.

Board of directors: The group that manages a corporation.

Boutique practice: Law office that specializes in a particular area of law.

Certificate of incorporation: Document filed with the local secretary of state to create a corporation.

Director of administration: Person in charge of administrative aspects of the office.

Director of marketing: Person in charge of finding new clients for the office.

Financial director: Person in charge of the monetary aspects of operating an office.

General counsel: Head of a government or corporate law division.

In-house counsel: Attorney employed by a corporation as a full-time employee.

Large-size firm: Generally, a law office with more than 75 attorneys.

Legal clinic: Law office designed to provide low-cost or no-cost legal services.

Limited liability company (LLC):   Unincorporated association permitted in several jurisdictions, providing limited personal liability for its members.

Management committee: Group in charge of managing a large-size law office.

Managing partners: Senior attorneys who oversee a law office's management committee.

Medium-size firm: Law office consisting of between 25 and 75 attorneys.

Office manager: Person responsible for the law office's administrative decisions.

Open space concept: Design structure in which work areas are shared by persons performing similar functions rather than placing them in individual offices.

Paralegal coordinator: Person in charge of hiring paralegals and assigning their workloads.

Partnership: An association of two or more persons engaged in business as co-owners.

Partnership agreement: Document signed by partners detailing their rights and liabilities.

Personnel director: Person in charge of hiring and firing staff.

Practice management: Method of accepting and distributing workload.

Professional corporation: Corporation owned exclusively by licensed professionals.

Small firm: Law office consisting of up to 25 lawyers.

Sole practitioner: Attorney operating a law office on his or her own.

Sole proprietorship: Method of owning and managing a business by just one person who has unlimited personal liability for the obligations of the business.

Statute of limitations: Law designating the time limit in which a lawsuit may be instituted.

Traditional office design: Design structure in which each person has an individual office.

War room: Design structure in which a particular space is designated for all work to be done on a specific project.

Cases for Analysis

The following cases are presented to highlight some of the concepts discussed in the text. Bane v. Ferguson discusses the responsibilities of law partners to each other, and Johnson v. Shaines & McEachern, PA discusses the problems incident to the legal structure of a law office.

Bane v. Ferguson
890 F.2d 11 (7th Cir. 1989)

POSNER, Circuit Judge.

The question presented by this appeal from the dismissal of the complaint is whether a retired partner in a law firm has either a common law or a statutory claim against the firm's managing council for acts of negligence that, by causing the firm to dissolve, terminate his retirement benefits. It is a diversity case governed by the law of Illinois, rather than a federal-question case governed by the Employee Retirement Income Security Act, 29 U.S.C. §§1001 et seq., because ERISA excludes partners from its protections.

Charles Bane practiced corporate and public utility law as a partner in the venerable Chicago law firm of Isham, Lincoln & Beale, founded more than a century ago by Abraham Lincoln's son Robert Todd Lincoln. In August 1985 the firm adopted a noncontributory retirement plan that entitled every retiring partner to a pension, the amount depending on his earnings from the firm on the eve of retirement. The plan instrument provided that the plan, and the payments under it, would end when and if the firm dissolved without a successor entity, and also that the amount paid out in pension benefits each year could not exceed five percent of the firm's net income in the preceding year. Four months after the plan was adopted, the plaintiff retired, moved to Florida with his wife, and began drawing his pension (to continue until his wife's death if he died first) of $27,483 a year. Bane was 72 years old when he retired. So far as appears, he had, apart from social security, no significant source of income other than the pension.

Several months after Bane's retirement, Isham, Lincoln & Beale merged with Reuben & Proctor, another large and successful Chicago firm. The merger proved to be a disaster, and the merged firm was dissolved in April 1988 without a successor—whereupon the payment of pension benefits to Bane ceased and he brought this suit. The suit alleges that the defendants were the members of the firm's managing council in the period leading up to the dissolution and that they acted unreasonably in deciding to merge the firm with Reuben & Proctor, in purchasing computers and other office equipment, and in leaving the firm for greener pastures shortly before its dissolution. The suit does not allege that the defendants committed fraud, engaged in self-dealing, or deliberately sought to destroy or damage the law firm or harm the plaintiff; the charge is negligent mismanagement, not deliberate wrongdoing. The suit seeks damages, presumably the present value of the pension benefits to which the Banes would be entitled had the firm not dissolved. . . .

Bane has four theories of liability. The first is that the defendants, by committing acts of mismanagement that resulted in the dissolution of the firm, violated the Uniform Partnership Act, Ill. Rev. Stat. ch. 106½, ¶9(3)(c), which provides that "unless authorized by the other partners . . . one or more but less than all the partners have no authority to: Do any . . . act which would make it impossible to carry on the ordinary business of the partnership." This provision is inapplicable. Its purpose is not to make negligent partners liable to persons with whom the partnership transacts (such as Bane), but to limit the liability of the other partners for the unauthorized act of one partner. See Hackney v. Johnson, 601 S.W.2d 523, 525 (Tex. Civ. App. 1980). The purpose in other words is to protect partners. Bane ceased to be a partner when he retired in 1985.

Nor can Bane obtain legal relief on the theory that the defendants violated a fiduciary duty to him; they had none. A partner is a fiduciary of his partners, but not of his former partners, for the withdrawal of a partner terminates the partnership as to him. Adams v. Jarvis, 23 Wis. 2d 453, 458, 127 N.W.2d 400, 403 (1964). Bane must look elsewhere for the grounds of a fiduciary obligation running from his former partners to himself. The pension plan did not establish a trust, and even if, notwithstanding the absence of one, the plan's managers were fiduciaries of its beneficiaries (there are myriad sources of fiduciary duty besides a trust), the mismanagement was not of the plan but of the firm. There is no suggestion that the defendants failed to inform the plaintiff of his rights under the plan or miscalculated his benefits or mismanaged or misapplied funds set aside for the plan's beneficiaries; no funds *were* set aside for them. Even if the defendants were fiduciaries of the plaintiff, moreover, the business-judgment rule would shield them from liability for mere negligence in the operation of the firm, just as it would shield a corporation's directors and officers, who are fiduciaries of the shareholders. See Cottle v. Hilton Hotels Corp., 635 F. Supp. 1094, 1099 (N.D. Ill. 1986).

That leaves for discussion Bane's claims of breach of contract and of tort. The plan instrument expressly decrees the death of the plan upon the dissolution of the firm, and nowhere is there expressed a commitment or even an undertaking to maintain the firm in existence, whether for the sake of the plan's beneficiaries or anyone else. Contracts have implicit as well as explicit terms, see, e.g., Foster Enterprises, Inc. v. Germania Federal Savings & Loan Assn., 97 Ill. App. 3d 22, 28, 52 Ill. Dec. 303, 308, 421 N.E.2d 1375, 1380 (1981); Wood v. Duff-Gordon, 222 N.Y. 88, 118 N.E. 214 (1917) (Cardozo, J.), and one can imagine an argument that the plaintiff was induced to retire by an implied promise that the managing council would do everything possible to keep the firm going—that without such an implied promise he would not have retired, given his dependence on the firm's retirement plan for his income after he retired. But Bane does not make this argument and anyway it is hopeless. The plan required partners to retire by age 72, an age Bane had already reached when the plan was adopted. Were there no such requirement the question would be whether, by the creation of the retirement plan, the partnership impliedly undertook to insure the retired partners, out of the *personal* assets of the members of the managing council, against any cessation of retirement benefits that was due to mismanagement by the council which contributed to the demise of the firm. To state the question is to answer it. See Cowles v. Morris & Co., 330 Ill. 11, 161 N.E. 150 (1928). . . .

We are sorry about the financial blow to the Banes but we agree with the district judge that there is no remedy under the law of Illinois.

Affirmed.

Johnson v. Shaines & McEachern, PA
835 F. Supp. 685 (D.N.H. 1993)

Order

LOUGHLIN, Senior District Judge.

This action was filed on April 30, 1993 by plaintiff Peter A. Johnson, general partner of Grassy Knoll Associates, a limited partnership, for alleged legal malpractice against the defendants Shaines & McEachern, P.A., and the G & M Law Group. Jurisdiction in this court is founded upon 28 U.S.C. §1332(a)(1). Presently before the court is G & M Law Group's Motion to Dismiss pursuant to Rules 12(b)(2), 12(b)(5) and 12(b)(6) of the Fed. R. Civ. P.

Facts

Plaintiff Peter Johnson (hereinafter Johnson), a resident of Florida, is the general partner of Grassy Knoll Associates, a limited partnership with a principal place of business in Florida. This partnership was formed for the purpose of acquiring and leasing the former Town of Londonderry dump site as a sanitary landfill. In 1984, Johnson retained defendant Shaines & McEachern, P.A. of Portsmouth, New Hampshire (hereinafter "Shaines") to represent Johnson in a legal action to recover damages stemming from a lease with SCA Disposal Services of New England (hereinafter SCA). The lease pertained to the landfill site on Auburn Road, Londonderry, New Hampshire.

In August 1984, Shaines filed two state court actions against SCA, both of which were removed to this court. Johnson's claim involved SCA's obligation to correct hazardous waste problems on the landfill site. SCA allegedly failed to fulfill its obligation and the property was thereafter placed on the Environmental Protection Agency's National Priorities List in 1983. Johnson contends that in August 1984 Shaines failed to plead as a part of Johnson's damages the costs of remediation of the hazardous waste at the site. On March 13, 1986 Shaines was contacted by the EPA and was informed that remedial action would be taken and that Johnson as the current owner was potentially liable for response costs under CERCLA, 42 U.S.C. §9606 et seq. Plaintiff contends that despite both having knowledge of these facts and being questioned on the issue by Johnson, Shaines did not file a motion to amend its pleadings to include a $10,000,000 claim for clean-up costs until well after the deadline for such pleadings had passed. On October 22, 1986 the trial court denied the motion to add the clean-up count as untimely filed. After trial, the jury returned a verdict for plaintiff in the amount of $620,000.

On August 3, 1988 Shaines initiated a second diversity action against SCA on behalf of Johnson to recover remediation and associated costs resulting from EPA's investigation. On May 7, 1990 the trial court granted summary judgment for SCA thereby dismissing the action holding that the action was barred by *res judicata*. This ruling was appealed to the First Circuit which upheld the judgment of the trial court.

Johnson claims in the present action that Shaines breached its duty of reasonable care by failing to include in the original action the claim for remediation costs thus giving rise to the present action for legal malpractice. Johnson alleges that shortly after Shaines undertook representation of Johnson, Shaines became affiliated with Goldstein and Manello, P.C. of Boston, Massachusetts (hereinafter Goldstein) and the two firms were referred to as the G & M Law Group. Doc. 8, Affidavit of Peter A. Johnson, para. 3. Johnson alleges Shaines specifically advised Johnson of the merger and informed Johnson that the legal resources of Goldstein were available to Shaines in its representation of Johnson. Id. at para. 4. Johnson claims that this affiliation influenced Johnson to maintain the attorney-client relationship to its conclusion in May 1991. Id. at para 5.

Discussion

(1) *Personal Jurisdiction*

Defendant G & M Law Group, and, to the extent it is an intended defendant, Goldstein moved for dismissal under Fed. R. Civ. P. 12(b)(2). The basis of this motion is two-fold. First, defendants contend that G & M Law Group is not a professional corporation and has no legal existence. Second, defendants contend that Shaines has not merged with the G & M Law Group or with Goldstein and therefore there is no basis for jurisdiction over defendants.

Standard of Review

A motion to dismiss pursuant to 12(b)(2) involves the defense of lack of jurisdiction over the person. Plaintiff has the burden of proof to produce facts necessary to sustain jurisdiction over the defendant. . . .

Johnson's claim is one for legal malpractice which sounds in negligence and therefore jurisdiction under §293-A:121 must be established, if at all, on the basis of a tort committed in New Hampshire. Johnson contends that the firm of Goldstein & Manello, P.C. and Shaines & McEachern, P.A., through their joint venture agreement pursuant to which the firms were referred to as the "G & M Law Group," are either a partnership in fact or if such partnership did not exist then a partnership by estoppel existed under RSA §304-A:16, discussed below. The same legal rules apply to both joint ventures and partnerships "as the '[p]arties in a joint venture stand in the same relationship to each other as the partners in a partnership.'" Stone and Michaud Insurance, Inc. v. Bank Five For Savings, 785 F. Supp. 1065, 1069 (D.N.H. 1992).

As the rights and duties of partners are subject to the rules of agency, Goldstein, through its agent Shaines, would be subject to the personal jurisdiction of this court for the alleged tort committed by the partnership against Johnson in New Hampshire. See generally, 59A Am. Jur. 2d Partnerships §633 (1987).

> The general rule is that jurisdiction over a partner confers jurisdiction over the partnership . . . because a partner is deemed by law and contract to be the partnership's agent. . . . [T]he activities of the partner are generally attributed to the partnership and jurisdiction over the partnership follows from the partner's contacts, if sufficient, regardless of the independent contacts between the partnership qua entity and the forum. . . . [T]he actions of a partner within the scope of a general partnership's purposes necessarily become the actions of the partnership. To attribute the partner's scope-of-business contacts to the partnership, therefore, is not only permissible, but mandated. For this reason, any forum able to exercise personal jurisdiction over the partner by reason of those activities must also be able to exercise jurisdiction over the partnership.

Donatelli v. National Hockey League, 893 F.2d 459, 467 (1st Cir. 1990). This court's exercise of personal jurisdiction over Goldstein is therefore dependent upon Johnson's prima facie showing of the existence of a partnership relationship between the defendants.

Johnson contends that the relationship that existed between defendants was at the very least a partnership under New Hampshire RSA §304-A:16, entitled "Partner By Estoppel," which provides in relevant part:

> I. When a person, by words spoken or written or by conduct, represents himself, or consents to another representing him to any one, as a partner in an existing partnership or with one or more persons not actual partners, he is liable to any such person to whom such representation has been made, who has, on the faith of such representation, given credit to the actual or apparent partnership, and if he has made such representation or consented to its being made in a public manner he is liable to such person, whether the representation has or has not been made or communicated to such person so giving credit by or with the knowledge of the apparent partner making the representation or consenting to its being made.
>
> II. When a person has been thus represented to be a partner in an existing partnership, or with one or more persons not actual partners, he is an agent of the persons consenting to such representation to bind them to the same extent and in the same manner as though he were a partner in fact, with respect to persons who rely upon the representation. Where all the members of the existing partnership consent to the representation, a partnership act or obligation results; but in all other cases it is the joint act or obligation of the person acting and the persons consenting to the representation.

New Hampshire RSA 304-A:16 (1991). Estoppel runs in favor of Johnson if he can show that he had knowledge of the holding out of defendants as a

partnership and that he relied on the apparent partnership to his detriment. See 59A Am. Jur. 2d Partnerships §678 (1987). The questions of
whether defendants are a partnership in fact or, in the alternative, whether
defendants have been held out as partners to Johnson so as to be estopped
from denying such relationship are ones of fact for the jury. Stone and
Michaud Ins., Inc. v. Bank Five for Savings, 785 F. Supp. 1065, 1069 (D.N.H.
1992); 59A Am. Jur. 2d Partnerships §685 (1987). . . .

(b)   Due Process

As the requirements of the long-arm statute have been met, the court
must now determine whether Goldstein has sufficient contacts with New
Hampshire so as to satisfy the requirements of due process. *Lex* at 404 (citing Papafagos v. Fiat Auto, S.P.A., 568 F. Supp. 692 (D.N.H. 1983)).

> . . . The court must engage in a two-step analysis to determine whether ju-
> risdiction over the defendant comports with due process: first, does the
> defendant have "minimum contacts" with the forum state, and, second,
> does assertion of personal jurisdiction offend traditional notions of fair
> play and substantial justice? International Shoe [Co. v. State, Office of Un-
> employment Compensation and Placement], 326 U.S. [310] at 316, 66 S. Ct.
> [154] at 158 [90 L. Ed. 95 (1945)].
>
>   Minimum contacts are established when a defendant "purposefully
> directs" his activities to residents of the forum state, Burger King [Corp. v.
> Rudzewicz], 471 U.S. [462] at 476, 105 S. Ct. [2174] at 2184 [85 L. Ed. 2d
> 528] (1985)] (citing Keeton v. Hustler Magazine, Inc., 465 U.S. 770, 774-75,
> 104 S. Ct. 1473, 1478-79, 79 L. Ed. 2d 790 (1984)), and the litigation results
> from alleged injuries that "arise out of or relate to" those activities, Id., 471
> U.S. at 472, 105 S. Ct. at 2182 (citing Helicopteros Nacionales de Colombia,
> S.A. v. Hall, 466 U.S. 408, 414, 104 S. Ct. 1868, 1872, 80 L. Ed. 2d 404 (1984)).

Lex at 404. Here, defendant Goldstein allegedly entered into a partnership
agreement or, at the very least, held itself out as a partner of the G & M
Law Group of which defendant Shaines was also a member. Also, as indicated by their Martindale-Hubbell listing, Goldstein & Manello is "A
Partnership including Professional Corporations" with a "Portsmouth
New Hampshire Affiliated Office: Shaines, McEachern, Goldstein &
Manello. . . ." See Doc. 8, Exhibit A. Thus it can be said that Goldstein pur-
posefully directed its activities to New Hampshire through its alleged
partnership relationship with Shaines. Moreover, taking as true Johnson's
contention that he was told that Goldstein & Manello would be involved
in his case, the present litigation necessarily results from the alleged injuries that arose out of or were related to Goldstein's activities as a partner
of Shaines. *Burger King,* supra, 471 U.S. at 472, 105 S. Ct. at 2182. By allegedly agreeing to enter into a partnership with Shaines, Goldstein
"should have reasonably anticipated being 'haled into court' here." *Lex* at
405 (quoting World-Wide Volkswagen v. Woodson, 444 U.S. 286, 297, 100 S.
Ct. 559, 567 62 L. Ed. 2d 490 (1980)). The alleged partners were on notice
that in such relationship "they all act on behalf of one another within the
scope of their partnership activity." *Donatelli* at 467 n.5.

The court also finds that assertion of personal jurisdiction over Gold-stein would not "offend traditional notions of fair play and substantial justice," *International Shoe,* supra, 326 U.S. at 316, 66 S. Ct. at 158. In so holding, the court has weighed the burdens on defendant Goldstein against New Hampshire's interest in redressing injuries that actually occur within the state, see *Omni Hotels* at 751; see also *Lex* at 405, and has found the latter to outweigh the former. The court concludes, therefore, that Goldstein's contacts with New Hampshire satisfy the requirements of due process and the court thus has jurisdiction over defendant Goldstein and the G & M Law Group. Defendants' motion to dismiss pursuant to Fed. R. Civ. P. 12(b)(2) and 12(b)(5) [is] therefore denied. . . .

Discussion

Defendant claims that the complaint does not allege that Goldstein had any duty to the plaintiff or that it had any role with respect to furnishing legal services to plaintiff; that Goldstein shared any responsibility for the conduct of plaintiff's case; or, that Goldstein agreed to assume any liability for the actions of Shaines. Defendant Goldstein concludes that the absence of any allegations creating any duty by Goldstein is fatal to plaintiff's claim.

In a suit against an attorney for malpractice, the plaintiff must prove, among other things, "the attorney-client relationship, or some other basis to establish the existence of a duty." Fairhaven Textile v. Sheehan, Phinney, Bass & Green, Professional Assoc., 695 F. Supp. 71, 73 (D.N.H. 1988). As discussed above, defendant's liability arises from its alleged partnership with Shaines. Plaintiff, through affidavits and other evidence discussed in detail above, has produced material facts as to which there is a genuine dispute, i.e. whether a partnership relationship among the defendants existed. Therefore, defendants' motion for summary judgment is denied.

Conclusion

Defendants' motion to dismiss pursuant to Fed. R. Civ. P. 12(b)(2), 12(b)(5) and 12(b)(6) [is] denied.

EXERCISES

1. Check your state statutes to determine whether a lawyer may form a limited liability company for his or her practice.
2. Check your state statutes to determine the requirements for creating a professional corporation.
3. Go to the law library and find a sample of a partnership agreement and analyze its provisions with respect to operating a law office.
4. Discuss which design structure of a law office you would prefer and indicate why and how this would improve your productivity.

5. Discover which local government agencies in your area have permanent legal staffs.
6. Briefly discuss the benefits or detriments of being a paralegal for a sole practitioner versus being a paralegal for a large law firm.
7. What factors would determine whether a large practice should be a professional corporation or a general partnership?
8. Examine the law office structure included in this chapter and discuss its benefits and detriments.
9. Find and compare advertisements for different law offices in your community.
10. Discuss how an office's image affects its client base.

SITUATIONAL ANALYSIS

Two lawyers wish to open a law practice together. The business of the practice will be estate planning and administration and in order to help provide effective services, the lawyers approach an accountant to join the firm. The accountant is willing to work with the attorneys but insists on an equal share of the business, including a say in management. In order to create the appropriate legal environment to further these ends, the lawyers and the accountant discuss various alternatives with respect to the legal structure of the office. They discuss the possibility of forming a partnership, a professional corporation, or a limited liability company.

What legal and ethical problems might be encountered by two attorneys and an accountant setting up a legal practice with any of the above-mentioned structures? Check your state statutes to determine what, if any, problems exist with respect to these arrangements.

2 People in a Law Office

Immediately upon entering a law office environment, the paralegal assumes a unique and heightened sense of responsibilities and due care towards the clients, attorneys, and other members of the legal community. As a legal professional, the paralegal's ethics are of paramount importance; the paralegal must continually act with candor, honesty, integrity and good faith throughout all machinations of the law.

> Anna C. Ermutlu, J.D.
> Director of Education
> The National Center for
> Paralegal Training
> Atlanta, Georgia

CHAPTER OVERVIEW

The preceding chapter discussed the external attributes of a law office—its organizational, legal, and design structures. This chapter will focus on the internal aspects of a law office—its people.

A law office is a business, just like any other profit-making venture, and its income-producing product is the service it provides the clients. Unlike a company that manufactures items for use or consumption, a law office is a service industry whose primary asset is its people. No matter how flashy the surroundings or carefully organized the structure, a law firm will not flourish if it provides inadequate or incompetent services. Consequently, the people in the office, the **legal team,** constitute the most important internal asset of the firm.

The legal team is headed by one or more attorneys who are assisted by a wide spectrum of support staff, from law clerks and legal assistants to secretaries, receptionists, and investigators. All these professionals working together toward a common goal of providing the best legal service possible is the true "law office."

This chapter will detail all of the personnel involved in operating a successful legal practice and discuss each person's function with respect to his or her contribution to the legal team.

Attorneys

The foremost member of the legal team is the attorney. Attorneys have the ultimate responsibility for the work performed by all the other professionals who assist them in the performance of the office's function. Only attorneys may offer legal advice and counsel, and it is their obligation to see that the work performed by the support staff meets all requisite legal standards.

In order to become an attorney most states require a person to obtain a bachelor's degree from an accredited four-year university and then attend law school for an additional three years. Upon the successful completion of law school one receives a degree known as a **Juris Doctor (J.D.)** or a **Bachelor of Laws (LL.B.)**, depending on the designation given by the law school. After receiving the law degree, a state **bar exam** must be passed, and all of the ethical requirements established by the highest judicial authority in the state must be met. Once all of these requirements have been attained, one is sworn in to the state bar and is now permitted to be called an attorney. All attorneys, after the swearing in, are considered to be officers of the court and as such are held to a high standard of ethical care.

Persons who have achieved all of the above are known as **attorneys, attorneys-at-law, counselors-at-law,** or **lawyers.** The terms are interchangeable and at best reflect stylistic differences. At this point the attorney is permitted to give legal advice and may represent clients in a court of law.

EXAMPLE:

Ruth attended her state university and received a bachelor's degree in English. She then continued her studies at a law school located in her state capital and received a J.D. degree three years later. In the July following her law school graduation she took the bar exam, and three months later was notified that she passed. After a check into her background, Ruth was admitted to her state bar. Ruth is now an attorney.

In all law offices other than those of sole practitioners, attorneys are classified and titled according to the position they hold in the hierarchy of the office. The most typical appellations appear below.

Partners/Shareholders

In a law office operating as a professional corporation all the attorneys who have purchased an interest in the business are called **shareholders.** As a shareholder, the attorney is entitled to a portion of the profits of the office, the percentage depending on the number of shares he or she owns. Generally, attorneys join an office as a staff attorney (see below) and after a number of years may be invited to become a shareholder by purchasing shares, or they may arrive from another firm and immediately buy into the professional corporation. Being a shareholder also entitles the attorney to a say in the management of the corporation. Once again, the amount of management rights the attorney may exercise is determined by the number of shares the attorney owns.

If the law office is operated as a general partnership, the attorney who has management rights in the operation of the enterprise is called a **partner.** Typically, after a number of years staff attorneys may be invited to become partners, or outside attorneys may be invited to join, for monetary consideration, immediately as a partner. A partner has a voice in the control of the entire operation of the law office.

There is a hierarchy even in the category of partner. An **equity partner** is one who not only receives compensation for the services he or she performs but also is entitled to share in the profits and losses of the office. "Equity" indicates an ownership right in a business. Conversely, a **nonequity partner** may be entitled to some management control of the office but only receives a salary for services performed. The nonequity partner does not share in the profits or losses of the firm.

The partners may be further classified into senior, junior, and managing partners. A **senior partner** is an attorney who, because of length of association with the office, is given a greater voice in management and a greater percentage of the office's profits. A **junior partner** typically is a newly created partner whose tenure with the firm as a partner is of shorter duration than that of the senior partners. As a junior partner the attorney is given less say in management and a smaller percentage of the profits. The **managing partner** is usually a senior partner who is given the responsibility for overseeing the administration of the law office itself.

 EXAMPLE:

The firm of Smith and Jones is operated as a general partnership. Smith and Jones are both senior partners, as are Wilkes and Booth, two attorneys who have been with the firm for over 25 years. Guizling has been with the office for 10 years and has just been invited to become a partner. Guizling is a junior partner, entitled to a smaller percentage of the profits than Smith, Jones, Wilkes, or Booth.

Staff Attorneys

All attorneys who regularly work for a law office but who do not have any say in the management of the business are considered **staff attorneys.** There are three categories of staff attorney:

1. associate
2. senior associate
3. contract attorney

Associate

An **associate** is an attorney who works for the office for a salary and who, presumably, will someday become a partner or shareholder in the office. All newly hired attorneys in a law office are usually considered associates.

Typically, an associate will work as a staff attorney for a period of years while the partners evaluate his or her work. At the end of this period the managing attorneys may ask the associate to join as a partner or shareholder. This is the primary employment goal for most attorneys working in a law firm.

EXAMPLE:

Kevin and Stan have just graduated from law school and have passed their bar exams. They are hired by a law firm as associates.

Senior Associate

If the associate is not invited to join as a partner or shareholder (termed "making partner"), he or she may stay on at the firm as a **senior attorney** or **associate,** someone who is not going to be a partner but has seniority in the firm. Many attorneys who do not make partner usually leave the firm to form their own partnerships or find employment elsewhere but may remain at the office for a period of time before leaving.

EXAMPLE:

After working at the law office for ten years, Kevin is asked to join as a partner. He is thrilled and accepts, and is now considered a junior partner. Stan, meanwhile, has not been asked to become a partner but remains at the office as a senior attorney.

Contract Attorney

When a special legal problem or project arises, a law office will often hire an outside attorney who has special knowledge or skill in the problem area. This **contract attorney** is only hired for a specified period of time and is never really considered part of the permanent legal staff. This attorney acts as a legal consultant to the office, and the position is totally determined by the contract that the attorney has with the law office.

EXAMPLE:

Arlene has been practicing law for over 12 years and has developed a certain expertise in elder law. A law firm's major client has become involved in a lawsuit involving elderly employees, and the firm hires Arlene as a contract attorney to supervise the office staff in representing the client in this particular matter.

Other Attorneys

There are two other types of attorney classification that may be encountered in a law office. The first is the attorney who is considered to be **of counsel.** "Of counsel" is really a very loose term and has no specific legal definition. Generally, an attorney who is considered Of Counsel is connected with the law office but does not share in the profit, loss, or management of the firm. Sometimes partners who retire will be made Of Counsel in order to maintain some connection with the firm. Or, as a preliminary step to inviting an attorney who has not worked for the office to become a partner, the office may designate the attorney Of Counsel to see how well the attorney works with the office legal team. Usually attorneys who are Of Counsel have some special knowledge or expertise that the offices wishes to have associated with its name.

EXAMPLE:

A former United States president decides he wishes to maintain some contact with the legal community, having been a lawyer before he became president. His former law firm designates him Of Counsel, and he is given office space and support staff. His name appears on the office letterhead and he handles particularly sensitive lawsuits for the firm.

Second, there are a small group of attorneys who maintain no steady connection with any category of law office and do not maintain their own offices as sole practitioners. These attorneys **freelance**—that is, they are employed on a temporary basis by many different law offices that, because of unusual workloads, have a need for additional attorney support for a short period of time. These attorneys are a subset of the contract attorneys mentioned above, but usually have less specific expertise and are given work typically meted out to associates in the office.

EXAMPLE:

Gail, a young attorney, likes her freedom and has decided to free-lance rather than open her own office or work for someone else. She signs on with an agency that finds temporary legal staff for various law firms in the area. Gail is an example of a freelance attorney, and her work varies depending on each office that employs her.

Law Clerks

Law clerks typically are law students who work for a law office part-time while they are in school and before they pass the bar exam. Law clerks are the primary professional assistants to the attorneys; because of the specialized knowledge they are learning in law school, law clerks are given legal research assignments and may assist the attorney in client interviews and court proceedings. The law clerk is not an attorney and may not give any legal advice. The law clerk works under the supervision of an attorney, and the attorney is ultimately responsible for all work performed by the law clerk. Many law students clerk at law offices so that the attorneys may become familiar with their work and ask them to join the firm when they graduate from law school.

EXAMPLE:

Robert is in his second year at his state law school and has just been hired by a major firm in his city to work for 25 hours per week. Robert is now a law clerk, and his primary duties involve preliminary legal research for three attorneys to whom he has been assigned.

Paralegals

A **paralegal** or **legal assistant** is a person who is hired to assist an attorney in the preparation of legal documents. There are no specific educational requirements necessary to become a paralegal, although most law offices will only hire persons who have completed a course of study at an accredited paralegal institution or at two- or four-year colleges with paralegal programs.

The paralegal is not an attorney and may not give any legal advice. The paralegal typically assists the attorney in completing legal forms, editing the attorney's memoranda and briefs, filing documents with the court, and assisting in all aspects of organizing and documenting legal materials. All work performed by a paralegal must be supervised and signed off by an attorney. If the legal assistant gives any legal advice or prepares any legal documents unsupervised by an attorney, it is considered an **unauthorized practice of law,** and the person performing such acts may be fined and imprisoned. The primary responsibility of the legal assistant is to assist the attorney in all nonclerical legal matters.

 EXAMPLE:

Susan has just graduated from a paralegal school in her city and has received a paralegal certificate from the school. Susan may now be hired by an attorney to assist in providing legal services; Susan may not go out on her own to assist the public directly in the preparation of legal documents — that is an unauthorized practice of law.

Administrative and Secretarial Staff

In addition to the legal professionals described above, almost all law offices hire clerical professionals as part of the legal team. These clerical support professionals not only provide a service in freeing up the time of the legal professionals, but their work has a direct impact on the image of the office because they are the persons with whom the clients have the most contact. Four distinct categories of support professionals will be discussed below.

Office Manager

The **office manager** is generally the administrative head of a law office, the person responsible for appointing all nonlegal staff, assigning support personnel, and seeing that the office is adequately stocked with supplies. Many times the office manager may have discretion with respect to assigning office space, a major prerogative in any law office.

There is no specific educational requirement necessary to become an office manager, but a definite skill in administration is mandatory. In especially large law offices, the office manager may share some responsibility with a **paralegal coordinator** who is in charge of all the office's legal assistants. The office manager typically answers directly to the managing partner and is considered part of the senior management of the office.

 EXAMPLE:

After working as a secretary for ten years and a paralegal for five years, Dorothy has just been made office manager of her law office. Dorothy is now directly responsible for a staff of twenty secretaries, five paralegals, and three clerks. It is her job to see that the administrative side of the office runs smoothly.

Librarian

If the law office is particularly large, it may maintain its own law library for the use of its staff. The head of the law library is usually a librarian who has earned a bachelor's degree and a master's degree in library science (MLS). The **law librarian** is responsible for maintaining the library, purchasing reporters and services and keeping them up-to-date, and maintaining office files of research documents. The librarian may supervise a staff of library clerks. As with the office manager, the law librarian is considered a part of the senior management of the office.

 EXAMPLE:

After earning his master's in library science, Leo attends a paralegal school in order to become familiar with legal materials. He now feels prepared to look for a job in a law library and eventually hopes to become the law librarian of a major law firm.

Secretaries

Secretaries are responsible for all the filing and word processing in the law office. They are expected to be able to take dictation and to have a pleasant manner both personally and on the telephone because they are usually one of the first people clients encounter when they visit or call the law office.

Secretaries are either assigned to specific persons or are part of a secretarial pool, performing their work for whoever in the firm needs work done. Work in the secretarial pool may be assigned by the office manager.

The secretary is expected to be able to spell correctly and to be familiar with the general rules of grammar. He or she is expected to check and correct the spelling and grammar of the documents they type. Secretaries are usually considered one of the most important persons on the legal team. Because most legal work involves writing documents, the crucial work of typing and producing that writing in its final form is the function of the legal secretary.

 EXAMPLE:

Angela has just graduated from a vocational high school and has acquired excellent typing, word processing, and dictation skills. She is hired by a small law office to become part of its legal team.

Receptionist

The **receptionist** is the person who sits at the front desk of the law office. Again, the receptionist may create the first impression potential clients receive of the law firm. The receptionist is required to be friendly, to make clients or other visitors feel comfortable, and to act in a professional manner that reflects well on the office. The receptionist also answers the main telephone for the office, and therefore it is important that the receptionist be skillful in oral communication. The receptionist accepts packages and may be required to do some light typing. The receptionist serves as the primary advertisement for the office.

Other Staff

In addition to the administrative and secretarial staff discussed above, there may occasionally be additional support staff hired as part of the legal team, especially in larger law offices.

Clerks

In order to assist the administrative and secretarial staff, **clerks** may be used to file and retrieve documents, maintain the library and other support facilities, and run the general errands of the office. These persons must be eager and willing to work because most of the mundane aspects of running a business are left on their shoulders.

Security Personnel

As will be discussed in the next chapter, one of the most important elements of the attorney-client relationship is the confidential nature of this communication. As a consequence, it is imperative that all documents, records, and computer materials be kept secure and away from prying eyes. Not only will law offices invest in basic security systems such as locks, safes, and alarms, but many times guards are employed to maintain a secure office even if no other staff is present. These **security personnel** may or may not be licensed to carry guns and are usually **bonded**—that is, they have posted money to insure the faithful performance of their duties. Keeping all work physically secure is an issue whose importance in a law office cannot be overemphasized.

Investigators

Occasionally, law offices will hire private **investigators** if the need arises on a particular case; some very large law firms employ investigators on a full-time basis. Investigators are used to discover important evidence that an attorney will need in order to represent a client, including everything from document discovery, finding witnesses or parties, and maintaining surveillance. Law offices that are heavily involved in litigation practice are most likely to employ investigators.

EXAMPLE:

The law office represents an insurance company. One of the company's clients has put in a claim stating that she was in an accident and has permanently lost the use of her legs. The office sends out its investigator to maintain surveillance on the woman, and the investigator is able to photograph the woman dancing at a local nightclub. The investigator has performed an invaluable service for the office and its client.

People and Ethics

The major ethical concern arising out of the work of the legal team is the unauthorized practice of law. Legal advice may only be given by licensed attorneys, and no one else in the office may ethically proffer a legal opinion, regardless of how conversant he or she may be with the particular area of law. For a more detailed analysis of this ethical problem, read the cases appearing below.

CHAPTER SUMMARY

The key element of every law office is its legal team, the persons who compose the primary asset of the business. Because a law office is a service industry, its ability to perform and produce is totally dependent on the ability of its personnel.

Each member of the legal team provides an important portion of the whole effort. It is well to remember that everyone from the senior partner to the file clerk is a professional who provides professional services, and the team is only as good as each of its members.

The composition of the legal team falls into six major categories:

1. Partners or shareholders are the attorneys responsible for overseeing the entire operation. These people are licensed to practice law and may give legal advice.

2. Staff attorneys are also lawyers but with less seniority and experience than the partners. They receive a salary for work performed and have no equity interest in the law office.

3. Law clerks are law students who work for the office while in school. They generally provide legal research for the attorneys and are prohibited from giving legal advice. All of their work is supervised and signed by an attorney.

4. Paralegals are employed to assist attorneys in all nonclerical legal functions. They are not lawyers and may not give legal advice, and their work must be supervised by an attorney.

5. Administrative and support staff may consist of an office manager, librarian, secretaries, and receptionists. These people provide the clerical work support for the attorneys, law clerks, and paralegals.

6. Other staff, such as general clerks, security personnel, and investigators, provide additional administrative support for the legal team.

In most law offices, successful legal work is the result of the collaboration of every member of the legal team.

Key Terms

Associate: Salaried attorney working for a law firm.

Attorney: Person licensed to practice law.

Attorney-at-law: Alternative name for a person licensed to practice law.

Bachelor of Laws (LL.B.): The law degree awarded by some law schools.

Bar exam: State exam used to license lawyers.

Bond: Money posted to insure the faithful performance of specified duties.

Clerk: Person who provides general administrative support for an office.

Contract attorney: Lawyer hired by a law office because of his or her special expertise for a particular project.

Counselor-at-law: Attorney.

Equity partner: Partner in a law firm who has an ownership interest in the profits and losses of the business.

Freelance attorney: Lawyer who is hired on a casual basis by law offices to handle unusually heavy workloads.

Investigator: Person who provides investigative services for an office.

Junior partner: Partner in a law office who does not have seniority and therefore has less say in the management of the office.

Juris Doctor (J.D.): Law degree conferred by most law schools.

Law clerk: Law student providing legal assistance to attorneys in a law office.

Law librarian: Head of the library of a law office.

Lawyer: Attorney.

Legal assistant: Paralegal.

Legal team: The members of a law office working in collaboration with each other.

Managing partner: Law partner who is in charge of the administration of the office.

Nonequity partner: Partner who does not share in the profit and losses of the office.

Of counsel: Loose term indicating a lawyer with some permanent connection with a law office, but not a partner or associate.

Office manager: Person in charge of the administrative side of a law office.

Paralegal: Person who assists an attorney in all legal matters.

Paralegal coordinator: Person in charge of law office's legal assistants.

Partner: Lawyer who has management say and ownership rights in a law office.

Receptionist: Person in charge of the front desk of an office.
Secretary: Person hired to file, word process, and take dictation.
Security personnel: Guard hired to safeguard the office and its contents.
Senior attorney: Associate who has not been asked to be a partner in the
        law office but who has worked for the firm for a number of years.
Senior partner: Generally a controlling partner in a law office.
Shareholder: Attorney who has purchased an interest in a law office op-
        erating as a professional corporation.
Staff attorney: Lawyer employed full-time by a law office.
Unauthorized practice of law: Giving legal advice without a license.

Cases for Analysis

The following cases are included to expand some of the concepts discussed in the text. In Gautam v. De Luca the court discusses some of the
legal responsibilities of an attorney, both personally and in supervising the
legal team. The Florida Bar v. Furman highlights the unauthorized practice
of law by a paralegal.

Gautam v. De Luca
521 A.2d 1343 (N.J. Super. 1987)

Before Judges Pressler, Baime and Ashbey.
The opinion of the court was delivered by BAIME, J.A.D.
This is an appeal from a judgment of the Superior Court, Law Division, awarding both plaintiffs compensatory and punitive damages based
upon the alleged legal malpractice of defendant Samuel De Luca and his
associate Dominick Conte. The predicate for plaintiffs' claim was that their
former attorneys had negligently represented them in a prior medical malpractice case resulting in the dismissal of their complaint. Plaintiffs made
no effort to establish the viability or value of their underlying medical malpractice action. Rather, they sought to recover damages for the mental an-
guish and emotional distress allegedly caused by the legal malpractice of
defendant and Conte. The novel question presented by this appeal is
whether damages for emotional distress are recoverable in a legal malpractice action. Auxiliary questions concern whether the evidence was sufficient to support an award of punitive damages.
The salient facts can be recited briefly. Plaintiffs Narinder and Urmila
Gautam filed a two-count complaint in which they alleged that defendant
and Conte negligently prosecuted their claim for medical malpractice resulting in the dismissal of their complaint. In the first count, plaintiffs alleged that defendant and Conte were "negligent" in failing to exercise the
knowledge, skill and ability possessed by members of the legal profession.
They claimed that they "suffered injuries and damages" as a "direct and
proximate result" of such negligence. In the second count, plaintiffs alleged that defendant and Conte "deliberately or with reckless indiffer-

ence" failed to advise them of the fact that their medical malpractice claim had been dismissed. Plaintiffs alleged that such conduct warranted punitive damages.

At trial, plaintiffs testified that sometime prior to 1977 they engaged Conte to represent them in unrelated medical malpractice and workers' compensation actions. It is undisputed that Conte was a sole practitioner at this time. However, it is also uncontradicted that Conte joined defendant's law firm in the position of associate shortly thereafter. Conte filed and signed the medical malpractice complaint under defendant's name. Named as defendants were the Jersey City Medical Center, the City of Jersey City and Mrs. Gautam's treating physician.

Protracted discovery proceedings ensued. It is apparent that Conte was extremely dilatory in complying with the court's discovery orders. After lengthy delays and repeated motions, plaintiffs' complaint was ultimately dismissed on this basis on December 6, 1979. Despite plaintiffs' numerous requests for information, Conte never apprised them that their complaint had been dismissed.

In October 1980, plaintiffs received a letter from Conte advising them that he had become ill and could no longer serve as their attorney in the workers' compensation action. Because of the ambiguity of the letter, plaintiffs contacted various court officials and at that time first learned that their complaint in the medical malpractice action had been dismissed. Although Conte cooperated fully with plaintiffs' newly retained attorney, their efforts to have the complaint reinstated proved unavailing.

Both plaintiffs testified that they were greatly distressed by this experience. According to plaintiffs, Conte had told them that their case "had a potential value of $5,000,000." Over vigorous objection, plaintiffs' attorney was permitted to admit into evidence a notice of claim filed with the City of Jersey City demanding the sum of $5,000,000 as damages. Both plaintiffs testified that they developed various psychological problems because of their dashed expectations. Mr. Gautam stated that he suffered constant headaches and back pains and that his marriage began to deteriorate. In similar fashion, Mrs. Gautam testified that she developed insomnia and began experiencing bladder control problems.

Both Conte and defendant testified. According to Conte's testimony, he began to suffer severe disabling headaches shortly after he commenced employment with defendant's firm. Eventually, this condition caused him to leave the office for substantial periods of time. Ultimately, Conte found it necessary to instruct many of his clients to retain other attorneys. According to his testimony, he sent a letter to plaintiffs in June 1980, advising them of his condition and suggesting that they engage another lawyer in the medical malpractice case. He testified that he sent plaintiffs another letter in October 1980 instructing them to retain another attorney in the workers' compensation action. Conte testified that he never received the order dismissing plaintiffs' complaint. When he was apprised of the dismissal, he cooperated fully with plaintiffs' attempt to have the complaint reinstated.

Defendant testified that he was totally unfamiliar with plaintiffs' case. He pointed out that Conte had been retained by plaintiffs prior to his association with his office. Although defendant maintained a "case registry" with appropriate references to all active files, plaintiffs' medical malpractice action had never been listed. With one minor exception, defendant never communicated with the Gautams. It is undisputed that on one occasion defendant answered the telephone and left a message for Conte at plaintiffs' request. Apparently, this was an extremely brief conversation. Plaintiffs' medical malpractice case was not discussed.

Defendant testified that he was aware of Conte's medical problems, but never felt it necessary to review or otherwise supervise his case load. Despite Conte's illness, defendant believed that he was fully able to accord proper attention to his cases. Defendant further testified that he first saw the order dismissing plaintiffs' complaint at the trial.

At the commencement of trial and following the presentation of evidence, both defendant and Conte sought dismissal of plaintiffs' action. Although phrased in a variety of ways, the principal thrust of their argument was that compensatory damages for emotional distress could not be recovered in a legal malpractice case. They contended that where an attorney is guilty of malpractice resulting in the dismissal of his client's complaint, the appropriate measure of damages is the amount of the judgment that could otherwise have been obtained against the primary defendant. Both defendant and Conte asserted that plaintiffs could not prevail in the absence of proof concerning the value of the claim that was lost because of their alleged malpractice. They further argued that punitive damages could not be recovered because plaintiffs failed to establish the underlying cause of action.

[Discussion regarding trial instructions deleted.]

We find no justifiable cause to remand the matter for a retrial. Our thorough review of the record convinces us that the evidence was wholly insufficient to support a recovery of either compensatory or punitive damages.

Legal malpractice suits are traditionally grounded in the tort of negligence. Although not a guarantor against errors in judgment, Morris v. Muller, 113 N.J.L. 46, 50, 172 A. 63 (E.&A. 1934), an attorney is required to exercise on his client's behalf the knowledge, skill and ability ordinarily possessed and employed by members of the legal profession similarly situated and to utilize reasonable care and prudence in connection with his responsibilities. Lamb v. Barbour, 188 N.J. Super. at 12, 455 A.2d 1122 [(App. Div. 1982)]. Under this professional standard, an attorney has an obvious duty to timely file and properly prosecute the claims of his client. Hoppe v. Ranzini, 158 N.J. Super. at 163-164, 385 A.2d 913 [(App. Div. 1978)]; Passanante v. Yormark, 138 N.J. Super. at 238-239, 350 A.2d 497 [(App. Div. 1975)]. Equally plain is the responsibility of an attorney to inform his client promptly of any information important to him. State v. Pych, 213 N.J. Super. 446, 459, 517 A.2d 871 (App. Div. 1986); Passanante v. Yormark, supra, 138 N.J. Super. at 238, 350 A.2d 497; RPC 1.1 to RPC 8.5. See also In re Lanza, 24 N.J. 191, 196, 131 A.2d 497 (1957). Obviously, this duty encompasses the responsibility to inform a client of the dismissal of his complaint.

The failure of an attorney to abide by these obligations plainly constitutes malpractice at least where there is no reasonable justification shown
to support the opposite conclusion. Hoppe v. Ranzini, supra, 158 N.J.
Super. at 164, 385 A.2d 913; Passanante v. Yormark, supra, 138 N.J. Super.
at 238-239, 350 A.2d 497. Although our research has disclosed no published
opinion bearing on the precise issue, we are equally convinced that an attorney's failure to properly supervise the work of his associate may constitute negligence particularly where, as here, the associate is hindered or
disabled by virtue of his illness. We need not dwell upon the subject. Suffice it to say, a reasonable trier of fact could conclude that defendant was
guilty of malpractice because he took no action to safeguard the rights of
his law firm's clients despite his knowledge of Conte's disabling sickness.

The general rule is that an attorney is responsible for the loss proxi-
mately caused the client by his negligence. Hence, the claimant must show
by a preponderance of the evidence what injuries he suffered as a proximate
consequence of the attorney's breach of duty. Lieberman v. Employers Ins.
of Wausau, 84 N.J. at 342, 419 A.2d 417 [(1980)]. In that context, the measure
of damages is ordinarily the amount that the client would have received but
for his attorney's negligence. Ibid. See also Hoppe v. Ranzini, supra, 158 N.J.
Super. at 164, 385 A.2d 191. Such damages are generally shown by introduc-
ing evidence establishing the viability and worth of the claim that was irre-
deemably lost. This procedure has been termed a "suit within a suit."
Lieberman v. Employers Ins. of Wausau, supra, 84 N.J. at 342, 419 A.2d 417.
See also Coggen, "Attorney Negligence . . . A Suit Within a Suit," 60 W. Va.
L. Rev. 225, 233 (1958); Annotation, "Attorney-Negligence-Damages," 45
A.L.R.2d 62, 63-67 (1956). The principle has been stated as follows:

> [P]laintiff has the burden of proving by a preponderance of the evidence
> that (1) he would have recovered a judgment in the action against the
> main defendant, (2) the amount of that judgment, and (3) the degree of
> collectibility of that judgment. [Hoppe v. Ranzini, supra, 158 N.J. Super. at
> 165, 385 A.2d 191.]

. . . We are nevertheless persuaded that emotional distress damages
should not be awarded in legal malpractice cases at least in the absence of
egregious or extraordinary circumstances. Whether viewed within the
context of the traditional concept of proximate cause, see People Exp. Air-
lines, Inc. v. Consolidated Rail, 100 N.J. 246, 252-253, 495 A.2d 107 (1985);
Robinson v. Gonzalez, 213 N.J. Super. 364, 369, 517 A.2d 479 (App. Div.
1986), or simply as a matter of sound public policy, Caputzal v. The Lind-
say Co., 48 N.J. 69, 75-78, 222 A.2d 513 (1966), we are convinced that damages should be generally limited to recompensing the injured party for his
economic loss. . . .

We also observe that the evidence presented at trial was clearly insufficient to warrant punitive damages against defendant. "The key to the right
to punitive damages is the wrongfulness" of the tortfeasor's act. Nappe v.
Anschelewitz, Barr, Ansell & Bonello, 97 N.J. at 49, 477 A.2d 1224. To warrant a punitive award, "the defendant's conduct must have been wantonly

reckless or malicious." Ibid. Stated another way, "[t]here must be a 'positive element of conscious wrongdoing.'" Berg v. Reaction Motors Div., 37 N.J. 396, 414, 181 A.2d 487 (1962), quoting McCormick, Damages §126 at 280 (1935). See also Di Giovanni v. Pessel, 55 N.J. 188, 191, 260 A.2d 510 (1970).

The evidence presented against defendant plainly did not satisfy this standard. The record is totally barren of any evidence which might reasonably support the conclusion that there was a "deliberate act or omission [by defendant] with knowledge of a high degree of probability of harm and reckless indifference to consequences." Berg v. Reaction Motors Div., supra, 37 N.J. at 414, 181 A.2d 487. At best, the evidence presented by plaintiffs established that defendant failed to properly supervise Conte's work. Plaintiffs utterly failed to prove that defendant was aware of the dismissal of their medical malpractice complaint. Whatever may be said with respect to the nature and quality of Conte's conduct, the evidence presented at trial did not warrant a recovery of punitive damages against De Luca.

In sum, we are convinced that the trial judge committed prejudicial error in his instructions to the jury and that the evidence did not warrant recovery of either compensatory or punitive damages. Accordingly, the judgment of the Law Division is reversed as to defendant De Luca.

The Florida Bar v. Furman
451 So. 2d 808 (Fla. 1984)

Per Curiam.

The Florida Bar filed petitions charging Rosemary W. Furman, d/b/a Northside Secretarial Service, with engaging in the unauthorized practice of law in the State of Florida, in contempt of this Court's order of November 1, 1979, as reported in The Florida Bar v. Furman, 376 So. 2d 378 (Fla. 1979), appeal dismissed, 444 U.S. 1061, 100 S. Ct. 1001, 62 L. Ed. 2d 744 (1980). The charges were assigned to a referee and a report returned for our consideration. We have jurisdiction under article V, section 15 of the Florida Constitution and The Florida Bar Integration Rule, article XVI.

A brief recitation of the prior history of this case is necessary. Respondent Furman is not and never has been a member of The Florida Bar (Bar) and is not licensed to practice law within this state. In 1977, the Bar filed petitions with this Court alleging that respondent had engaged in the unauthorized practice of law by giving legal advice and by rendering legal services in connection with marriage dissolutions and adoptions in the years 1976 and 1977. More specifically, the Bar alleged that respondent performed legal services by soliciting information from customers and by preparing legal pleadings for them in violation of Florida law and that, through advertising, respondent held herself out to the public as having legal expertise in Florida family law. We appointed a referee to receive evidence and to make findings of fact, conclusions of law, and recommendations as to the disposition of the case. In due course the referee submitted findings that respondent had engaged in the unauthorized practice of law and recommended that she be adjudged guilty of contempt of this Court. We found respondent guilty and permanently enjoined and restrained her from further engaging in the unauthorized practice of law, as specified, but did not find her guilty of contempt.

On September 28, 1982, and March 9, 1983, the Bar filed petitions alleging six and ten instances, respectively, wherein respondent had continued her unauthorized practice of law in contempt of this Court's order. We issued rules to show cause on November 30, 1982, and March 21, 1983, respectively, and appointed a referee to receive evidence and to make findings of fact, conclusions of law, and recommendations. The referee conducted pretrial hearings, consolidated the rules, and set evidentiary hearings for June 20 and 21, 1983. On June 20, 1983, we denied respondent's motions for a stay of the proceedings and for trial by jury. Respondent chose not to testify at the evidentiary hearings. The uncontradicted testimony of former customers of respondent was that she advised them to falsify information in marriage dissolution papers and to conceal relevant information from the courts acting on the dissolution petitions. Her purported reasons were various: it's none of their damn business, they don't pay any attention to the information, or you'll (either) get less or give more money in the dissolution judgment. In one instance, respondent advised a wife who had been married, divorced, and remarried to the same husband but could not remember the date of the remarriage to insert the date of the dissolved first marriage as the date of the second marriage in the petition for dissolution. Another couple who disagreed on whether their stipulation on child custody provided for $35 per week or $35 per child was advised that it didn't matter because the judge awarded whatever he wanted to anyway. In a particularly egregious instance, respondent assisted a husband seeking a marriage dissolution in preparing a stipulation in which he agreed to child custody by the wife. While the dissolution petition and child custody stipulation were pending before the court, the husband became aware that the wife was abusing the children, took actual custody of the children, and consulted respondent about withdrawing his stipulated agreement on child custody. Respondent advised him not to do so because this would require "starting over" on the dissolution petition and he should let the social agency (HRS) handle the child abuse and custody problem.

At the conclusion of the evidentiary hearings, the referee scheduled briefing and the case was orally argued on August 15, 1983. Both parties were given an opportunity thereafter to submit proposed orders for the referee's consideration. On September 28, 1983, the referee set a hearing for October 10, 1983, to announce his findings and recommendations and to hear arguments in aggravation or mitigation, if appropriate. At the beginning of the hearing, the referee distributed draft copies of his prospective order and announced the highlights of the order from the bench. The draft recommended that respondent be held in indirect criminal contempt and that she be sentenced to unspecified terms of imprisonment. The referee then offered respondent an opportunity to present evidence and argument in mitigation and recessed the hearing for a short time to permit respondent to consider her options. Respondent chose not to testify or present evidence, but joined the Bar in presenting arguments, after which the referee entered the order under consideration. The order recommended concurrent four-month sentences in state prison.

Respondent raises . . . objections to the referee's report. . . .

We turn then to the referee's findings that respondent contemptuously continued the unauthorized practice of law in violation of our injunction. The referee found in pertinent part:

J. Ms. Furman prepared pleadings that went beyond just transposing information from an intake sheet to a form. She articulated that information in a fashion which raised justiciable issues regarding child custody, child support, division of property.

K. Ms. Furman explained legal remedies and options to litigating parties which affected the procedural and substantive legal rights, duties, and privileges of those parties.

L. Ms. Furman construed and interpreted the legal effects of Section 61.13, Florida Statutes, pertaining to shared parental responsibility.

M. Ms. Furman gave advice on how to construct and prepare a financial picture that would result in increased monetary benefits or decreased monetary obligations as the case may be for the one seeking her advice, without regard for the truth, in some instances.

N. Ms. Furman, as part of her comprehensive legal assistance, gave advice and direction on how and where to file documents with instructions on how to technically prepare and litigate the case in Court.

O. Ms. Furman was available to her customers to correct erroneous or legally deficient pleadings that she had prepared, and to remedy problems experienced by her customers during the dissolution hearing which otherwise frustrated a conclusion thereto.

P. Ms. Furman professed to her customers to have knowledge of the weight and credibility that judges attach and give to legal documents and crucial legal information and evidence.

Q. Ms. Furman participated in oral dialogues with her customers regarding such issues as money for the support of children, safety of children from abusing parents, the placement of children with the most deserving parent, available remedies and options for litigating parties, her interpretation and understanding of legal documents and pertinent statutes, the financial status of husbands and wives as they bore on their need or ability to receive or pay, the ability of her customers to comply with financial Court-ordered obligations, the importance of Court orders and complications therewith, and corrective procedures for defective dissolution proceedings.

R. Ms. Furman, in each case, was paid a monetary fee ranging up to $100.00.

Of the sixteen alleged instances of unauthorized practices of law, four were nolle prossed by the Bar. The referee's findings were based on a case-by-case examination and analysis of the twelve instances where evidence of unauthorized practice of law was introduced. The evidence consisted of the testimony of the customers involved in the specific instance and relevant documents or forms that respondent had prepared for the customer. This evidence was almost entirely uncontradicted except for cross examination. We have reviewed the findings on these twelve charges and find that they are supported by the evidence. We find no error and approve the findings of the referee. . . .

Respondent's objection is that the referee erred in failing to dismiss the second rule to show cause because of procedural irregularities. Reports of the unauthorized practice of law are investigated and disposed of in accordance with Integration Rule, article XVI. Local committees are established throughout the state to receive and investigate such reports and to forward them to The Florida Bar for further investigation, processing, and disposition. There is also a Standing Committee on Unauthorized Practice of Law which functions statewide to oversee the local committees and perform various other duties. These duties include submitting recommendations to the Bar's Board of Governors on instituting litigation, supervising such litigation, and conducting investigations of unauthorized practice on its own behalf or in concert with local committees. The charges contained in the first petition or rule were investigated by the local committee, forwarded to the Standing Committee, considered and approved by the Standing Committee, and a recommendation made to the Board of Governors that litigation be initiated. The Board of Governors approved the litigation and the chairman of the Standing Committee prepared and signed a petition to this Court which commenced the litigation against respondent. The respondent does not contest the propriety of the procedures followed in filing the first petition or that the litigation was properly initiated. . . .

Turning to the referee's recommendations, we approve the findings that respondent has violated the terms of our order enjoining and restraining her from performing the specific acts therein prohibited. We hold her in contempt of court. We, however, do not accept the referee's recommendation that she be imprisoned in the state prison for two concurrent four-month terms. Under the facts of this case, we find it more appropriate to sentence respondent to the Duval County jail for a single term of 120 days. We suspend 90 days of the 120-day term of imprisonment. When this opinion becomes final, the sheriff of Duval County is authorized and directed to take respondent into custody and to imprison her for 30 days. If respondent does not violate the terms of our continuing injunction for a period of two years, the suspended term of 90 days shall be deemed satisfied.

The terms and provisions of our previous order permanently enjoining and restraining respondent remain in effect.

Costs of these proceedings are taxed against the respondent, Rosemary Furman.

It is so ordered.

EXERCISES

1. Not every jurisdiction requires attorneys to have attended law school. Research your state to determine whether someone may become an attorney without going to law school and, if so, what are the requirements?
2. How does your state define the "unauthorized practice of law"?
3. Some states permit paralegals to represent clients without attorney supervision in very limited circumstances. Is this so in your jurisdiction and, if so, under what circumstances?
4. Discuss the distinguishing characteristics between a law clerk and a paralegal.
5. Write a job description for a legal secretary.
6. What factors would you consider in evaluating the abilities of a person who has applied for the position of paralegal?
7. Do you agree or disagree with the court's decision in The Florida Bar v. Furman?
8. What is your opinion of providing punitive damages to clients who have been injured by an attorney's malpractice?
9. In addition to the ethical concerns regarding the unauthorized practice of law, what other ethical considerations may be involved in working on a legal team?
10. Do you prefer to work alone or as a member of a team? Indicate how this preference would affect your value to a law office.

SITUATIONAL ANALYSIS

Three paralegals decide to open an office and name it Rent-A-Para. Its purpose is to provide paralegal services on a temporary basis to various lawyers and law offices in their community.

After two years of working together, the office has become well-known and respected. However, two potential problems have arisen. First, several of the lawyers who have hired the office have become so confident of the paralegals' abilities that they no longer supervise or check the work they assign. Second, several clients of the lawyers who have hired the office have started calling the paralegals directly in order to request help in filling out simple legal forms. Some clients have even asked the paralegals to represent them in small claims court.

What ethical and legal difficulties do you see Rent-A-Para facing? How could the potential problems be rectified without injuring the office's business?

3 Law Office-Client Relationship

Rules of confidentiality are set forth in the Code of Ethics and there are unwritten rules, principles and images. Be aware of all of them — I think the issue can be loaded with potential for misinterpretation; therefore, more than anywhere else, here I would err on the side of appearing too scrupulous in avoiding breaches of confidentiality and the tarnishing of anyone's image. Being meticulous will ensure that when the chips are down the client is always the winner in fact, as it should be, and I am also the winner on principle, as I must be.

Maria Montgomery
Legal Assistant
Stroock & Stroock & Lavan
New York, New York

CHAPTER OVERVIEW

The two preceding chapters have dealt with the internal organization of a law office. It is now time to focus on the relationship of the office to outside persons, that is, the clients. As indicated previously, all of the structural and personnel elements of an office combine to form the **image** of the particular firm — the way outsiders view the office. A law office's image is probably the most important factor in its ability to generate work.

Because of the relatively large number of rival lawyers and law offices, it is imperative that a firm present a competent and caring image in order to attract potential clients over competing firms. The reputation that an office develops is based on the actual and perceived ability of its personnel, and in this way business is developed for the firm.

This chapter will concentrate on the interpersonal relationships that should exist between the law office and potential and current clients. Because of the service nature of a legal practice, public relations dominate its ability to attract and retain clients. Every member of the office must be aware of this and present the office in every situation in its most favorable light.

Concepts of Public Relations

Public relations can be defined as the manner in which a particular person or business makes the general public aware of its image. It is a subdivision of the broader concept of advertising. However, the law is a service industry and offers no physical product to potential buyers. The "product" for a law firm is its personnel, and the manner in which the firm collectively presents itself is how a law office attracts clients.

The second most important attribute of a law office—the first being legal competence—is its ability to provide customer service and satisfaction. This means that the office personnel must be able to communicate effectively with clients not only to ascertain their needs, but also to allay their fears and see that their emotional and intellectual needs with respect to their particular legal problems are met. For a law office, communication is the key to its public relations. Most clients find the law a strange and formidable arena, and one of the functions of the law office is to ease the clients' concerns.

 EXAMPLE:

A client comes to a law office because her neighbor fell on her property, thereby breaking his leg, and is now suing for one million dollars. The client is afraid of the lawsuit and believes that the result of the litigation will bankrupt her. It is the function of the law office to calm her and assure her that the likelihood of her neighbor actually receiving one million dollars for a broken leg is unrealistic.

In order to present the office in the most attractive light, all office personnel must be able to communicate effectively with the firm's clients. Effective communication takes into consideration the emotional, physical, and intellectual needs of each client as an individual. A method of communication that is effective for one client may be totally ineffective when presented to another client.

 EXAMPLES:

1. Marian is a lawyer who needs to be represented in a personal injury case in which she is the injured party. The attorney in charge of the case explains the situation to Marian as one lawyer to another,

using all of the appropriate legal terms. Marian is satisfied that the office will do a competent job in protecting her interests.

2. Philip is a clothes designer who needs to be represented in a personal injury case in which he is the injured party. The attorney in charge of the case explains the situation by using complex legal terminology. Philip is totally lost and feels that the attorney's presentation is condescending.

All office personnel must be aware of certain **communication barriers** that may affect dialogue with a client. One example of a communication barrier is the language usage illustrated above. Using only technical terms in speaking to clients unfamiliar with those terms cuts off communication, as would using any specific language with which the client is uncomfortable.

  EXAMPLE:

Sandra is a paralegal working for a large, conservative law office. Sandra grew up using "street language" and slang as a regular method of communication. When she speaks to the office's corporate clients, they do not understand her jargon and worry about the ability of the office to understand their problems.

Another barrier to effective communication is noise or unusual visual distractions. Having loud music playing in an office may interfere with the client's ability to hear what the office personnel are saying. Unusually colored walls or designs that are large and distracting may also interfere with the client's ability to focus on what is being said. All external aural and visual distractions should be kept to a minimum to reduce or eradicate barriers to effective communication.

As indicated above, all communication can be divided into verbal and nonverbal methods of communication. **Verbal communication** concerns language skills, either oral or written. Using words incorrectly, speaking ungrammatically, employing slang, or having a limited vocabulary or even a heavy accent all affect communication. In order to present the appropriate office image, all members of the firm must speak and write clearly and effectively, and avoid errors in speech that the client would find disturbing. It should go without saying, of course, that the use of expletives is always incorrect.

  EXAMPLE:

Mario was born outside the United States and came to America as an adult. Mario, who has a very heavy foreign accent, works as a paralegal in a law office. When he speaks to the clients, many find it hard to understand him. Although Mario's verbal skills are excellent in every other respect, it might be beneficial if he could minimize his foreign intonation so that the clients can understand what he is telling them.

Nonverbal communication refers to every method of expression other than words. Nonverbal communication manifests itself in such ways as dress, eye contact, body language, and voice quality.

In terms of public relations, the first impression that a person or office makes on an outsider is by means of nonverbal communication, principally dress and grooming. As the saying goes, you only have one chance to make a first impression, and that impression is made long before any word is uttered.

Every law office presents a different nonverbal image in the manner of dress adopted by its members. As a generalization, older corporate law firms favor conservative dress and somber colors, whereas entertainment law firms or those specializing in criminal defense prefer more fashionable or more casual attire. Every member of the office should present a fairly consistent visual image, one that reflects the attitude of the office. Regardless of the specific manner of dress, all members of the office must be well-groomed, clean, and neat.

 EXAMPLE:

Cheryl works as a secretary for a law office that represents many different unions. Cheryl prefers to dress elegantly but the clients are very down-to-earth, and the office staff tends to dress casually to put the clients at ease. Cheryl tempers her wardrobe during working hours.

Nothing is more distracting than trying to listen to a person who is constantly fidgeting or looking all around the room. It is important to focus attention directly on the client, listen to what he or she says, and keep body movements to a minimum. Words are the lifeblood of the law, and therefore anything that interrupts or distracts the flow of verbal communication can be a barrier to the effectiveness of the office.

 EXAMPLE:

Lillian is a law clerk and has been asked to get some information from a client. During the interview, Lillian constantly plays with her rings and bracelets, distracting the client. At the end of the interview the client does not feel that Lillian really heard a word that he said.

A well-modulated voice is probably one of the most impressive communication skills that a person can develop. As radio and television advertisers have known for years, the quality of a voice can be extremely effective in communicating information to the public. It can seduce an unwary listener into total agreement. Developing an even-tempered tone can be a valuable asset in presenting a positive image of an office.

EXAMPLE:

A client is very nervous about an upcoming court appearance. The senior attorney in the office has a beautiful, well-modulated tonal quality to her voice, and as she explains the court process, the client is calmed because of the soothing quality of the attorney's voice. The image presented by the senior attorney is one of competence and care.

To present an appropriate office image by means of communication, always listen and ask questions. No one wants to talk into a vacuum, and any indication to a client that the people in the office are not attentive listeners creates a negative impression. The most effective method of letting a client know that her words are receiving attention is by asking questions that relate directly to what the client is saying. Asking questions for the sake of asking questions is an obvious ploy and may have a negative effect on the client, but well-thought-out questions relating directly to the client's problems demonstrate interest and concern. Also, the best way to acquire knowledge is by asking questions. The distinguishing characteristic between an effective and an ineffective listener is the person's ability to listen intently and ask pertinent questions.

Furthermore, every member of the legal team must listen to what the client is *truly* saying and not simply the verbatim account of the client's words. This is known as emphatic listening, a genuine understanding of the meaning the speaker is attempting to convey.

EXAMPLE:

A client is in the office to determine the appropriateness of filing bankruptcy. Throughout the interview he makes constant reference to his children's schooling. To the careful listener it is clear that this client's primary concern is his continued ability to educate his children if he files bankruptcy, and that this issue should be addressed first rather than the other, more immediate, legal problems.

Several guidelines should be kept in mind in order to present a positive public image of the office to the clients:

1. Speak correctly, avoiding all slang, expletives, and verbal space fillers.
2. Avoid or minimize noise.
3. Avoid having distracting colors or objects in the room.
4. Dress appropriately for the image the office wishes to project and always be well-groomed.
5. Maintain eye contact with the client and don't fidget.
6. Avoid emotional exchanges and have a well-modulated voice.
7. Listen carefully to what is being said.
8. Ask pertinent questions.
9. Consider the particular needs of each individual client.

Confidentiality

One of the most important factors in the office-client relationship is the office's responsibility to keep all information received from the client confidential. **Confidentiality** means that clients are assured that anything they tell an attorney or any member of the office will be kept in strict confidence and not be divulged to anyone, including the friends and loved ones of the office staff. Not only is there an expectation of privacy and confidentiality on the part of clients when they communicate with a law office, but the law office itself recognizes this expectation of privacy as a legal right.

The right of a client to keep all information divulged to a law office confidential is known as the **attorney-client privilege.** This is a legal privilege belonging to the client, which grants the client the right to prevent his or her attorney, or anyone working for the attorney, from divulging any information the client has passed on. The only possible exception to this right would occur if the client is going to testify under oath and, because of information previously given to the attorney, the attorney realizes that the client is going to commit perjury. The attorney is prohibited, as an officer of the court, from contributing to the commission of a crime — namely, false testimony.

The expectation of confidentiality and the right to keep all information privileged extend to each and every member of the office. Because so many people are included on the legal team, every person in the office has access to and is required to work on confidential matters. The law office would soon be out of business if clients could not rely on the discretion of each and every member of the firm.

 EXAMPLE:

A corporate client of the law office is planning to take over another corporation. The office has been working for several months on all of the details. One of the file clerks, while copying some material, reads the details of the takeover. The file clerk is prohibited from divulging the information because of the expectation of confidentiality and the attorney-client privilege.

Personnel-Client Relationships

Each and every member of the law office is an ambassador representing the office to outside persons, especially clients. In order to attract and keep clients, and to attract additional business by means of client referrals, it is the duty and responsibility of every member of the legal team to be cooperative and attentive to the needs of the client. The public relations value of the relationship that is created between the client and all personnel in the office cannot be too strongly stressed. The key to good office-client relations is providing appropriate service, and to attain this objective the following concepts should be borne in mind.

The client always comes first. As a service profession, a law office must remember that the client is the reason why the office exists. The adage "the customer is always right" applies to law offices as well as other commercial ventures. Remember—no client, no business, no office!

EXAMPLE:

On Friday afternoon a client decides he must have a complicated will drawn up before he leaves for vacation Sunday night. Despite weekend plans, the attorney stays late Friday and works all Saturday morning in order to have the will prepared before the client's departure. The personal wishes of the attorney must take a back seat to the professional needs of the client.

Treat each client as if he or she is the only client. This is primarily a subset of remembering that the client always comes first, but it is important to stress this personal relationship that must exist between the office and the client. Each and every client must be made to feel special and important not only for the purpose of public relations but because, in fact, he or she is.

Always keep promises to clients. This means that all telephone calls must be returned, copies of all documents must be sent to the client, and the client must be kept constantly informed of the progress of his or her case. Clients need constant attention in order to feel that the office cares about their legal problems, and more clients are lost because of unreturned calls and lack of updates about the progress of their case than for any other reason. Many times the client doesn't necessarily need to hear from a particular person but simply needs to obtain information from the office as it arises. Always be sure that the client is kept abreast of what is going on.

EXAMPLE:

The office is handling a relatively simple lawsuit for a client. During discovery a pretrial motion is filed and a hearing date is set for one month from the filing of the motion. The hearing is postponed twice, and three months have passed. The client should be kept informed of what is happening, even if what is happening is a delay. The client's uncertainty about the progress of the case translates into a conviction that the office does not care about its progress.

Always be courteous and polite but avoid becoming overly personal with the client. A law office is a professional arena, and every member of the staff must be conscious of maintaining a professional manner with all clients. It is never a good idea to become too personally involved with a client because the client may begin to view the law office as a place to meet friends rather than to acquire professional assistance. This could result in the long run in losing clients who think their "friends" should help them out for free.

EXAMPLE:

An associate with the office begins to develop an overly friendly relationship with a client. One day the client asks the associate to "look over" a 30-page contract and becomes incensed when the office sends a bill. The client thought the associate would read the document as a friend extending a favor and not as an attorney whose only income-producing asset is time and knowledge.

Always document all communications with the client, and word the documentation clearly. Letters and other writings sent out by the office represent part of the verbal communication with the client. If the document is sloppy, unclear, or ambiguous, it presents a negative image of the office to the client. Additionally, documentation is always important in order to avoid problems later on when trying to ascertain exactly what has transpired between the office and the client.

EXAMPLE:

After incorporating a client, the attorney tells the client to check with his accountant as to the appropriateness of filing for Subchapter S tax treatment. The conversation is not documented, the client forgets, and two years later the client sues the attorney for malpractice claiming that he paid more taxes than he had to because the attorney failed to alert him to the Subchapter S election. A simple letter at the time of incorporation to confirm the conversation would have reminded the client and avoided the problem.

Client Relationships and Ethics

The major ethical consideration involved in the law office-client relationship is the responsibility of the entire legal team to maintain the confidentiality of client records and communications. As stated above, confidentiality is not only an expectation, it is the legal right of the client, and it is considered a major ethical breach for any member of the legal team to disclose information received from or by a client in confidence.

Of course, a problem may arise when there is a conflict between the attorney's responsibility of maintaining client confidentiality and the attorney's position as an officer of the court. The attorney may not permit a client to perjure herself under oath, but rather than forgo the expectation of confidentiality, many attorneys attempt to convince the client to refuse to take the witness stand or to refuse to make statements under oath. Should the client resist the attorney's argument, the attorney's greater ethical responsibility belongs to the court, as the representative of all the people, rather than to the individual client.

CHAPTER SUMMARY

All members of a law office must be concerned at all times with the image they project. Because a law office is nothing more than the sum of each member of the legal team, the image that the team creates will determine how potential and current clients view the firm.

In order to project a positive image the office must be cognizant of public relations by maintaining appropriate contact with firm clients. The presentation that the office makes through both verbal and nonverbal communication will influence a person's decision to retain the professional services of the office. Because of the abundance of law practices, public relations is the primary method whereby one office distinguishes itself from its competition. To promote effective communication, the office must avoid all barriers to communication, such as a noisy environment, distracting decor, and inappropriate language.

Each member of the law office must maintain all information gathered from the client in strictest confidence. Any breach of this expectation of confidentiality is not only a violation of law and ethics but will, without question, result in the loss of business for the office if the public perceives that its personnel cannot keep client matters to themselves.

Finally, a law office must always remember that it is in the business of providing a service, and as such the wishes of the client must always take precedence. No one wants to be treated in an offhanded or uncaring manner, especially if he or she is paying for service and professional treatment.

Key Terms

Attorney-client privilege: Legal right of a client to prevent disclosure of any information given to an attorney or members of the attorney's office incident to the attorney providing legal representation.

Communication barriers: Anything that hinders effective client communication, such as noise, incorrect grammar, physical distractions, and so on.

Confidentiality: Maintaining the secrecy of anything a client tells any member of a law office.

Image: Characteristic attitude and appearance presented to clients of a law office by the members of the legal team.

Nonverbal communication: All methods of communication other than words, such as body language, voice tone, and so on.

Public relations: Method of projecting an office's image to the general populace.

Verbal communication: Method of communication by words, oral or written.

Cases for Analysis

The following cases, In re National Mortgage Equity Corp. Mortgage Pool Certificates and People v. Mitchell, underscore some of the problems incident to the confidential nature of the attorney-client relationship.

In re National Mortgage Equity Corp. Mortgage Pool Certificates
120 F.R.D. 687 (C.D. Cal. 1988)

TASHIMA, District Judge.

These consolidated actions involve, inter alia, charges of fraud on a massive scale against National Mortgage Equity Corporation, its president David A. Feldman (collectively "NMEC"), Lord, Bissell & Brook and Leslie A. Michael (collectively "LBB"). NMEC was the originator, assembler, marketer and (at times) servicer of a program to sell mortgage-backed certificates. See National Mortgage Equity Corp. Mortgage Pool Certificates Sec. Litig., 636 F. Supp. 1138 (C.D. Cal. 1986) ("*NMEC I*"), and *NMEC II*, 682 F. Supp. 1073 (C.D. Cal. 1987). During the period relevant to these actions, LBB was NMEC's attorneys, including at least during a portion of the period its attorneys on securities and securities offerings matters. Both client and attorney have been charged by numerous third-parties in these consolidated actions with securities fraud and other wrongdoing.

LBB has long made known its belief that it has a right to disclose otherwise confidential attorney-client communications over the client's (NMEC's) objection to the extent necessary to LBB's self defense in these actions. After the resolution of a number of other discovery disputes over an extended period, including a ruling that the crime or fraud exception to the attorney-client privilege has vitiated NMEC's invocation of the attorney-client privilege for a substantial portion of the period involved in this action, see *NMEC III,* 116 F.R.D. 297 (C.D. Cal. 1987) (preliminary ruling on crime-fraud exception issue); *NMEC IV,* 849 F.2d 1166 (9th Cir. 1988) (dismissing appeal), LBB informed NMEC of its intent to disclose certain privileged documents pursuant to the self defense exception. NMEC promptly moved for a protective order under F.R. Civ. P. 26(c), to prevent such disclosure.

Because of the need for a prompt ruling, at the hearing on the motion the Court denied the motion, holding that LBB, as attorneys charged with wrongdoing, were entitled under the self defense exception to disclose otherwise confidential attorney-client communications between it and NMEC, to the extent necessary to defend against such allegations.

Whether or not there is, or should be, a self defense exception to the attorney-client privilege in the circumstance here is a question of first impression in this Circuit. For that reason, the Court deems it appropriate fully to explicate the reasons for its holding.

The self defense exception lies at the congeries of two seemingly unrelated but important legal doctrines: the law of evidentiary privileges and the rules which govern the ethical conduct of lawyers. Because these consolidated cases invoke both federal and state claims, under F.R. Evid. 501, whether or not such an exception exists is an issue of federal law. This issue also involves the ethical standards which govern the conduct of lawyers. With respect to the standards which govern such conduct, under Local Rule 2.5.1, members of the bar of this Court are bound to comply with the Rules of Professional Conduct of the State Bar of California. However, those rules contain no provision specifically governing an attorney's conduct in this area. In such a situation, the Court may look to the American Bar Association ("ABA") Model Rules of Professional Conduct (1983) (the "Model Rules") as an appropriate standard to guide the conduct of members of its bar. See Securities Inv. Protection Corp. v. Vigman, 587 F. Supp. 1358, 1362-63 (C.D. Cal. 1984).

The leading case on this issue is Meyerhofer v. Empire Fire & Marine Ins. Co., 497 F.2d 1190 (2d Cir. 1974), cert. denied, 419 U.S. 998, 95 S. Ct. 314, 42 L. Ed. 2d 272 (1975). *Meyerhofer* involved an attorney disqualification motion based on asserted wrongful disclosure of confidential information obtained from the client. The disclosure was made (successfully) in order to avoid being named as a defendant in a securities fraud action. The Second Circuit held that no ethical impropriety had been committed, including of Canon 4 of the Code of Professional Responsibility because Disciplinary Rule 4-101(C)(4) permitted a lawyer to reveal "Confidences or secrets necessary . . . to defend himself . . . against an accusation of wrongful conduct." Id. at 1194-95.

As can be seen, *Meyerhofer* was not a privilege case, but involved attorney sanctions under the Disciplinary Rules for asserted improper professional conduct. The privilege issue was squarely confronted in First Fed. Sav. & Loan Assn. v. Oppenheim, Appel, Dixon & Co., 110 F.R.D. 557 (Mag. S.D.N.Y. 1986). In a well reasoned opinion, the Magistrate held that an attorney, impleaded as a third-party defendant in a securities action by a third-party plaintiff other than the client had the right under the self defense exception to disclose without client consent, otherwise privileged attorney-client communications to the extent reasonably necessary to the attorney's defense. Id.

Another persuasive source, neither relied on nor discussed in *First Fed.*, also strongly counsels in favor of recognizing the self defense exception.

Model Rule 1.6(b)(2) provides:

> A lawyer may reveal such information [relating to representation of a client] to the extent the lawyer reasonably believes necessary:
>   (2) . . . to establish a defense to a . . . civil claim against the lawyer based upon conduct in which the client was involved, or to respond to allegations in any proceeding concerning the lawyer's representation of the client.

Earlier versions of Model Rule 1.6 would have limited the lawyer's right to disclose to disciplinary proceedings or to respond to allegations made by the client. ABA, The Legislative History of the Model Rules of Professional Conduct: Their Development in the ABA House of Delegates (ABA 1987) ("Legislative History of the Model Rules") at 50-51. The comment to Rule 1.6, as adopted, makes clear the lawyer's right to make disclosure in the circumstances which obtain here:

> If the lawyer is charged with wrongdoing in which the client's conduct is implicated, the rule of confidentiality should not prevent the lawyer from defending against the charge. Such a charge can arise in a civil . . . proceeding, and can be based . . . on a wrong alleged by a third person; for example, a person claiming to have been defrauded by the lawyer and client acting together.

Id. at 54. See also Subin, "The Lawyer as Superego: Disclosure of Client Confidences to Prevent Harm," 70 Iowa L. Rev. 1091, 1135-44 (1985). Although the commentary does not speak directly to the relationship between Rule 1.6 and the attorney-client privilege, it does state: "Whether another provision of law supersedes Rule 1.6 is a matter of interpretation beyond the scope of these Rules, but a presumption should exist against suppression." Cf. *Wilkinson*, 111 F.R.D. at 438 (exclusionary rules and privileges to be strictly construed, quoting Trammel v. United States, 445 U.S. 40, 50, 100 S. Ct. 906, 912, 63 L. Ed. 2d 186 (1980)).

The Court has been cited to no case decided since the seminal *Meyerhofer* case which, either on ethical or evidentiary grounds, disallowed invocation of the self defense exception to defend against third-party allegations of wrongdoing. *Meyerhofer, First Fed.* and Model Rule 1.6(b)(2) argue strongly for recognition of the self defense exception. The Court finds these authorities to be persuasive and agrees with *First Fed.* that the federal common law of privilege should recognize a self defense exception to the attorney-client privilege in the circumstances of these cases.

On the issue of the extent of the disclosure, both Model Rule 1.6(b) and its commentary recognize that "disclosure should be no greater than the lawyer reasonably believes is necessary to vindicate innocence. . . ." Legislative History of the Model Rules at 54. See also *First Fed.,* 110 F.R.D. at 567 (applying Rule 1.6 standard). The Court has made an *in camera* review of the self defense materials and finds that their disclosure is reasonably necessary, i.e., "as a practical matter, [the materials] seem likely to provide significant assistance to [the attorney's] defense." Id. The same standard applies to deposition testimony by members of LBB. Id.

In this regard, the Court rejects the suggestion made by some parties that "selective" disclosure should not be allowed, that if the exception is permitted to be invoked, *all* attorney-client communications should be disclosed. This suggestion is rejected as directly contrary to the reasonable necessity standard. The Court does agree that in order to avoid unfairness, all previously withheld communications which concern the same discrete subject matter (narrowly construed) as to which the self defense exception is invoked, should be disclosed. See *First Fed.,* id. at 567 ("all documents pertaining to the communications at issue"); cf. Weil v. Investment/Indicators, Research and Management, Inc., 647 F.2d 18, 24 (9th Cir. 1981) (voluntary waiver of attorney-client privilege of a "communication" "constitutes waiver of the privilege as to all other such communications on the subject" [citations omitted]). LBB has represented that the group of documents to be disclosed under the self defense exception meets this criterion and the Court has no reason to take that representation at less than face value.

Finally, the Comment to Model Rule 1.6 indicates that, because disclosure should be no greater than necessary, "appropriate protective orders . . . should be sought by the lawyer to the fullest extent practicable." The Court agrees with this suggestion. Therefore, an appropriate protective order shall issue limiting access to these materials to counsel for parties in the "Northern District" cases only. See *NMEC I,* 636 F. Supp. at 1143 n.2. Because LBB has, at least tentatively, settled with the Bank of America, see *NMEC III,* 116 F.R.D. at 299 n.2, no self defense disclosure is sought or is necessary in the Bank of American action.

It is ordered:

1. Pursuant to the self defense exception to the attorney-client privilege, LBB may disclose to all counsel of record in the Northern District cases, otherwise confidential attorney-client communication which LBB deems reasonably necessary to defend against said actions.

2. Disclosure of any attorney-client communication in self defense shall require that all such communications concerning the same discrete subject matter be disclosed.

3. All counsel to whom any disclosure is made pursuant to this order shall hold such disclosures (both documentary and testimonial) in

confidence and not disclose the same to any third-person, including their clients, except:

(a) As and only to the extent necessary in the prosecution of any claim or in defense thereof in any of the Northern District cases.
(b) Any person to whom disclosure is made shall be informed of this protective order and advised that he or she is bound by its terms.

4. Except to the limited extent granted above, NMEC's motion for a protective order is denied.

People v. Mitchell
448 N.E.2d 121 (N.Y. 1983)

SIMONS, Judge.

Defendant has been convicted after a jury trial of murder, second degree, for the stabbing death of a prostitute named O'Hare McMillon. He contends that his conviction must be reversed because it rests on evidence of privileged statements he made in his lawyer's office and statements improperly solicited by a police guard while he was in custody, and because the court's charge to the jury violated the rule in Sandstrom v. Montana, 442 U.S. 510, 99 S. Ct. 2450, 61 L. Ed. 2d 39. The Appellate Division affirmed the judgment by a divided court. The majority agreed with the trial court that defendant's statements made in the lawyer's office were not privileged and that his statements to the jail guard were spontaneous. It held that the court's charge though erroneous was harmless (People v. Mitchell, 86 A.D.2d 976, 448 N.Y.S.2d 352). The dissenter at the Appellate Division voted to reverse on the *Sandstrom* issue and to conduct a hearing on the question of privilege. There should be an affirmance.

Defendant was a resident of Waterloo, New York, and, at the time these events occurred, he was under indictment for causing the stabbing death of his girlfriend, Audrey Miller, in February, 1976. He was represented on that charge by Rochester attorney Felix Lapine. In January, 1977 defendant went to Rochester to take care of some personal matters and registered at the Cadillac Hotel. On the evening of January 5 while sitting at the hotel bar, he met O'Hare McMillon. They had two or three highballs and then were seen to leave the bar about 11:00 P.M. and take the elevator to the floor on which Mitchell's room was located. No one saw either of them leave defendant's room that night or the next morning, but in the afternoon of January 6, on a tip from attorney Lapine, the police went to defendant's hotel room and found the partially clad dead body of O'Hare McMillon on the bed. She had been stabbed 11-12 times in the face, chest and back. At least four of the wounds were sufficient to cause her death by exsanguination.

After leaving the hotel room that morning, defendant went to attorney Lapine's office. Lapine was not in but defendant met and spoke to a legal secretary, Molly Altman, in the reception area. She testified that he seemed nervous and as if he was looking for someone. Apparently he could not find whomever it was he was looking for so he left only to return a minute later and start telling her about what happened the night before. She testified that he said: "he wanted to go out and have a last fling . . . he had been out drinking and met a girl and then he woke up in the morning and she was dead. He had stayed there all night and then he walked out again."

While he was talking to Ms. Altman, Judith Peacock, another legal secretary, entered the reception area. She testified that defendant was kind of rambling on but he said that: "he had laid next to someone all night and they didn't move, and he [was] in a bar and . . . in a hotel . . . this person who he had laid next to was black and he was worried because when the black people found out about it, they protect their own and he would be in danger." She also testified that he muttered something about a knife.

Ms. Pope-Johnson entered the room. She asked defendant what was wrong and he told her: "that there was a dead body and he felt that he had done it and that the person was dead, that she was dead because of being stabbed."

Shortly thereafter, Lapine entered the office and talked privately with defendant. After defendant left Lapine called the police and had them check defendant's hotel room. The body was discovered, defendant's identification learned from the hotel registration and defendant found and arrested at a bar near the courthouse.

At the police station while defendant was waiting to be processed, he was placed in a room and guarded by a Sergeant Page. He had been given his *Miranda* rights, and attorney Lapine had visited him privately and advised the police not to interrogate his client. It was Page's testimony, credited by the trial court and the Appellate Division, that defendant, while so guarded, spontaneously asked Page if the police had found the knife and then stated: "I must have killed her like I did Audrey and I don't remember that either." "I picked her up in a bar last night." At trial the statements were redacted to eliminate the reference to Audrey and received by the court as spontaneous statements. That finding of fact was supported by the evidence (see People v. Lynes, 49 N.Y.2d 286, 294, 425 N.Y.S.2d 295, 401 N.E.2d 405; cf. People v. Lanahan, 55 N.Y.2d 711, 447 N.Y.S.2d 139, 431 N.E.2d 624). Molly Altman, Judy Peacock and Robin Pope-Johnson also testified at trial about defendant's inculpatory statements made in the law office after the court determined that the statements were not privileged.

I

The attorney-client privilege, developed at common law, is now contained in our statute (CPLR 4503, subd. [a]). Its purpose is to ensure that one seeking legal advice will be able to confide fully and freely in his attorney, secure in the knowledge that his confidence will not later be revealed to the public to his detriment or his embarrassment. The court recently formulated the elements of the privilege as follows:

First, it is beyond dispute that no attorney-client privilege arises unless an attorney-client relationship has been established. Such a relationship arises only when one contacts an attorney in his capacity as such for the purpose of obtaining legal advice or services. (CPLR 4503, subd [a]; see, e.g., People v. Belge, 59 A.D.2d 307, 309, 399 N.Y.S.2d 539; United States v. United Shoe Mach. Corp., 89 F. Supp. 357, 358-359; 8 Wigmore, §2292.) Second, not all communications to an attorney are privileged. In order to make a valid claim of privilege, it must be shown that the information sought to be protected from disclosure was a "confidential communication" made to the attorney for the purpose of obtaining legal advice or services. (Matter of Jacqueline F., 47 N.Y.2d 215, 219, 417 N.Y.S.2d 884, 391 N.E.2d 967; People ex rel. Vogelstein v. Warden of County Jail of County of N.Y., 150 Misc. 714, 717-718, 270 N.Y.S. 362; 8 Wigmore §2292.) Third, the burden of proving each element of the privilege rests upon the party asserting it. (Matter of Gavin, 39 A.D.2d 626, 628, 331 N.Y.S.2d 188; Matter of Grand Jury Empanelled Feb. 14, 1978, (3 Cir.), 603 F.2d 469, 474.) Finally, even where the technical requirements of the privilege are satisfied, it may, nonetheless, yield in a proper case, where strong public policy requires disclosure. (Matter of Jacqueline F., 47 N.Y.2d 215, 417 N.Y.S.2d 884, 391 N.E.2d 967, supra; People ex rel. Vogelstein v. Warden of County Jail of County of N.Y., 150 Misc. 714, 270 N.Y.S. 362, supra.)

(Matter of Priest v. Hennessy, 51 N.Y.2d 62, 68-69, 431 N.Y.S.2d 511, 409 N.E.2d 983.)

Defendant sought to foreclose the testimony of Pope-Johnson, Altman and Peacock, contending that because of Lapine's prior retainer by defendant for the homicide of his girlfriend there was an ongoing attorney-client relationship which made any statements of defendant uttered in Lapine's office or waiting room privileged. The court excused the jury and conducted a *voir dire* of Mr. Lapine and Robin Pope-Johnson, Lapine's paralegal, correctly ruling that defendant bore the burden of establishing that his statements were privileged. . . .

On this state of the record, we conclude that defendant has not met his burden of establishing that when he spoke to these unknown women in a common reception area, his statements were intended to be confidential and made to an employee of his attorney for the purpose of obtaining legal advice. The only evidence identifying the women came from Lapine who responded to a question whether he had "any female employees" by saying "Yes, Robin Pope-Johnson." She, it turns out, was the last woman in the office to hear defendant's inculpatory statements and even if statements made to her at the time could have been privileged, the privilege was lost because of the prior publication to nonemployees and the utterance of the statements to Pope-Johnson in front of the nonemployees (see People v. Buchanan, 145 N.Y. 1, 26, 39 N.E. 846; People v. Belge, 59 A.D.2d 307, 309, 399 N.Y.S.2d 539). Taking this view we need not consider whether the statements could be privileged because of an ongoing retainer between defendant and Lapine or if they could be privileged if made to the attorney's employee before a formal retainer was agreed upon. . . .

Accordingly, the order of the Appellate Division should be affirmed.

Cooke, C.J., and Jasen, Jones, Wachtler, Fuchsberg and Meyer, JJ., concur.

Order affirmed.

EXERCISES

1. Discuss what you believe to be the most important types of nonverbal communication and indicate why.
2. Discuss why the attorney-client privilege is an important legal right.
3. Discuss why image is important to the business of a law office.
4. Develop a "client manual" in which you indicate appropriate methods of maintaining office-client relationships.
5. Discuss why all members of the legal team are ambassadors for the law office.
6. Discuss some of the ramifications that could result from a breach of confidentiality.
7. Indicate various methods by which an office can present a specific image to the public.
8. Discuss the importance of emphatic listening to effective representation of a client.
9. Indicate some nonverbal body language that would detract from effective communication or would present a negative image.
10. Discuss why verbal skills are important for all members of the legal team.

SITUATIONAL ANALYSIS

An attorney in the law office is unusually overweight and tends to favor very vibrant colors in her clothing. She also wears a lot of makeup. The law office is a very old and established firm, and its clients are very conservative. Several clients have commented negatively on the attorney's appearance and have indicated that they do not believe that she can effectively represent their interests because of her appearance. The partners in the firm feel that the attorney's work is good and that she has potential, but are worried about losing business or being sued for unlawful discrimination. What avenues of approach can the partners take in order to rectify the situation?

4 Law Office Billing

Billing is a real pain. . . . A lot of my work involves representing indigent criminals as court appointed counsel, and I get paid by the court by submitting payment vouchers. The vouchers have to be submitted within 60 days of the final disposition of the case, and it's hard to find the time to prepare the vouchers. The vouchers can take 2 to 4 hours to complete (which is non-billable time), and when I'm busy it can become a question of doing legal work or doing billing. If I don't get the vouchers in by the due date, it's up to the discretion of the judge as to whether I get paid at all.

Carol Himmelfarb-Parker
Sole Practitioner
Washington, D.C.

CHAPTER OVERVIEW

The fundamental financial requirement of every business, law offices included, is to generate income. Simply performing the services is not enough; the clients must be billed for the work performed.

The concept of billing may appear at first glance to be fairly straight-forward, but in fact there are several types of different billing arrangements that all law firms may utilize, and the determination as to which method is most appropriate for each client is only the first step in the law office's billing process. Once the proper billing method has been agreed on with the client, the office must allocate all of its expenses between those that may be directly billed to the client and those items that represent **overhead**—general office operations—that are not separately billable but must be considered in determining the appropriate amount of the fee. Overhead is the law office's own expenses that must be met before any profit can be made.

In order to keep track of all costs incident to performing its legal services, the office must maintain strict control over the timekeeping records of its legal team. In terms of law office billing, time is money and records must be maintained indicating all time spent on each client's problems.

Once the fee has been determined and established, the office must create procedures for sending bills to clients and for keeping track of all money actually paid or amounts still **outstanding**—that is, billed but unpaid. No business can exist if its clients or customers do not pay for work performed.

In addition to the foregoing, a law office, unlike other forms of business, has certain ethical considerations that must be taken into account when establishing and determining fees. Under the American Bar Association's Model Rule of Professional Conduct 5.4(a) a lawyer may not share a legal fee. Sharing a legal fee is known as **fee splitting.** This means that a lawyer may only bill for legal work actually performed and may not pay or receive a fee simply for recommending a client to another attorney. An attorney is also prohibited from sharing a legal fee with a nonlawyer, such as an accountant or doctor, who may refer a client to the law office. Legal fees may only be received for legal work performed.

 EXAMPLE:

A lawyer who specializes in litigation has a client who wants to incorporate a business. The lawyer recommends a second lawyer to the client. When the second lawyer accepts the client, he or she is prohibited from paying the first attorney a fee; the first attorney merely made a recommendation but performed no legal work.

Rule 5.4(d) of the Model Rules of Professional Conduct also prohibits a professional corporation of attorneys from admitting nonlawyers as shareholders because this too would be considered sharing a fee. However, several jurisdictions do permit persons licensed in different professions to incorporate together as a professional corporation. In these states problems may arise between the corporate statute and the ethical rules.

This chapter will focus on all of the problems incident to establishing an appropriate fee, keeping track of time, and keeping the client informed of all expenses.

Types of Fees

Prior to determining which method of billing is most appropriate for a particular client, the entire spectrum of potential fee arrangements must be understood. There are six primary types of fees:

1. retainer
2. contingency fee
3. flat or fixed fee
4. hourly fee
5. court-awarded fee
6. prepaid legal services

Retainer

A retainer is probably the most traditional method of billing clients and represents money paid at the beginning of the attorney's legal representation of the client. Retainers fall under two classifications: those that are unearned and those that are earned. An **unearned retainer** is a sum of money that the client gives to the attorney that is then placed into a trust account. As the attorney performs work for the client, the attorney bills the client and withdraws the appropriate amount from the trust account. This type of unearned retainer is known as a **cash advance retainer** and represents money paid by the client against future billing. It is considered unearned because the attorney only has the right to the funds once the legal work is performed. With this type of billing the attorney is guaranteed that there will be funds available for the work that he or she performs.

 EXAMPLE:

A client gives an attorney a cash advance retainer of $2,000 as payment against litigation expenses. The attorney places this amount in a trust account, and at the end of the first month the attorney bills the client for $500 for work performed and then withdraws $500 from the trust account. The case is settled during the second month, and the attorney's work for the second month is billed at $300. The attorney withdraws $300 from the trust account, and $1,200 is returned to the client.

An **earned retainer** is a retainer that belongs to the attorney at the moment of payment by the client. The funds are immediately available for use by the law office, and no trust account need be established. There are three types of earned retainers:

1. pure retainer
2. case retainer
3. retainer for general representation

Pure Retainer

A pure retainer is a sum of money paid by a client to a lawyer or law office to ensure that the attorney will be available to the client throughout the year, and that the office will not accept any client whose interests are adverse to those of the client who paid the retainer. It is a method of ensuring the availability of legal representation.

EXAMPLE:

A very wealthy client is involved in a multiplicity of legal problems. In order to ensure that the law office will be available to represent the client when the need arises, the client pays the law office a $10,000 pure retainer for one year. This money immediately belongs to the office, and the client will be billed separately for legal work actually performed. The retainer guarantees the office's availability to the client.

Case Retainer

A case retainer is a nonrefundable fee that a client pays to a law office as an inducement to perform legal work for the client. This type of retainer is a "bonus" paid to convince the office to accept the client.

EXAMPLE:

A member of a terrorist group is being sued and is having difficulty finding legal counsel. In order to induce a particular attorney to represent him, the terrorist pays the attorney a case retainer. The retainer immediately belongs to the attorney and is not dependent on the work eventually performed.

Retainer for General Representation

A retainer for general representation is a retainer paid in contemplation of all ongoing representation except for actual litigation. Many corporate clients use the retainer for general representation in order to avail themselves of the constant services of a particular law firm. The office's billable time is offset by the retainer, but the money belongs to the office immediately upon payment.

EXAMPLE:

A corporate client pays the law office a retainer of $5,000 per month for general representation. This money immediately belongs to the office. Even if the work the office performs during the month is only equal to $3,000 in fees, the full $5,000 remains with the firm. The next month the client pays another $5,000 for general representation.

The determination as to whether a retainer is unearned or earned depends on the wording of the contract that exists between the law office and the client. All lawyers are required to establish their fee arrangements with their clients in writing in order to protect the client, and the writing becomes the representation contract between the parties. As a consequence, dependent on the specific language, any of the above-discussed earned retainers may be considered unearned. The reasons for the retainer remain the same but the availability of the funds for use by the law office may vary.

Contingency Fee

A contingency fee is a method of payment in which the attorney's fee is a percentage of the ultimate award granted to the client. If the client loses, the attorney receives no fee. The plaintiffs in most personal injury cases hire lawyers under a contingency fee arrangement.

Under Model Rule 1.5(c) all contingency fee agreements must be in writing. A contingency fee agreement does not cover actual expenses, such as court costs, transcription fees, and filing fees, and the client is responsible for these costs. Generally the attorney will advance these costs against the ultimate outcome, but if the client loses, the client is still responsible for these expenses. Additionally, states place maximum percentages on the amount of the contingency fee. The written contingency agreement alerts the client to these guidelines.

Rule 1.5(d) prohibits contingency fee arrangements in criminal or domestic relation matters.

EXAMPLE:

The law office enters into a contingency fee agreement with a client in a personal injury case. The agreement states that the office will be entitled to one-third of any amount awarded to the client, plus actual expenses. The case is settled for $20,000. The law office has advanced $3,444 in court fees, stenographer fees, postage, and so on. The law office will receive $10,000 and the client will receive $10,000 under the agreement.

A selection of retainer forms follows. The first agreement represents the personal injury case in the preceding example.

Exhibit 1: Contingency Fee Agreement

The Undersigned, residing at _____, hereby retains _____, having offices at _____, to represent the Undersigned in a claim arising from _____

_____

on the ____ day of ____, 199__ against _____. The Undersigned hereby gives _____ the exclusive right to take all legal steps to enforce the said claim and hereby further agrees not to settle this action in any manner without _____'s written consent.

In consideration of the legal services rendered and to be rendered, the Undersigned hereby agrees to pay and hereby authorizes _____ to retain out of any moneys that may come into hand by reason of the above claim Thirty-three and one-third (33⅓) percent of the sum recovered, whether recovered by suit, settlement or otherwise.

Such percentage shall be computed on the net sum recovered after deducting from the amount recovered expenses and disbursements for expert testimony and investigative or other services properly chargeable to the enforcement of the claim or prosecution of the action. In computing the fee, the cost as taxed, including interest upon a judgment, shall be deemed part of the amount recovered. For the following or similar items there shall be no deduction in computing such percentages: liens, assignments or claims in favor of hospitals, or for medical care and treatment by doctors and nurses.

Exhibit 2: Contingency Fee Agreement
(Straight Percentage)

T 540—Contingent retainer straight 33-⅓ percent—
1st and 2nd Dept., App. Div. 3-93

JULIUS BLUMBERG, INC.
PUBLISHER, NYC 10013

To .... **Retainer**

....

.... , Attorney

The undersigned, Client, residing at ....

hereby retains you to prosecute or adjust a claim for damages arising from—

personal injuries sustained by   ....

....

loss of services of ....

property damage to ....

on ....19...........through the negligence of ....

... .

or other persons.

The Client hereby gives you the exclusive right to take all legal steps to enforce this claim through trial and appeal. The attorney shall have the right but not the obligation to represent the client on appeal.

In consideration of the services rendered and to be rendered by you, the Client agrees to pay you and you are authorized to retain out of any moneys that may come into your hand by reason of the above claim:

Thirty three and one-third percent ($33\frac{1}{3}\%$) of the sum recovered, whether recovered by suit, settlement or otherwise.

Such percentage shall be computed on the net sum recovered after deducting from the amount recovered expenses and disbursements for expert testimony and investigative or other services properly chargeable to the enforcement of the claim or prosecution of the action. In computing the fee, the costs as taxed, including interest upon a judgment, shall be deemed part of the amount recovered. For the following or similar items there shall be no deduction in computing such percentages: liens, assignments or claims in favor of hospitals, for medical care and treatment by doctors and nurses, or self-insurers or insurance carriers.

If the cause of action is settled by Client without the consent of Attorney, Client agrees to pay Attorney the above percentage of the full amount of the settlement for the benefit of Client, to whomever paid or whatever called. The attorney shall have, in the alternative, the option of seeking compensation on a *quantum meruit* basis to be determined by the court. In such circumstances the court would determine the fair value of the service. Attorney shall have, in addition, Attorney's taxable costs and disbursements. In the event the Client is represented on appeal by another attorney, Attorney shall have the option of seeking compensation on a *quantum meruit* basis to be determined by the court.

Client

Dated..................... .... 19........... .... (L.S.)
Signature - Print name beneath

Witness. . .   .. (L.S.)
Signature - Print name beneath

Forms may be purchased from Julius Blumberg, Inc., NYC 10013, or any of its dealers. Reproduction prohibited.

Exhibit 3: Contingency Fee Agreement (Sliding Scale)

To...   **Retainer**

....

.... , Attorney

The undersigned, Client, residing at   ....

hereby retains you to prosecute or adjust a claim for damages arising from

personal injuries sustained by

....

loss of services of   ....

property damage to   ....

on ....19.........through the negligence of...........................

....

or other persons.

The Client hereby gives you the exclusive right to take all legal steps to enforce this claim through trial and appeal. The attorney shall have the right but not the obligation to represent the client on appeal.

In consideration of the services rendered and to be rendered by you, the undersigned agrees to pay you and you are authorized to retain out of any moneys that may come into your hand by reason of the above claim:
(A) Fifty per cent on the first one thousand dollars of the sum recovered,
(B) Forty per cent on the next two thousand dollars of the sum recovered,
(C) Thirty-five per cent on the next twenty-two thousand dollars of the sum recovered.
(D) Twenty-five per cent on any amount over twenty-five thousand dollars of the sum recovered; whether recovered by suit, settlement, or otherwise.

Such percentage shall be computed on the net sum recovered after deducting from the amount recovered expenses and disbursements for expert testimony and investigative or other services properly chargeable to the enforcement of the claim or prosecution of the action. In computing the fee, the costs as taxed, including interest upon a judgment, shall be deemed part of the amount recovered. For the following or similar items there shall be no deduction in computing such percentages: liens, assignments or claims in favor of hospitals, for medical care and treatment by doctors and nurses, or self-insurers or insurance carriers.

In the event extraordinary services are required you may apply to the court for greater compensation pursuant to the Special Rules of the Appellate Division regulating the conduct of attorneys.

If the cause of action is settled by Client without the consent of Attorney, Client agrees to pay Attorney the above percentage of the full amount of the settlement for the benefit of Client, to whomever paid or whatever called. The attorney shall have, in the alternative, the option of seeking compensation on a *quantum meruit* basis to be determined by the court. In such circumstances the court would determine the fair value of the service. Attorney shall have, in addition, Attorney's taxable costs and disbursements. In the event the Client is represented on appeal by another attorney, Attorney shall have the option of seeking compensation on a *quantum meruit* basis to be determined by the court.

Client

Dated   ....19.........

                                                        Signature - Print name beneath   (L.S.)

Witness   ....

                                                        Signature - Print name beneath   (L.S.)

Forms may be purchased from Julius Blumberg, Inc., NYC 10013, or any of its dealers. Reproduction prohibited.

Exhibit 4: Retainer Agreement
(Medical or Dental Malpractice)

To ....   **Retainer**

....

.... , Attorney

The undersigned, Client, residing at ....
hereby retains you to prosecute or adjust a claim for damages arising from

personal injuries sustained by ....

....

loss of services of ....

property damage to ....

on ....19..........through the negligence of..

....
or other persons.

The Client hereby gives you the exclusive right to take all legal steps to enforce this claim through trial and appeal. The attorney shall have the right but not the obligation to represent the client on appeal.

In consideration of the services rendered and to be rendered by you, the undersigned agrees to pay you and you are authorized to retain out of any moneys that may come into your hand by reason of the above claim:
(i)   30 percent on the first $250,000 of the sum recovered,
(ii)   25 percent on the next $250,000 of the sum recovered,
(iii)   20 percent on the next $500,000 of the sum recovered,
(iv)   15 percent on the next $250,000 of the sum recovered,
(v)   10 percent on any amount over $1,250,000 of the sum recovered; or,

Such percentage shall be computed on the net sum recovered after deducting from the amount recovered expenses and disbursements for expert testimony and investigative or other services properly chargeable to the enforcement of the claim or prosecution of the action. In computing the fee, the costs as taxed, including interest upon a judgment, shall be deemed part of the amount recovered. For the following or similar items there shall be no deduction in computing such percentages: liens, assignments or claims in favor of hospitals, for medical care and treatment by doctors and nurses, or self-insurers or insurance carriers.

In the event extraordinary services are required you may apply to the court for greater compensation pursuant to the Special Rules of the Appellate Division regulating the conduct of attorneys.

If the cause of action is settled by Client without the consent of Attorney, Client agrees to pay Attorney the above percentage of the full amount of the settlement for the benefit of Client, to whomever paid or whatever called. The attorney shall have, in the alternative, the option of seeking compensation on a *quantum meruit* basis to be determined by the court. In such circumstances the court would determine the fair value of the service. Attorney shall have, in addition, Attorney's taxable costs and disbursements. In the event the Client is represented on appeal by another attorney, Attorney shall have the option of seeking compensation on a *quantum meruit* basis to be determined by the court.

Client

Dated.. 19..........   ....(L.S.)
                                                 Signature - Print name beneath

Witness..   ....(L.S.)
                                                 Signature - Print name beneath

Forms may be purchased from Julius Blumberg, Inc., NYC 10013, or any of its dealers. Reproduction prohibited.

Exhibit 5: Retainer Agreement (Matrimonial Action)

 A 455—Retainer Agreement, Matrimonial Rules, based upon clauses approved by N.Y. Chapter of American Academy of Matrimonial Lawyers and Family Law Section of N.Y.S Bar Association. 12-93.

JULIUS BLUMBERG, INC.,
PUBLISHER, NYC 10013

RETAINER AGREEMENT

1. Names and Addresses of parties entering into agreement.
THIS AGREEMENT FOR LEGAL SERVICES by and between

(you, the Client), and

(the Law Firm)
constitutes a binding legal contract and should be reviewed carefully.

2. Nature of the services to be rendered.
(a) This Retainer Agreement confirms that you have retained this firm as your attorneys to represent you in negotiating an agreement with your husband/wife, if that is reasonably possible; or, if not, to represent you in a matrimonial action.

(b) It is further understood that: (1) The retainer fee does not include any services rendered in Appellate Courts or any actions or proceedings other than the action for which this office has been retained; (2) With respect to the matter which is specified above, this Retainer Agreement and any sums paid to this firm pursuant hereto, do not cover any services relative to any appeal or any other services which might be required following the entry of a final judgment or order, including but not limited to such matters as enforcement or modification. Our representation shall terminate with the entry of final judgment in your matter, unless extended by mutual agreement between us in writing.

(c) The Client authorizes the Law Firm to take any steps which, in the sole discretion of the firm, are deemed necessary or appropriate to protect the Client's interest in the matter.

3. Amount of the advance retainer, if any, and what it is intended to cover.
(a) In order for us to begin our representation you have agreed to pay us and we have agreed to accept a retainer payment of $. This retainer payment does not necessarily represent the amount of the overall fee which you may incur by virtue of our services. The amount of our eventual fee will be based upon our regular schedule of established hourly time charges, along with any out-of-pocket disbursements (such as court costs, messenger services, transcripts of proceedings, long distance telephone calls, telefaxes, process service fees, mileage, deposition and court transcripts, and excess postage) which are incurred in your behalf.

(b) The Client further understands that the hourly rates apply to all time expended relative to the Client's matter including but not limited to, office meetings and conferences, telephone calls and conferences, either placed by or placed to the client, or otherwise made or had on the Client's behalf or related to the Client's matter, preparation, review and revision of correspondence, pleadings, motions, disclosure demands and responses, affidavits and affirmations, or any other documents, memoranda, or papers relative to the Client's matter, legal research, court appearances, conferences, file review, preparation time, travel time, and any other time expended on behalf of or in connection with the Client's matter.

4. The circumstances under which any portion of the advance retainer may be refunded. Should the attorney withdraw from the case or be discharged prior to the depletion of the advance retainer, the written retainer agreement shall provide how the attorney's fees and expenses are to be determined, and the remainder of the advance retainer shall be refunded to the client.
(a) In the event that we obtain a disposition of your matrimonial matter, either by way of a settlement agreement (termed separation agreement or stipulation of settlement) or by judgment by the court of the issues involved in your case, the aforementioned retainer fee [or the sum of $] shall also be the minimum fee charged to you, i.e., there will be no refund of the retainer fee [or the sum of $]. However, notwithstanding the above, if you discontinue our services prior to a disposition of your matter by agreement or judgment of the court, or if this firm is relieved as your attorneys by court order, any unearned portion of the retainer fee you advanced to this firm shall be refunded to you.

An example of how the minimum fee operates is as follows: If the Law Firm resolves the matter with the expenditure of only 4 hours of time by a partner, and 6 hours of time expended by an associate attorney, there would be no refund to the client even though the time charges add up to less than the minimum fee.

Notwithstanding the above, if the attorney-client relationship is terminated without your matter having been concluded, e.g., if you and your spouse were to reconcile and the action was discontinued, or if you were to discharge the Law Firm as your attorneys, or if the Law Firm were to withdraw its representation, a fair and reasonable fee would be determined in accordance with legally accepted standards. At present, the legally recognized elements of a reasonable fee, as set forth in the Code of Professional Responsibility, are as follows:
• The time and labor required, the novelty and difficulty of the questions involved and the skill requisite to perform the legal services properly.
• The likelihood, if apparent or made known to the client, that the acceptance of the particular employment will preclude other employment by the lawyer. (You should know that the Law Firm, by accepting retention as your attorney, is clearly precluded from representing the opposing party against you.)

Exhibit 5: *(continued)*

- The fee customarily charged in the locality for similar legal services.
- The amount involved and the results obtained.
- The time limitations imposed by the client or by circumstances.
- The nature and length of the professional relationship with the client.
- The experience, reputation and ability of the lawyer or lawyers performing the services.
- Whether the fee is fixed or contingent. (You should know that the Code of Professional Responsibility provides: "A lawyer shall not enter into an arrangement for, charge or collect...[a]ny fee in a domestic relations matter, the payment or amount of which in contingent upon the securing of a divorce or upon the amount of maintenance, support, equitable distribution, or property settlement...")

5. The client's right to cancel the agreement at any time; how the attorney's fee will be determined and paid should the client discharge the attorney at any time during the representation.

(a) You have the absolute right to cancel this Retainer Agreement at any time. Should you exercise this right, you will be charged only the fee expenses (time charges and disbursements) incurred within that period, based upon the hourly rates set forth in this Retainer Agreement, and the balance of the retainer fee, if any, will be promptly refunded to you.

6. How the attorney will be paid through the conclusion of the case after the retainer is depleted; whether the client will be asked to pay another lump sum.

(a) You agree to pay us such additional fees and to reimburse us for our advances on your behalf that may be due from time to time not later than   days from the date that we shall submit a bill to you for same. If an amount due to us is not paid within   days after our statement to you of the amount due, interest at the rate of   % per annum (or interest at the prevailing statutory rate as set forth in the Civil Practice Law and Rules) shall be added to the balance due to us.

7. The hourly rate of each person whose time may be charged to the client; any out-of-pocket disbursements for which the client will be required to reimburse the attorney. Any changes in such rates or fees shall be incorporated into a written agreement constituting an amendment to the original agreement, which must be signed by the client before it may take effect.

(a) The retainer fee shall be credited toward an hourly rate of $ per hour for time I expend; $ per hour for time other partners expend; $ per hour for time expended by associates in this office, and $ per hour for the time expended by paralegals in this office.

(b) In addition to the foregoing, your responsibility will include direct payment or reimbursement of this firm for disbursements advanced on your behalf, the same to include, but not necessarily be limited to, court filing fees, recording fees, charges of process servers, travel expenses, copying costs, messenger services, necessary secretarial overtime, transcripts and the customary fees of stenographers referable to examinations before trial in the event such examinations are utilized.

(c) The hourly rates set forth in this Retainer Agreement will remain in effect throughout the period of our representation for the matter set forth in this Retainer Agreement, unless changed by mutual consent of you and our firm, in which event any modification of the hourly rates shall be reduced to writing and signed by you and the Law Firm.

8. Any clause providing for a fee in addition to the agreed-upon rate, such as a reasonable minimum fee clause, must be defined in plain language and set forth the circumstances under which such fee may be incurred and how it will be calculated.

[SEE CLAUSES UNDER NO. 4, supra]

9. Frequency of itemized billing, which shall be at least every 60 days; the client may not be charged for time spent in discussion of the bills received.

You will be billed periodically, generally each month but in no event less frequently than every 60 days. Included in the billing will be a detailed explanation of the services rendered, by whom rendered, and the disbursements incurred by our firm in connection with your matter. Upon receipt of our bill, you are expected to review the bill and promptly bring to our attention any objections you may have to the bill. While we strive to keep perfectly accurate time records, we recognize the possibility of human error, and we shall discuss with you any objections you raise to our bill. You will not be charged for time expended in discussing with us any aspect of the bill rendered to you.

10. Client's right to be provided with copies of correspondence and documents relating to the case, and to be kept apprised of the status of the case.

(a) We shall keep you informed of the status of your case, and agree to explain the laws pertinent to your situation, the available course of action, and the attendant risks. We shall notify you promptly of any developments in your case, including court appearances, and will be available for meetings and telephone conversations with you at mutually convenient times. We do insist that appointments be made for personal visits to our offices. Copies of all papers will be supplied to you as they are prepared (unless you request to the contrary), and you will be billed a reasonable photocopy charge (at present,   cents per page) for these materials which will be included in your periodic billing.

11. Whether and under what circumstances the attorney might seek a security interest from the client, which can be obtained only upon court approval and on notice to the adversary.

Exhibit 5: *(continued)*

(a) While we expect to be paid the fees due us in timely fashion, in situations where the Client does not have funds readily available to pay additional fees as they accrue, we may, as an accommodation, agree to take a security interest in property in lieu of immediate payment. A security interest may take the form of a confession of judgment, promissory note, or mortgage upon specified property. In either event, a lien will attach to your property. In the case of your marital residence, any such security interest shall be nonforeclosable, i.e., we shall not force a sale of your home but would be paid at the time you sell the premises. You are advised that any such security interest can be granted to us only with the permission of the justice assigned to your case upon an application on notice to the opposing party, and after an application has been made for your spouse to pay the outstanding fees.

(b) In the event such application for payment of counsel fees by your spouse and a security interest for the fees due this firm is made to the Court, the Client agrees to cooperate in connection with such application and to consent to the relief being requested from the Court. Failure on the part of the Client to so cooperate and consent shall be deemed as a basis for withdrawal by the Law Firm from representation of the client.

12. Under what circumstances the attorney might seek to withdraw from the case for nonpayment of fees, and the attorney's right to seek a charging lien from the court.

(a) You are advised that if, in the judgment of this firm, we decide that there has been an irretrievable breakdown in the attorney-client relationship, or a material breach of the terms of this Retainer Agreement, we may decide to make application to the court in which your action is pending to be relieved as your attorneys. In such event, you will be provided with notice of the application and an opportunity to be heard. Should any fees be due and owing to this firm at the time of our discharge, we shall have the right, in addition to any other remedy, to seek a charging lien, i.e., a lien upon the property that is awarded to you as a result of equitable distribution in the final order or judgment in your case. No such lien may attach to maintenance or child support payments.

(b) In the event that any bill from the Law Firm remains unpaid beyond a _____ day period, the Client agrees that the Law Firm may withdraw its representation, at the option of the firm. In the event that an action is pending, and absent your consent, an application must be made to the Court for such withdrawal. Where the fee is unpaid for the period set forth above, the Client acknowledges that in connection with any such withdrawal application, that the account delinquency shall be good cause for withdrawal.

13. Should a dispute arise concerning the attorney's fee, the client may seek arbitration, which is binding upon

both attorney and client; the attorney shall provide information concerning fee arbitration in the event of such dispute or upon the client's request.

While we seek to avoid any fee disputes with our clients, and rarely have such disputes, in the event such a dispute does arise, you are advised that you have the right, at your election, to seek arbitration to resolve the fee dispute. In such event, we shall advise you in writing by certified mail that you have 30 days from receipt of such notice in which to elect to resolve the dispute by arbitration, and we shall enclose a copy of the arbitration rules and a form for requesting arbitration. The decision resulting from arbitration is binding upon both you and the Law Firm.

ADDITIONAL DISCRETIONARY PROVISIONS

1. Application for Fees.

(a) Under prevailing law, an application may be made to the court in which your action is pending, either prior to trial or at the trial, for your spouse to pay all or part of your legal expenses incurred and/or to be incurred in this matter. There is no certainty that any such recovery may actually occur, as the application rests in the discretion of the court. In the event such an award of fees is made and collected, the amount collected shall be credited to your bill. At the end of your case (i.e. a final judgment in the matrimonial action) any amount collected that exceeds your billing will be refunded to you. Conversely, you shall remain liable for any balance due to us after crediting any amount collected from your spouse.

2. Appeal (flat fee).

(a) This Retainer Agreement confirms that you have retained this firm to prosecute an appeal to the Appellate Division, Judicial Department, from the judgment (order) granted by Justice of the Supreme Court, _____ County, dated _____

(b) Our fee for legal services on this appeal to the Appellate Division is $ _____ , payable upon your signing of this Retainer Agreement. Disbursements are in addition to the above-mentioned fee and include, but are not limited to, an appellate filing fee of $ _____ ,the cost of obtaining trial transcripts, an appellate printer, process servers, messenger service, transportation and photocopies. Disbursements will be billed to you periodically as they are incurred.

(c) The above fee covers only this one appeal to the Appellate Division and not other or further appeals. No motions in any court or any other proceedings are included in the fee.

(d) You understand that your (former) spouse may cross-appeal from all or any part of the judgment (order) of the Supreme Court from which (s)he feels aggrieved. (S)he may also make a claim against you for legal services and expenses in connection with the appeal.

3. Retention of Experts.

(a) This Law Firm may engage, on your behalf, and with your prior consent, the services of an accountant in connection with an examination of the financial circumstances attendant upon your matrimonial action or proceeding. In addition, such other professionals may be utilized as may be required, with your prior consent, including, but not limited to, real estate appraisers and investigators.

Exhibit 5: *(continued)*

With regard to the charges which may be levied by such professionals, the same shall be your responsibility, either directly to such professionals or in reimbursement of this firm.

(b) In order for us to properly protect your interests, and in light of our experience in matrimonial litigation, it is important that we select or at least consent to the experts being retained in your matter. Accordingly, you agree to procure our consent relative to the retention of any experts for your case.

4. Other Attorneys in Firm Rendering Services.

(a) The client understands that no one particular member of the Law Firm is being retained but, rather, the Law Firm, as an entity, is undertaking legal representation of the client pursuant to this Retainer Agreement and that the Law Firm reserves the right to assign and delegate all aspects of such representation as the Law Firm, in its sole discretion, deems appropriate.

(b) Such assignment and delegation may include, but is not limited to, preparation of pleadings, motions, disclosure demands and responses, settlement negotiations, preparation of agreements, preparation and conduct of examinations before trial, court appearance, trial work, and any other matter deemed by the Law Firm to be appropriately delegated.

(c) Likewise, law clerks and paralegals are often called upon to assist in document production, file organization, preparation and review of financial statements and data, and such other duties as are assigned by the Law Firm.

5. Acknowledgement and Understanding.

(a) The client acknowledges that he or she has read this Retainer Agreement in its entirety, has had full opportunity to consider its terms, and has had full and satisfactory explanation of same, and fully understands its terms and agrees to such terms.

(b) The client fully understands and acknowledges that there are no additional or different terms or agreements other than those expressly set forth in this Retainer Agreement.

(c) The client acknowledges that he or she was provided with and read the Statement of Client's Rights and Responsibilities, a copy of which is attached to their Retainer Agreement.

6. Certifications.

We have informed you that pursuant to court rule, we are required, as your attorneys, to certify court papers submitted by you which contain statements of fact, and specifically to certify that we have no knowledge that the substance of the submission is false. Accordingly, you agree to provide us with complete and accurate information which forms the basis of court papers and to certify in writing to us, prior to the time the papers are actually submitted to the court, the accuracy of the court submissions which we prepare on your behalf, and which you shall review and sign.

7. No guarantees.

It is specifically acknowledged by you that the Law Firm has made no representations to you, express or implied, concerning the outcome of the litigation presently pending or hereafter to be commenced between you and your spouse. You further acknowledge that the Law Firm has not guaranteed and cannot guarantee the success of any action taken by the firm on your behalf during such litigation with respect to any matter therein, including without limitation issues of spousal and/or child support, custody and/or visitation, exclusive occupancy of the marital premises, equitable distribution of marital assets, the declaration of separate property, counsel fees and/or a trial.

8. Closing.

You are aware of the hazards of litigation and acknowledge that the Law Firm has made no guarantees in the disposition of any phase of the matter for which you have retained this office.

You acknowledge that pursuant to court rule, a copy of this Retainer Agreement is required to be filed with the court in which your action is pending. You indicate your understanding and acceptance of the above by signing below where indicated.

Dated:

Client: **Law Firm:**

I HAVE READ AND UNDERSTAND THE ABOVE,
RECEIVED A COPY AND ACCEPT ALL OF ITS TERMS:

by ....

PRINT OR TYPE CLIENT'S NAME BELOW

Flat or Fixed Fee

A flat or fixed fee is a set dollar amount that the client is charged for a particular legal service. Typically, items such as drafting a will or a contract or representation in a fairly small and straightforward problem are billed on a flat rate. Clients generally like flat fees because they know at the outset what their entire legal cost will be. Law offices have to be careful that when they establish a flat fee the money will, in fact, cover the actual time the problem takes.

EXAMPLE:

A client wishes to have an employment contract reviewed. The law office charges the client a flat fee of $500. The client knows exactly what the legal cost will be, and the law office intends that the time spent will justify the fee charged.

Hourly Fee

An hourly fee is a method of billing clients for all time actually spent on their legal problem. The more time spent, the greater the fee. This is the most common method of billing currently used, and it requires careful and detailed time recordkeeping. The client must receive regular itemized bills of all work performed, including expenses.

If an hourly fee is used, there are three methods of establishing the rate:

1. attorney hourly rate
2. client hourly rate
3. blended hourly rate

Attorney Hourly Rate

The attorney hourly rate indicates a specific hourly rate for each attorney, law clerk, and paralegal in the office. Each person may charge at a different rate, and the total for each billing period will depend not only on the amount of work performed but also on who performed the work.

EXAMPLE:

The senior partner in the office bills at $800 per hour; the associates bill at $250 per hour. At the end of the month the senior partner has spent three hours working on the client's problem and the associates have spent ten hours. The client is billed $4,900.

Client Hourly Rate

A client hourly rate is a set hourly fee that the client is billed regardless of who performs the work on his or her behalf. Under this method a paralegal's time and a senior partner's time are billed at the same rate. For the client this means that bills are only dependent on the hours of work performed; for the law office it means that work can be performed by the least expensive member of the legal team because billing is dependent on the work, not the person.

EXAMPLE:

The law office and the client agree on a client hourly rate of $200. During the month all work for the client was performed by a paralegal. The paralegal's billable hourly fee is $75, and ten hours of work were performed for the client. The client's bill is $2,000. The bill would be the same even if the work had been performed by the senior partner who bills at $600 per hour.

Blended Hourly Rate

A blended hourly rate establishes one hourly rate for each category of professional: one rate for all senior partners, one for all junior partners, one for all associates, and one for all paralegals (in some states a law office may not bill a paralegal's time on an hourly rate). Therefore, regardless of the hourly rate of any one particular professional, the client is billed by class rather than by person.

EXAMPLE:

A law office and a client agree to the following blended hourly rate:

> $300 per hour for all partners
> $250 per hour for all associates
> $100 per hour for all law clerks and paralegals

During the month a partner whose personal hourly rate is $500 spends two hours on the client's problem, an associate whose personal rate is $200 per hour spends five hours on the problem, and a paralegal whose rate is $75 per hour spends two hours on the client's work. The client is billed $2,050 under the blended hourly rate agreement. This saves the client $100 in fees that would have been billed under the attorney hourly rate discussed above.

Exhibit 6: Hourly Rate Bill

Invoice submitted to:
Date:
Invoice No.:

Professional Services:

Date	Service	Hours	
6/28	Phone conference	.2	
6/29	Court appearance	1.5	
			Amount
		1.7	$323.00

Additional Charges:

6/28	Photocopies	.40
	Litig. cover	.30
6/29	Transportation	2.50
		3.20

TOTAL AMOUNT OF THIS BILL: $326.20

Court-Awarded Fee

In criminal or quasi-criminal matters the court may appoint counsel to represent persons who cannot afford private legal representation. Many attorneys go to court each day in order to have cases assigned to them, and several state bar associations require attorneys to be available to represent indigents if no attorneys volunteer. In these circumstances the court establishes a fee for the work performed, and the fee is paid by the state. The attorney will submit a bill based on an hourly rate, and the court will determine its appropriateness.

Additionally, several different types of legal problems have statutorily set fees, such as estate work in which the fee is statutorily established at a set percentage of the total estate. As part of a lawsuit one side will sometimes request attorneys' fees, and the court will set the fee as part of the judgment.

In all the above situations the attorney must accept whatever fee the court establishes.

EXAMPLE:

An attorney volunteers to represent an indigent client in a drunk driving suit. After the trial the attorney submits a bill for $450 to the court. The court finds the fee excessive, and sets the fee at $325. The attorney will receive $325 from the state.

Prepaid Legal Services

Many legal clinics and other organizations have created what amounts to legal representation insurance known as prepaid legal services. For a yearly payment, the client is entitled to so many hours of legal counsel in set areas of law. Although this is considered a new concept, in fact it is really just a form of a retainer agreement created for lower-income clients and persons who would not normally seek legal counsel even though legal advice might be warranted. These arrangements serve a valuable purpose in assisting people who need legal advice but would not normally attempt to obtain it.

EXAMPLE:

A law office obtains an 800 telephone number and sells prepaid legal services to the public. For $75 per month all subscribers can call the 800 number for legal advice for up to three hours of total telephone time per month.

Now that the different types of billing arrangements have been detailed, it is time to discuss the methods used to determine the appropriate fee.

Determining Fees

As stated in the preceding section, all fee arrangements must be in writing. The writing acts not only as evidence of the agreement reached but affords clients the opportunity of seeing in black and white what they will be charged.

When a law office establishes its fees, it must take into consideration two general concepts: financial needs and ethical problems. By blending these two factors, an appropriate fee can be determined.

Financial Needs

The obvious reason for establishing a fee is the law office's need to make money and stay in business. However, if an office charges a fee that is excessively high, clients will go to other firms; if it charges fees that are too small, the office itself will be unable to stay open. Consequently, the ideal is to find the perfectly reasonable fee.

Pursuant to Model Rule of Professional Conduct 1.5 certain factors must be taken into consideration in establishing a fee.

Time Involved.   One aspect of fee setting is to determine in advance approximately how much time will be involved with the case. Of course, time can only be estimated in advance, but the fee should try to reflect the average time the problem should take.

Difficulty.   The more complex the legal matter, the more appropriate it is to charge a higher fee. For example, a simple will for a small estate is far easier to draft than a will for a multimillion-dollar estate with various inheritance problems. The fee should reflect the legal complexity of the problem.

Chance of Success.   If the chance of success is limited, not only should the client be forewarned, but the fee should not add an additional burden to a client with a losing problem.

Customary Fees in the Area.   Because expenses vary with geographic location, each locality has fees that are usual for the area. For instance, attorneys in New York City may charge $300 an hour, whereas attorneys in a similar practice with a similar background in a small farming community in Minnesota may charge $100 an hour. The legal fee should approximate the prevailing rates in the particular location.

Fixed or Contingent Fee.   The percentage of the contingency fee is usually established by statute, but fixed fees should represent a reasonable rate of return for the work the attorney actually performs.

In making the determination of what constitutes a reasonable fee, the law office must also decide its **minimum billable hours,** the number of hours of work it must bill each month in order to meet its salaries and expenses. There are only so many hours in a day, and the office must understand how many hours of work are devoted to meeting costs and how many hours are left over to make a profit. The fee must reflect this practical consideration of operating the law office.

Ethical Prohibitions

Besides financial concerns, there are several ethical concerns that must be taken into consideration when a law office determines its fees. The following is a short summary of some of these ethical questions.

Double Billing.   Double billing means charging two clients for the same work. For instance, suppose that two different clients request some information with respect to a new law. The office is only researching once; may it bill the full amount of time spent to each client? The answer is no. The fee is divided between the two clients.

Mistakes.   If a law office makes a mistake, is it entitled to charge the client for the firm's error? The answer is no, and the time spent on the mistake must be lost to the office as unreimbursable time.

Efficiency.   No two professionals work at the same rate of speed. If a problem would take an average attorney three hours to solve, but a particular attorney is more efficient and solves the problem in one hour, may he or she charge for three hours' worth of time? There is a financial cost to being efficient.

Work Assignments.   If the client is billed at an attorney hourly rate, should the firm assign the least or most expensive attorney to the case? If the client is paying a blended fee, should the office assign the least expensive professional to the client so as to make the greatest profit? There are no definite answers to these questions.

Billing Overhead.   As will be discussed below, **overhead** represents the general costs of keeping the office open. As a general rule these costs cannot be directly billed to the client, but they must be taken into account when establishing the actual dollar amount of the fee.

Remember that a law office is a business and must make a profit in order to continue its existence. The way that a law office or any other enterprise makes money is by **leverage,** making a profit from the work of others. For example, if an attorney works 16 hours a day, his total income can only be 16 times an hourly fee. However, if the attorney employs a paralegal whose cost to the attorney is $60 per hour but whose work can be billed to the client at $75 per hour, the attorney has increased his total income by $240 per day (16 times $15). A law office's financial success is based on its ability to charge a reasonable fee to its clients that can be leveraged by its cost of maintaining its legal team.

Costs and Overhead

As mentioned above, overhead represents the expenses that must be met just to keep an office open. Typical overhead expenses are rent, utilities, secretarial services, and repairs. These items must be met regardless of whether the office has any clients.

Costs, on the other hand, represent expenses that are incurred exclusively or predominantly to further a client's business. Some examples of costs are court filing fees, faxes, messenger services, and depositions. These items are directly billable to the client because they would not have been incurred but for the client's needs.

Every law office must make a careful examination of all expenses for a given period to determine whether the item represents overhead or a client's costs. Attorneys are prohibited from billing clients directly for their own overhead.

EXAMPLE:

In a given month a law office receives a telephone bill of $800. Long-distance calls made on behalf of the firm's client account for $730 of the charges. Thus, $70 worth of the bill is the office's overhead, and $730 is directly billable to the client whose work engendered the expense.

Timekeeping

A crucial aspect of billing is the maintenance of an accurate timekeeping system. Keeping track of the actual time spent by the members of the legal team for each client's problems helps the office determine whether the hourly fee charged represents an appropriate return for the time spent, whether the flat fee actually covers the costs of doing the work, and whether the contingency fee truly compensates the office for the work performed. The setting of an appropriate fee is a direct function of ascertaining the time the work will take.

Every law office requires all of its professional staff to keep detailed **timesheets** or **timeslips** that divide the day into segments, usually at ten-minute intervals. Each minute of time must be recorded, indicating the client on whose work the time was spent. This information is mandatory in order to verify the fees charged to the client.

The attorneys, law clerks, and paralegals must determine for each segment of time whether the work performed represents billable or nonbillable time. **Billable time** is time spent directly benefiting a particular client. **Nonbillable time** is general office time, including work breaks, staff meetings, and so forth, for which work time is spent but is not chargeable to any client. This time accounts for a portion of the firm's overhead expenses previously discussed. Also, as mentioned in conjunction with the ethical considerations incident to office billing, the office may not charge as billable time any time spent inefficiently or mistakenly. This too must be considered part of the office overhead.

As part of their public relations policies or because of the desires of the staff, many offices devote several hours per week to **pro bono** work. Pro bono work is charitable, nonbillable time that the staff spends to help provide legal services for indigents or for public causes. This work must also be recorded on the timesheets with indications that it represents the charitable efforts of the office.

Although many law firms still maintain timesheets by a **manual time system** (handwritten or typed by the staff), many others now utilize a **computerized time system** in which each member of the team enters individual time information into his or her computer terminal, which then automatically records the information in the main computer and divides up the time among the clients indicated (see Chapter 10). For computerized offices, the staff must prepare **timeslip verification forms** that keep track of the time for the computer-generated time reports.

Keeping track of one's time in ten-minute intervals throughout the day may seem overly burdensome, but the time reports generated by this information are used by the office management to determine the efficiency of the office as a whole and that of each staff member in particular, and form the basis for making financial projections and keeping track of income and expenses. Without accurate time reports, a law office would soon find itself in deep financial trouble.

See the following exhibits for examples of timesheets.

Exhibit 7: Daily Time Report

DAILY TIME REPORT

NAME:_____   #:_____   DATE:_____

Work Codes: 1-Billable   2-CLE   3-Pro Bono   4-Recruiting   5-Client Develop.
             6-Com. Mtgs. 7-Admin.   8-Vacation   9-Ill/Pers.

DESCRIPTION:

1)
   CLIENT #_____ MATTER #_____

   CLIENT NAME_____

   MATTER NAME_____

   WORK CODE_____ HOURS_____

2)
   CLIENT #_____ MATTER #_____

   CLIENT NAME_____

   MATTER NAME_____

   WORK CODE_____ HOURS_____

3)
   CLIENT #_____ MATTER #_____

   CLIENT NAME_____

   MATTER NAME_____

   WORK CODE_____ HOURS_____

4)
   CLIENT #_____ MATTER #_____

   CLIENT NAME_____

   MATTER NAME_____

   WORK CODE_____ HOURS_____

5)
   CLIENT #_____ MATTER #_____

   CLIENT NAME_____

   MATTER NAME_____

   WORK CODE_____ HOURS_____

6)
   CLIENT #_____ MATTER #_____

   CLIENT NAME_____

   MATTER NAME_____

   WORK CODE_____ HOURS_____

Exhibit 8: Sample Timesheet

CLIENT		CLIENT NO.	MATTER NO.
MATTER			

PERIOD ENDED	ATTORNEY'S TIME										TOTAL	INVOICED	
	①	②	③	④	⑤	⑥	⑦	⑧	⑨	⑩		DATE	AMOUNT

JULIUS BLUMBERG, INC. NYC 10013

REORDER NO T 5028

Forms may be purchased from Julius Blumberg, Inc., NYC 10013, or any of its dealers. Reproduction prohibited.

Billing Procedures

Once the appropriate fee has been determined and agreed to by the client, all costs and overhead expenses have been ascertained, and all timesheets have been prepared, it is time for the office to send bills to the clients. One nonfinancial, but important, aspect of the billing procedure is the physical appearance of the bill itself. Regardless of whether the bill is manually typed or computer-generated, it should always look neat, be readily understandable, and be presented in a professional manner. There are several guidelines that should be kept in mind when preparing and sending bills to clients.

1. Always discuss payment procedures with a client at the start of the office's representation, and be sure that the billing procedures have been presented to the client in writing. This minimizes problems later on, and the clients know from the outset what potential costs they may be likely to encounter.

2. Always send bills at regualar intervals; do not send out bills haphazardly. Most law offices send bills at the end of each month, and this provides clients with some concept of regularity with respect to their legal representation. If there is ongoing representation and no work is performed for a client during a particular month, the client should still receive a bill from the office indicating no charges are due.

3. The billing format used should be easy for the client to read and understand, and all charges must be specifically itemized. In this fashion, if there are any questions, individual items can be addressed immediately.

4. Always indicate a payment date on the bill. Having a payment date indicates to clients that they must pay when the fee is due and cannot pay randomly. Additionally, by having a payment due date the office can keep track of **aged accounts receivable,** work billed but unpaid by the due date. This helps the office maintain strict financial controls on its operations. See Chapter 5.

5. Enclose a self-addressed return envelope in the bill. This makes it easier for clients to make their payments promptly.

Once payment has been received (and the check clears at the bank), report the payment with the check number in the computer and in the client's file. This will avoid double billing and inaccurate assumptions that payment has or has not been made, and will keep the books of the office up-to-date. Keep in mind that receiving payment from clients for bills sent is the only way the law office generates actual income.

Should a problem arise with respect to a client not making timely payments, the office can always work out a repayment schedule or agree to a slight reduction or discount on the bill. Although this is not an appropriate way to operate in each and every situation, partial payment is better than no payment at all. Always be ready to speak to the client about payment and always maintain a friendly manner.

Fee Collection

Regardless of how careful the law office may be with respect to billing, there are times when a client simply refuses to pay a bill. The law office is prohibited ethically from withholding work it has performed for the client as a method of forcing the client to pay the bill if such withholding would adversely affect the client's legal rights, the work withheld has already been paid for, or the client has become financially unable to pay.

The office always has the right to sue the client for work performed and to assert a lien over the client's files (provided such lien does not significantly harm the client's legal rights with respect to the represented matters), and many law offices resort to the use of collection agencies. However, the office should be aware that in many instances courts do not look favorably on lawyers suing clients for fees, and the best course of action is always to attempt to avoid such problems by specifying all billing procedures to the client in advance of taking on the representation and to work out payment schedules if a financial hardship arises.

CHAPTER SUMMARY

In terms of financial well-being, the most important function of a law office is to prepare and send appropriate bills to its clients for work performed. Without billing, the office would be unable to generate income and stay in business.

The first step in creating an appropriate billing procedure is to determine the type of fee that is going to be charged to each client. The most common forms of fees are hourly rates and contingency fees, but many firms still charge retainers and fixed fees, and many fees are established by court or statutory authority. Be aware that several states not only set statutory fees but also set fee limitations by statute as well, thereby limiting the amount that the client will have to pay. Regardless of the types of fee chosen, the office must make sure that the fee is explained to the client, both orally and in writing.

In order to determine the appropriate amount to charge, the law office must be conversant with all of its overhead expenses and the time involved in furthering each client's interests. If the amount of the fee does not represent the office's actual costs, it will soon be out of business.

Finally, as work is performed for the client, the office must prepare and mail accurate bills to the client, bills that the client can readily comprehend. If the client is not billed at regular intervals, or the bill is so confusing that the client balks at payment, the office will not generate sufficient income to maintain its operations. Billing itself can become an element of the public relations of the office, especially the manner of preparing the bill and explaining it to the client. Happy and cared-for clients are more likely to pay their bills on time. Unhappy clients who believe that they are getting shortchanged by the firm will create billing problems.

Key Terms

Aged accounts receivable: Amounts billed but unpaid by the payment due date.

Attorney hourly rate: Hourly fee set for each individual legal professional.

Billable time: Work time actually spent on a client's problem for which the client may be billed.

Blended hourly rate: Hourly fee set for each category of legal professional.

Case retainer: Nonrefundable fee paid to an attorney as an inducement to represent the client.

Cash advance retainer: Money paid to an attorney to offset future billing.

Client hourly rate: Hourly fee set for all legal work performed regardless of the person or category of professional who actually does the work.

Contingency fee: Fee based on a percentage of the eventual award granted to the client.

Costs: Money expended directly on behalf of a client, billable to that client.

Court-awarded fee: Legal fee established by a court.

Double billing: Billing two clients for the same work, considered unethical.

Earned retainer: Fee immediately available for use by the office; not dependent on actual work performed.

Fee splitting: Unethical practice of sharing a fee with someone who did not perform any legal work for the client.

Fixed fee: Set dollar amount established to perform a specific legal task regardless of the time involved.

Flat fee: Fixed fee.

Hourly fee: Legal fee dependent on the time the work takes.

Leverage: Method of making a profit from the work of others.

Minimum billable hours: The least amount of hours an office has to bill in a given period in order to meet its expenses.

Nonbillable time: Work time that cannot be charged to any client.

Outstanding accounts: Fees billed but unpaid.

Overhead: Operating expenses of an office.

Prepaid legal services: Method of acquiring legal representation, similar to health insurance; a premium is paid for a set amount of legal service time.

Pro bono: For free; charitable legal work.

Pure retainer: Money paid to ensure the availability of the law office's services.

Retainer for general representation: Money paid in contemplation of ongoing representation outside of litigation.

Timesheet: Form used to keep track of work time.

Timeslip: Timesheet.

Timeslip verification form: Document used to check accuracy of computer timesheets.

Unearned retainer: Money paid that is not yet available for use by the office.

Cases for Analysis

The following cases highlight some legal problems that a law office may encounter with respect to its billing procedures. In Cluett, Peabody & Co. v. CPC Acquisition Co., the court discusses the appropriateness of the law office's billing rates. In In re Union Carbide Corp. Consumer Product Business Securities Litigation, problems with court-awarded fees are underscored.

Cluett, Peabody & Co. v. CPC Acquisition Co.
863 F.2d 251 (2d Cir. 1988)

MAHONEY, Circuit Judge:

Appellants Paul A. Bilzerian, Bilzerian & Brodovsky and CPC Acquisition Company, Inc. (collectively "Bilzerian") appeal from a judgment of the United States District Court for the Southern District of New York, Leonard B. Sand, Judge, entered in favor of appellee Latham & Watkins in the amount of $354,569 for legal services rendered in connection with that law firm's representation of Bilzerian during his attempted takeover of Cluett, Peabody & Co., Inc. ("Cluett").

We affirm.

Background

This action arises from a dispute concerning the legal fees charged to Bilzerian by the law firm Latham & Watkins, a California partnership with offices in Los Angeles and Manhattan, among other locations, for services rendered in connection with Bilzerian's bid to acquire control of Cluett. In May, 1985, Bilzerian retained Latham & Watkins in connection with his acquisition of Cluett stock. Bilzerian and Latham & Watkins entered into a verbal agreement whereby Latham & Watkins was to be paid at the unitary rate of $150 per hour for legal services related to the takeover.

Between May and November, 1985, Latham & Watkins rendered a variety of legal services commonly performed during the course of an attempted acquisition of a corporation. These services included the preparation and filing of a voluminous number of documents with the appropriate state and federal governmental agencies, the preparation and control of all press releases and advertisements, negotiations with certain subordinated debtors, review of credit arrangements with various financial institutions, and litigation related thereto.

On October 16, 1985, in attempting to carry out his plan to take control of Cluett, Bilzerian initiated a tender offer for the acquisition of Cluett's outstanding shares. On that same day, in connection with Bilzerian's tender offer, Latham & Watkins commenced an action in the United States District Court for the Eastern District of California against Cluett, which was opposed to the tender offer, seeking both to enjoin Cluett from implementing a "poison pill" defensive tactic and damages from Cluett's directors for breach of fiduciary duty in attempting to implement the "poison pill." Approximately one week later, Cluett filed suit in the United States District Court for the Southern District of New York to enjoin Bilzerian's tender offer. Shortly thereafter, Bilzerian's California action was transferred to the Southern District of New York and the two actions were consolidated. The parties cross-moved for temporary and permanent injunctive relief in the district court. The district court issued a temporary restraining order against all parties.

On November 4, 1985, prior to the disposition of the remaining motions, Cluett agreed to be acquired by a third party, West Point-Pepperell, Inc. As part of the acquisition, West Point-Pepperell agreed to purchase all Cluett shares held by Bilzerian. The effect of that agreement was thus to moot the Bilzerian-Cluett litigation. Bilzerian realized a $7.5 million profit on his sale of Cluett stock, and also received $5 million in reimbursement for fees and expenses incurred during his attempted acquisition of Cluett, including Latham & Watkins' legal fees. On January 14, 1986, the parties entered into a stipulation dismissing with prejudice the actions related to the tender offer.

On or about November 15, 1985, however, a dispute arose over the amount Latham & Watkins had billed Bilzerian for services rendered. On that date, Latham & Watkins received a letter from David A. Tallant, Bilzerian's personal attorney, which stated that Bilzerian would pay only approximately sixty percent of Latham & Watkins' fees and disbursements billed through October 31, 1985, based upon Bilzerian's belief that he had been charged excessively. The letter further stated that such payment would constitute full satisfaction of all sums due and owing, including November attorney time and disbursements not yet billed, and charges for continued representation until all matters concerning the transaction were completed.

On November 19, 1985, Job Taylor III, a member of Latham & Watkins, informed Mr. Tallant that despite the existence of several outstanding matters connected with the Cluett transaction, Latham & Watkins would no longer continue to represent Bilzerian without payment of the fees and disbursements previously incurred and assurance satisfactory to Latham & Watkins with respect to the payment of future fees and disbursements. On November 27, 1985, Latham & Watkins moved for permission to withdraw as Bilzerian's counsel in the Southern District litigation. The district court granted that motion on December 3, 1985.

On December 10, 1985, Bilzerian filed a declaratory judgment action in California state court seeking a determination of the amount of legal fees owed to Latham & Watkins. Shortly thereafter, Latham & Watkins moved that the district court in the instant action exercise its ancillary jurisdiction over the fee dispute and determine the fees owed. That motion was referred to a magistrate by Judge Sand. On May 1, 1986, the district court adopted the magistrate's report, which recommended, as a matter of discretion, that ancillary jurisdiction be exercised over the fee dispute.

Following lengthy motion practice, the action was tried to a jury in May, 1987. The jury returned a verdict in favor of Latham & Watkins in the amount of $354,569, and judgment was entered thereon on July 21, 1987. This appeal followed.

Discussion

Bilzerian raises two claims on this appeal. First, he argues that the billing of certain law firm employees not yet admitted to the bar of any jurisdiction at the same hourly rate as licensed attorneys, without disclosure to the client, is improper and fraudulent, requiring a determination that Bilzerian owes nothing to Latham & Watkins. [Second claim omitted.]

A.   The Fraud Claim

Bilzerian's first claim is a novel one, never before put to this court. He contends that by billing certain associates not yet admitted to the bar of any state at the same hourly rate as attorneys who had been admitted to practice, Latham & Watkins attempted to defraud him, and that this court must put a stop to such a deceptive and corrupt billing practice by denying any recovery to Latham & Watkins. We conclude that his claim is utterly devoid of merit.

The facts pertinent to this issue are largely undisputed. Bilzerian and Latham & Watkins entered into a verbal contract whereby Bilzerian was to be billed at a unitary rate of $150 per hour. Bilzerian subsequently learned that three Latham & Watkins "employees" who had graduated from law school, but had not yet been admitted to practice in any jurisdiction, performed approximately a hundred hours of work on the Cluett transaction for which he was billed at the $150 rate. Although Latham & Watkins knew that these "employees" were unadmitted, the firm never disclosed that fact to Bilzerian. This, Bilzerian claims, constitutes fraud on the part of Latham & Watkins.

Specifically, Bilzerian argues that the trial court incorrectly instructed the jury that the billing of unlicensed attorneys at attorneys' rates could not even be considered as a basis for fraud. Judge Sand charged in pertinent part:

I also instruct you that although you have heard testimony with respect to the billing for legal services rendered by first year associates not yet admitted to the bar, I instruct you that although you may consider Latham & Watkins billing for the services of not yet admitted attorneys in considering the fair and reasonable value of Latham & Watkins services you may not base a finding of fraud on this practice which defendant's expert has testified is the uniform practice in this community — that is, the inclusion in legal services of time spent by first year associates not yet admitted. . . .

As I have stated, a finding of fraud or bad faith requires a finding that the attorney is not entitled to any compensation or fee.

Under New York law, it is well settled that intent to deceive is an essential element of fraud. Kalisch-Jarcho, Inc. v. City of New York, 58 N.Y.2d 377, 385 n.6, 448 N.E.2d 413, 417 n.6, 461 N.Y.S.2d 746, 750 n.6 (1983); Mallis v. Bankers Trust Co., 615 F.2d 68, 80 (2d Cir. 1980), cert. denied, 449 U.S. 1123, 101 S. Ct. 938, 67 L. Ed. 2d 109 (1981); Irving Trust Co. v. Gomez, 550 F. Supp. 773, 774 (S.D.N.Y. 1982). The district court determined that any evidence regarding Latham & Watkins' intent to deceive Bilzerian with respect to the rates billed for unlicensed associates was insufficient as a matter of law to warrant a jury instruction on the issue. The record amply supports that conclusion.

Judge Sand noted that the only evidence relevant to the fraud issue was the testimony of Daniel P. Levitt, a partner at a New York law firm and *Bilzerian's expert witness.* Mr. Levitt testified:

I think it is a standard practice in this community for law firms where they charge for their time to charge for the time of unadmitted associates at the same rate they would charge when they are admitted at the entry level billing.

Bilzerian offered no evidence to controvert the testimony that this was the custom and practice of New York law firms. Judge Sand accordingly stated at the charging conference:

Your claim is fraud. The requirements of fraud are very clear. An intentional misrepresentation made to deceive and relied upon.

What evidence is there to show, given Mr. Levitt's testimony, and the universal practice in this community, that the billing practice was with the intent to deceive?

I'm going to strike the claim of fraud insofar as it relates to unadmitted attorneys.

That conclusion was wholly appropriate.

Bilzerian nonetheless contends that bar associations across the country have declared such a practice to be improper and fraudulent, and that this court should therefore adopt that rule.

In support of this argument, Bilzerian relies primarily upon three ethics opinions by local bar associations; two from the State of New York and one from California.

In addition to the fact that such ethics opinions are merely advisory and not binding on this court, Bilzerian's reliance thereon is further misplaced because all three opinions are inapposite to the facts before us. Bilzerian cites New York City Bar Association Ethics Opinion No. 837, which states the general proposition that "it is not professionally proper for members of the Bar to represent an employee to be a member of the Bar when the employee has not in fact been admitted to the Bar." This opinion, however, concerns the responsibilities that may be entrusted to an unadmitted first year law student, and nowhere addresses billing practices with respect to law school graduates. It is thus irrelevant to the case at bar.

New York County Lawyers' Association Opinion No. 666 is similarly irrelevant. That opinion discusses the tasks in which an unadmitted law school graduate may engage on behalf of a law firm. Again, billing practices were not considered in the opinion.

Los Angeles Bar Association Ethics Committee Formal Opinion No. 391 is equally unavailing, since it only applies to billing practices with respect to law clerks, paralegals and secretaries. While it specifically states that the services of such employees should normally be billed at a lower rate, the overall description of these services is "non-attorney time." Although the opinion is less than completely clear, there is no indication that it is intended to apply to billing for the services of law school graduates. To the extent it might be read as applicable to the instant situation, we decline to follow it as setting a standard for New York attorneys.

As a last resort, Bilzerian argues that The T. J. Hooper, 60 F.2d 737 (2d Cir. 1932), requires this Court to reject Latham & Watkins' custom and practice defense. The T. J. Hooper, however, dealt with the propriety of a custom and practice defense in a negligence setting, and has no application here where Bilzerian is required to establish intent to deceive.

We conclude that the district court was clearly correct in its refusal to charge the jury that Latham & Watkins' billing practice with respect to unadmitted associates was a basis to return a fraud verdict against Latham & Watkins. . . .

Conclusion

The time has come for Bilzerian to disgorge to Latham & Watkins a relatively minuscule portion of the five million dollars which Bilzerian was paid by West Point-Pepperell, Inc. to cover the expenses of his tender offer for Cluett. The judgment of the district court is affirmed.

In Re Union Carbide Corp. Consumer Product
Business Securities Litigation
724 F. Supp. 160 (S.D.N.Y. 1989)

BRIEANT, Chief Judge.

In a decision dated July 13, 1989, 718 F. Supp. 1099, this Court approved, pursuant to Fed. R. Civ. P. 23(e), a settlement in the amount of $31,739,917 (the Settlement Fund) between the class members and defendants Union Carbide Corporation (Union Carbide) and Morgan Stanley & Co. as set forth in the Stipulation of Settlement dated December 22, 1988. . . .

The terms of the Stipulation of Settlement provide that the legal fees of counsel who produced the settlements for plaintiffs shall be paid out of the Settlement Fund in an amount to be fixed by the Court. At the time that we issued the findings and conclusions approving the settlement of these actions, this Court believed that it would be improvident to make a determination concerning legal fees and disbursements, at least until the final judgment approving the settlement achieved appellate finality. Accordingly, the Court severed the issue of the attorneys' fees and deferred resolution of the fee request pending appellate finality of the judgment entered on July 25, 1989 on the July 13, 1989 findings and conclusions.

The Court also believed that, in the interest of fairness, plaintiffs' counsel should submit supplemental applications for reimbursement of additional expenses incurred before the Settlement Fund is distributed to authorized claimants, in order to account for time expended by plaintiffs' attorneys from March 10, 1989, the cut-off date used by counsel initially in calculating their lodestar, at least through July 25, 1989, the date of this Court's order approving the settlement, or, if the case was appealed, through the date of the Court of Appeals' judgment. . . .

Plaintiffs' attorneys, with the exception of Harvey Greenfield, now jointly request an award of attorneys' fees in the amount of $6,026,073 to be paid from the Settlement Fund, together with reimbursement of expenses in the amount of $460,956.40, which includes amounts expended for the retention of experts. Based on the 1988-89 non-contingent hourly rates of plaintiffs' law firms, the lodestar amount is $2,348,230 for the 11,208 hours plaintiffs' counsel expended on this litigation over the past three years.

The requested fee is 2.57 times the lodestar, representing a composite multiplier of 2.6 for the time expended by members of plaintiffs' steering committee, and 2 for the time expended by other counsel. With the exception of Harvey Greenfield, plaintiffs' counsel have agreed to allocate the aggregate fees awarded among themselves in relation to the amount of work and the responsibilities undertaken, the risks sustained, and the relative contributions of the various law firms towards the settlement. Mr. Greenfield has made his own separate application for fees and disbursements. . . .

The Supreme Court has long recognized that, when a plaintiff-representative successfully establishes or protects a fund in which the other class members have a beneficial interest, the costs of litigation may be spread among the fund's beneficiaries. Trustees v. Greenough, 105 U.S.

527, 15 Otto 527, 26 L. Ed. 1157 (1882); Mills v. Electric Auto-Lite Co., 396 U.S. 375, 90 S. Ct. 616, 24 L. Ed. 2d 593 (1970); Alyeska Pipeline Service Co. v. The Wilderness Society, 421 U.S. 240, 95 S. Ct. 1612, 44 L. Ed. 2d 141 (1975). Under the "equitable fund" doctrine, attorneys for the successful party may petition for a portion of the fund as compensation for their efforts. As the Supreme Court stated in Boeing Co. v. Van Gemert, 444 U.S. 472, 100 S. Ct. 745, 62 L. Ed. 2d 676 (1980):

> [A] litigant or lawyer who recovers a common fund for the benefit of persons other than himself or his client is entitled to a reasonable attorney's fee from the fund as a whole.

Id. at 478, 100 S. Ct. at 749. . . .

Accordingly, the starting point for this Court's determination of a just and adequate fee to be paid to class plaintiffs' counsel in this case is the number of hours expended in prosecution of the litigation, or the lodestar. Our review of the record and our familiarity with this entire case shows that the hours expended by all counsel, as adjusted with respect to Mr. Greenfield, were reasonable, and reasonably necessary for the litigation. The time spent by jointly petitioning counsel was reasonably and efficiently allocated among senior partners, partners, associates and paralegals of each firm to provide high quality work at a lower cost, and was directly related to the prosecution of the class claims in this action. As to Mr. Greenfield, the Court finds that a lodestar of $93,200.00 is appropriate. This accepts the agreed figure of $90,000, with one day in court at $3,200 incurred thereafter. His additional work after the original fee submission, other than the appearance in court, seems essentially duplicative and unnecessary.

In arriving at their lodestar, class plaintiffs' counsel used current hourly rates as of year-end 1988 and 1989, rather than historic billing rates. Courts in this District have approved the use of current billing rates in calculating the lodestar amount, in order to "compensate for the delay in receiving compensation, inflationary losses, and the loss of interest." In re Generics Corp. of America Securities Litigation, [1980 Transfer Binder] Fed. Sec. L. Rep. (CCH) ¶97,719, 98,770 (S.D.N.Y. 1980). The holding of the Court of Appeals in New York State Assn. for Retarded Children, Inc. v. Carey, 711 F.2d 1136 (2d Cir. 1983), further supports the propriety of using current (1988-89) hourly rates here. As the Second Circuit noted, "[i]f the services were rendered over two or three years, relevant figures for the current year will normally still be appropriate." Id. at 1152-53.

In light of the use of current rates, and the award of a multiplier, it seems inappropriate to add pre-judgment interest. Interest will be allowed from the date of the judgment to be entered hereon, to the date of payment at the net rate of return earned by the Settlement Fund.

Included in the requested lodestar are the hourly charges for paralegals' time. In United States Football League v. National Football League, 887 F.2d 408, 416 (2d Cir. 1989), an antitrust case, our Court of Appeals, quoting Missouri v. Jenkins, — U.S. — , 109 S. Ct. 2463, 105 L. Ed. 2d 229 (1989), held that "'the prevailing practice in a given community' is to govern whether paralegals' time is billed separately, and whether it is billed at cost or at market rates."

The Court of Appeals in *United States Football League* drew an inference "that the practice of New York law firms is to bill paralegal time at hourly or market rates," and concluded that "the hourly market rate for paralegal service in New York City is includable in the attorney's fees award in this case. We agree that billing for a paralegal's time in this manner 'makes economic sense' and encourages cost effective delivery of legal services." Id.

This Court believes that the inference drawn by the Court of Appeals in *United States Football League* as to the New York custom and practice of billing the time of paralegals is well-founded, and we are confident that any law firms which are not billing their paralegal services at an hourly rate, will do so forthwith upon reading that decision. The practice does make economic sense, if for no other reason than to do otherwise creates a disincentive to use paralegals. We conclude therefore, in light of *United States Football League* that the inclusion of the paralegals' time within the lodestar is proper, and that the paralegals' time is entitled to such multiplier as the Court may award for the lawyers.

This litigation involved multiple claims against multiple defendants for violations of the federal securities laws and the common law in connection with Union Carbide's issuance of the Rights and the manner in which it calculated the payments Rightsholders were entitled to receive from the sale of Union Carbide's Consumer Products Division. Considering the multitude of issues and the substantial defenses asserted by each of the defendants, class plaintiffs were at risk that they would be unable to obtain any meaningful recovery at trial.

Class counsel's efforts throughout this litigation were performed on a wholly contingent basis, with counsel also advancing the many thousands of dollars of necessary disbursements. If, after trial, class plaintiffs were unsuccessful, due to the contingent nature of the lawsuit, class plaintiffs' counsel would have received no compensation. This contingent fee risk is the single most important factor in awarding a multiplier; perhaps it is the only remaining valid basis now recognized by the caselaw of multipliers. In In re Agent Orange Product Liability Litigation, 818 F.2d 226, 236 (2d Cir. 1987), the Court of Appeals held:

> We have labelled the risk-of-success factor as "perhaps the foremost" factor to be considered under the second prong of the lodestar analysis. *Grinnell I*, 495 F.2d at 471. The multiplier takes into account the realities of legal practice by rewarding counsel for those successful cases in which the probability of success was slight and yet the time invested in the case was substantial.

The concept of awarding multipliers based also on the quality of the work and exceptional skills in the litigation and settlement negotiations, is described in *Agent Orange* as having been "severely restricted." 818 F.2d at 234. This restriction is said to have been imposed by Blum v. Stenson, 465 U.S. 886, 897, 104 S. Ct. 1541, 1548, 79 L. Ed. 2d 891 (1984), a case which considered the effect of a statute which called for a reasonable attorney's fee "adequate to attract competent counsel, but . . . [that does] not produce windfalls to attorneys." It is not entirely clear to this Court that Blum v. Stenson has been or should be lifted bodily into the caselaw concerning compensation of attorneys from a common fund. However, the later decision in Pennsylvania v. Delaware Valley Citizens' Council, 478 U.S. 546, 106 S. Ct. 3088, 92 L. Ed. 2d 439 (1986), awarding a fee authorized by a statute using the word "reasonable" in a case involving a non-monetary recovery, held at page 565, 106 S. Ct. at 3098:

> Expanding on our earlier finding in Hensley [v. Eckerhart, 461 U.S. 424, 103 S. Ct. 1933, 76 L. Ed. 2d 40 (1983)] that many of the Johnson [v. Georgia Highway Express Inc., 488 F.2d 714, 717-719 (5th Cir. 1974)] factors "are subsumed within the initial calculation" of the lodestar, we specifically held in *Blum* that the "novelty [and] complexity of the issues," "the special skill and experience of counsel," the "quality of representation" and "results obtained" from the litigation are presumably fully reflected in the lodestar amount, and thus cannot serve as independent bases for increasing the fee award. 465 U.S. at 898-900 [104 S. Ct. at 1548-49]. Although upward adjustments of the lodestar are still permissible, id. at 901 [104 S. Ct. at 1550], such modifications are proper only in certain "rare" and "exceptional" cases, supported by both "specific evidence" on the record and detailed findings by the lower courts. See id. at 898-901 [104 S. Ct. at 1548-49].

Without intending in any way to criticize the reasoning employed by our Supreme Court, we note that implicit in the entire American tradition of the contingent fee lawyer, is the concept that the advocate would have a stake in the outcome, which interest would induce the lawyer to invest, or gamble, his or her time and often considerable disbursements [in actual practice seldom paid by losing contingent fee clients], hoping to share in the benefits which the client would enjoy as a result of the attorney's professional skill, quality of work and success in outcome. Fees based solely on lodestars, with multiples awarded solely with reference to risk, will destroy this traditional motivation that has served the clients, the profession and society so well and for so long. . . .

The perceived problem of unconscionability in contingent fees relates in part to economy of scale. Obviously, it is not ten times as difficult to prepare, and try or settle a ten million dollar case as it is to try a one million dollar case, although the percentage contingent fee will return ten times as much. This fact, and a perception of possible abuse, drove the Courts to the use of the lodestar followed by a multiple. Experience has shown that this is not an ideal way to fix fees, although it may be required by current caselaw. We are fortunate, indeed, in this case that the lodestar appears to be both reasonable and accurate. However, needless duplication of hours, and a temptation to re-invent the wheel at the expense of the client or common fund are often found in major litigation. In the final analysis after adjusting the lodestar to conform to reality where necessary, and after a reasonable multiplier has been developed, and all is said and done, a

Court essentially makes no more than a qualitative assessment of a fair legal fee under all the circumstances of the case, just as if it had applied the twelve amorphous criteria set forth in Johnson v. Georgia Highway Express, Inc., 488 F.2d 714, 717-719 (5th Cir. 1974), or the six equally amorphous criteria of *Grinnell I,* cited earlier.

On September 27, 1989 a panel in the Ninth Circuit in the case of Paul, Johnson, Alston & Hunt v. Graulty, 886 F.2d 268 (9th Cir. 1989), considered the compensation due counsel under the common fund doctrine. Reversing a lodestar award representing 7% of the common fund that was created through the efforts of the appellant attorneys while acting concurrently for private parties under a one-third contingent fee, the Court of Appeals held:

> This reward represents a paltry seven percent of the common fund that was created . . . through the efforts of [counsel]. We consider this figure to be too low and therefore an unreasonable reward.
>
> We leave to the district court the task of determining what would be reasonable compensation for creating this common fund, but we add the following advice. A task force commissioned by the Third Circuit has recommended that compensation for creating common funds be calculated by a percentage of the funds created. See Court Awarded Attorney Fees, Report of the Third Circuit Task Force, 108 F.R.D. 237, 254-59 (1985); see also Blum v. Stenson, 465 U.S. 886, 900 n.16 [104 S. Ct. 1541, 1550 n.16, 79 L. Ed. 2d 891] (1984) (noting that the percentage basis method is grounded in tradition and therefore an acceptable way of calculating the fee award). This method stands in contrast to other courts who apply the "lodestar method," which calculates the fee award by multiplying the number of hours reasonably spent by a reasonable hourly rate and then enhancing that figure, if necessary, to account for the risks associated with the representation. [Citations omitted.] We believe that either method may, depending upon the circumstances, have its place in determining what would be reasonable compensation for creating a common fund. [Citations omitted.] . . .
>
> The sole remaining issue is what percentage of the common fund would provide [counsel] reasonable compensation. The answer to that question, of course, depends on the individual circumstances of this case with which the district court is more familiar than we are. Ordinarily, however, such fee awards range from 20 percent to 30 percent of the fund created. . . .

Adoption of a policy of awarding approximately 30% of the fund as attorneys' fees in the ordinary case is well-justified in light of the lengthy line of cases which find such an award appropriate and reasonable before or after superimposing the Lindy [Bros. v. Am. Radiator & Standard Sanitary Corp., 487 F.2d 161 (3rd Cir. 1973)] or Kerr [v. Screen Extras Guild, Inc., 526 F.2d 67 (9th Cir. 1975)] factors. Several years of this practice and the body of case law across the circuits validate this approach. The Supreme Court has accepted it. In Blum v. Stenson, 465 U.S. 886, 900 n.16 [104 S. Ct. 1541, 1550 n.16, 79 L. Ed. 2d 891] (1984), the Court noted approvingly the use of a percentage of the common fund to set attorneys' fees in common fund cases. In fact, the language of the note appears to assume that the percentage approach is routine. . . .

This Court concludes that the contingency risk normally considered by the Courts in awarding a multiplier, warrant some multiplier here. However, the Court does not find the plaintiffs' risk so great (or the success so exceptional) as to justify fee multipliers in the amount requested. Counsel should be compensated over and above their normal hourly rates where they have taken significant litigation risks and thereby produced a substantial benefit in an action to enforce rights "worthy of judicial encouragement," which this is. See In re "Agent Orange" Product Liability Litigation, 818 F.2d 226, 28 (2d Cir. 1987).

In approving the settlement of this action for $31,739,917, this Court considered the uncertainty of the outcome of the *Nicholson* case, then pending in the New York State Supreme Court, and what we believed at the time would be an inevitable delay in its resolution. While the ink was scarcely dry on our interlocutory judgment, however, the *Nicholson* litigation between Union Carbide and the company's dividend equivalent holders was settled for $15 million paid by Union Carbide, together with a rewriting of the instruments under which dividend equivalent holders receive their dividend equivalents, so as to guard against future disputes. If our case had not settled prior to *Nicholson,* the plaintiff Rightsholders class here would have then received the difference between the sum of $27,000,000 withheld for the *Nicholson* claimants, less the $15,000,000 finally paid to them, and reasonable transactional costs, which this Court estimates at $500,000 or less.

Since defendants' counsel asserted at our settlement hearing that any reversionary interest of our class in the $27 million withheld from the Rightsholders to await the outcome of *Nicholson* was factored into the sum offered and accepted in settlement of this litigation, the net result is now that the Rightsholders' many other claims for securities fraud, etc. were, at least from an economic point of view, settled for $20,239,917, and not $31,739,917 as would appear. This is so because once *Nicholson* was settled, our plaintiff class would have been entitled to the unexpended portion of the $27,000,000 which was withheld ($11,500,000), and this even in the absence of this lawsuit.

Based on the foregoing analysis and applying the court's informed judgment to the award of legal fees, the Court hereby awards the plaintiffs steering committee counsel a lodestar amount of $2,187,688.75 which in the Court's discretion will be augmented by a multiplier of 2.3, leading to a total fee of $5,031,684.

Petitioning counsel other than the steering committee are hereby allowed a lodestar in the amount of $169,041, which in the Court's discretion will be augmented by a multiplier of 1.5 to be applied to the lodestar, leading to a total fee award of $253,561. The application of Mr. Greenfield will be disposed of in the same fashion by awarding a lodestar as noted above of $93,200, enhanced by a multiplier of 1.5, making a total award to Mr. Greenfield of $139,800.

The Court notes that these fees amount to approximately 27% of the true economic recovery which is in keeping with the custom and practice in awarding fees in common fund cases in this District, said to range typically from 15% to 30% of the recovery. See Weseley v. Spear, Leeds &

Kellogg, 711 F. Supp. 713, 718 (E.D.N.Y. 1989); see also In re Warner Communications Securities Litigation, 618 F. Supp. 735, 749-50 (S.D.N.Y. 1985);
see also *Paul, Johnson,* supra, finding a 20% to 30% range in the Ninth Circuit. Such an award is consistent with the new learning (old wine in a new
bottle) announced by the Ninth Circuit in *Paul, Johnson,* supra, which new
learning we believe will proceed from West to East and take us back to
straight contingent fee awards bereft of largely judgmental and time-wasting computations of lodestars and multipliers. These latter computations,
no matter how conscientious, often seem to take on the character of so
much Mumbo Jumbo. They do not guarantee a more fair result or a more
expeditious disposition of litigation.

The disbursements as requested all appear proper and they are
hereby allowed.

The foregoing constitutes findings and conclusions of the Court on
the matter of the legal fees and disbursements. Settle a final judgment on
notice, which shall stay payment pending appellate finality.

So Ordered.

EXERCISES

  1. Check your state statute to determine how your jurisdiction regulates attorneys' fees.
  2. Find a recent case from your jurisdiction in which the court was
      presented with a law office billing problem.
  3. Discuss under which circumstances a law office would prefer a
      contingency fee to a fixed or hourly fee.
  4. Analyze the sample bill (page 78) for clarity and appropriateness.
  5. Discuss the importance of maintaining accurate timesheets.
  6. Discuses some methods of collecting a fee from a recalcitrant
      client.
  7. How does the court determine a "just and adequate fee" in the
      Union Carbide case (page 94)?
  8. Discuss some ethical considerations in determining a client's
      fees.
  9. Discuss the paralegal's role with respect to effective office billing
      procedures.
  10. Analyze the various fee agreements appearing in this chapter.

SITUATIONAL ANALYSIS

The law office has presented a bill to a client after the successful completion of a lawsuit. The office was working on a contingency fee agreement with the client that specified that the office would receive 30 percent
of the award for services rendered plus costs. The office is including in its
costs the overhead attributable to the client's representation as well as the

cost of the paralegal who worked on the case. The client refuses to agree to the total, claiming that overhead and paralegal salaries are not "costs" under a contingency fee agreement.

1. Argue the case for the law office.
2. Argue the case for the client.

5 Law Office Accounting

During my career I have worked for the Internal Revenue Service, major corporations, and small businesses and law firms. What I have discovered is that the businesses that succeed in the long run are those that pay careful attention to all of their financial accounts, both in inputting the data and in analyzing the records. It is the small details that make a business successful.

Sara C. Pfau
Accountant
New York, New York

CHAPTER OVERVIEW

One of the cornerstones of every successful business is the preparation and maintenance of accurate financial records. Not only is this recordkeeping necessary for taxation purposes, but it also provides the owner with a perspective on how the business is doing and where it should be going.

A law office, just like any other business, must be concerned with keeping a clear record of its finances. Regardless of the type of entity — professional corporation, partnership, sole proprietorship, or limited liability company — the law office needs accurate records in order to reach basic business decisions with respect to the operation of the enterprise: fees to charge, employees to hire (or fire), and maintenance of as low an overhead as possible.

There are four basic financial activities with which the law office must be concerned: (1) preparing financial statements, (2) accounting for credit and accounts payable and receivable, (3) managing costs, and (4) preparing a payroll. The paralegal will be responsible for some or all of the preparation of these financial documents that are needed to assist the attorney in reaching business decisions.

All financial documents are prepared according to what is known as the **accounting cycle.** The "cycle" involves the recording, classifying, and summarizing of financial information. Paralegals, as well as all other employees of the office, must keep accurate records of their time, supplies used, and other expenses involved in performing their jobs. These records must then be classified and allocated according to client workload and eventually encapsulated for client files and billing purposes. Each of these functions of the cycle must be completed at the end of every **accounting period,** a certain space of time in which financial data is summarized. Typically, businesses will summarize their financial records every month for internal purposes, every quarter (three months) for tax purposes, and at the end of the year for both tax and planning purposes (the **fiscal year**). The fiscal year is the annual date at which all financial records are closed, and is determined either by the calendar year or some other definite date approved by the IRS.

A law office, just like any other business, is concerned with the **bottom line** — making a profit. All monies coming into the office are not profit. From the general income the attorney must subtract all of the office's expenses; this results in the **gross profit** for the period (income less expenses). If the expenses exceed the income, the office has suffered a **gross loss** for the period. From the gross profit the attorney must further deduct all taxes due on that income, giving a **net profit** for the enterprise. This net profit indicates how well the office is doing.

This chapter introduces all of the financial documents that must be prepared by the law office in order to determine its financial health. It details basic recordkeeping concepts, such as bookkeeping entries and the balance sheet, as well as indicating how to create a budget. The budget will take into consideration how often money comes in and goes out of the business. The chapter concludes with a short explanation of how financial documents can be read and interpreted.

Client Funds

Before considering all of the details involved in maintaining the accounting records of a law office, it is imperative to understand that not all funds that come into the office either belong to or may be used by the attorney. An attorney, as a fiduciary for the client, will receive funds from various sources that must be held for the benefit of the client. A **fiduciary** is a person who is expected to meet a higher standard than ordinary care, and he or she is responsible for acting in the best interest of the person to whom the duty is owed. Attorneys typically receive funds for clients as part of the settlement of a lawsuit, the result of a judgment from a court or arbitrator, or as payment from an insurance company. As a fiduciary the attorney is expected to hold these funds exclusively for the benefit of the client.

Funds received on behalf of the client may not be placed in the ordinary accounts of the law office. Rule 1.15(a) of the American Bar Association Model Rules of Professional Conduct expressly prohibits an attorney from **commingling** client funds with those of the attorney. All funds coming to the attorney in his or her fiduciary capacity must be placed in special bank accounts known as **trust** or **escrow accounts** that legally belong to the client. Separate trust accounts must be maintained for each client, and these funds are not subject to the claims of any creditors of the attorney.

Trust accounts do not appear on the books of the law office. As stated above, these accounts belong to the client, not the attorney, and the attorney is strictly prohibited from using these funds for his or her personal or business purposes. It may be very tempting to use the money to cover a short-term financial need of the office, but Rule 1.15(b) of the Model Rules of Professional Conduct prohibits using the trust account funds to pay office or personal expenses. The interest that accrues on these accounts belongs to the client as well, except for certain states that provide that such interest go to the state bar association to provide funds for the defense of indigents or other projects of the association.

EXAMPLE:

A law firm settles a personal injury case for a client for $300,000. All of this money must be placed in an escrow account for the client, even though the client has agreed to pay the firm one-third of the monetary remedy she receives. Only when the client authorizes it may the funds be released for use by the law office.

When dealing with client trust accounts, withdrawals should only be made by check signed by the attorney handling that client's case, and no check should be drawn until all deposits have cleared. Because some states require that any person who is responsible for dealing with trust accounts must be bonded, each state's requirements must be individually checked.

EXAMPLE:

Continuing the above example: In order to release the funds to the client and retain its fee, the law office sends the client a statement of account indicating how much is in the trust account and the amount due to the law office for services rendered. When the client agrees in writing, the attorney handling the case draws two checks from the account, one for the client and one for the firm. At this time the firm is free to use the money it receives for its fee for office use.

Keep in mind that all client trust funds belong to the client, not the law office. These funds do not appear as part of the financial books of the office and may not be used for law office purposes.

Basic Bookkeeping Concepts

The first step in maintaining financial records is to create a bookkeeping system for the office. **Bookkeeping** is simply the process of recording all money that comes in and goes out of the office. All money coming in is called **inflow,** and all money going out is called **outflow.** This information is placed in a book known as a **journal** and is indicated in chronological order.

 EXAMPLE:

Date	Item	Inflow	Outflow
June 1	Fee from Client A	300.00	
June 1	Buy Supplies		25.00
June 2	Pay Utilities		136.00
June 3	Fee from Client B	875.00	

The inflow and outflow to and from the office are also known as the **debit** and **credit.** Debit is the inflow, or increase, in funds to the office, and credit is the outflow, or decrease, in funds from the office. The practice of debiting and crediting accounts is known as **double-entry bookkeeping.**

 EXAMPLE:

Date	Item	Debit	Credit
June 1	Fee from Client A	300.00	
June 1	Buy Supplies		25.00
June 2	Pay Utilities		136.00
June 3	Fee from Client B	875.00	

Rather than keep a journal of accounts, many offices maintain a slightly different kind of document called a **ledger.** A ledger is similar to a journal; however, instead of making all entries for the business in one book in chronological order, a ledger maintains a separate book, or account, for each client and expense. With a journal the entire financial history of the office appears in one document; with a ledger each item of income and expense is separately noted, and the totals represent the financial history of the office.

EXAMPLE:

Ledger Summary

	Debit Accounts	Credit Accounts	
Date	Clients	Utilities	Supplies
June 1	300.00 (Client A)		
June 1			25.00
June 2		136.00	
June 3	875.00 (Client B)		

Every time a number is entered in the ledger it is called a **posting.** Periodically, these records are totaled to come up with a **trial balance** to see how the office is doing until a final summary is done at the end of the accounting period.

At the end of a given period the "books are closed," meaning that all of the items entered are totaled and no new entries are posted. All of the credit items are then subtracted from the debit items, and the gain (or loss) for the period can be determined. This summary forms an initial financial statement for the office and indicates how well the office is doing financially.

In order to prepare a simple financial statement from the books of the office, the following steps should be taken:

1. Enter all inflow and outflow in the office journal.
2. Post the figures from the journal into a ledger of accounts.
3. Maintain a trial balance on either a daily or weekly basis.
4. Close the books.
5. Prepare a financial statement summarizing all of the inflow and outflow.

These simple financial statements form the basis for accounting concepts and provide the information necessary to create a balance sheet for the office.

Basic Accounting Concepts

The Balance Sheet

The basic financial document associated with accounting is known as the **balance sheet.** The balance sheet is the written summary of the **basic accounting equation: Assets = Liabilities + Equity.** In every business, regardless of whether it makes a profit, the balance sheet will balance.

A balance sheet is a method of taking all of the data obtained from the bookkeeping methods discussed above and placing it into accounts that correspond to the accounting equation for a given period. As long as the journal and ledger are properly maintained, the balance sheet can be completed in a fairly straightforward manner. However, always bear in mind that the balance sheet is the primary financial document used to determine the financial health of an enterprise; the journal and ledger merely aid in the coordinating process by which the necessary financial information is gathered.

Assets represent all of the accounts signifying the income and property of the business. The asset accounts are subdivided into those that are **current** (one year), **fixed** (permanent), and **receivables.** Examples of current assets are the money in the office checking account, office supplies, and any services for which the office has prepaid, such as cleaning services or a service contract on electronic equipment. Prepaid services are an asset because they represent something of value to which the office is entitled. Fixed assets are the office property itself if it is owned as opposed to rented, as well as all equipment such as computers, fax machines, and the like. Finally, and most important, receivables represent all work the office has performed for which it has billed clients; receivables are monies that the office is owed.

EXAMPLE:

ASSETS

   Current

Checking Account	13,875.00
Office Supplies	920.00
Prepaid Insurance (3 mos)	2,000.00
Prepaid Maintenance (1 mon)	500.00

   Fixed

Computers	8,500.00

   Receivables

Client A	3,000.00
Client B	250.00
Client C	640.00

Additionally, because businesses are allowed to **depreciate** business property — that is, take a deduction for the annual use of an item that can only be used for a limited number of years before it wears out or becomes obsolete — assets may also include an item of **depreciation,** indicating this use of a fixed asset. The number of years a fixed asset may be used before it becomes worthless is known as its **useful life.** The depreciation reduces the value of the fixed asset as it appears on the balance sheet over time.

Liabilities represent all items of expenses for which the office must pay. Expenses that appear in this column are known as **payables,** meaning that the office owes money on those accounts. Payables includes all typical expenses such as payroll, rent, utilities, and taxes.

EXAMPLE:

LIABILITIES

Rent Payable	3,500.00
Utilities Payable	136.00
Supplies Payable	25.00
Payroll	10,000.00

A more detailed discussion of receivables and accounts payable appears below.

Equity, the third and final item of the balance sheet, represents the ownership interest in the business. Equity is generally subdivided into two basic areas: capital and retained earnings. **Capital** represents all monies received by the business from persons who bought an interest in the business. In a professional corporation this would be the amount each shareholder attorney paid for his or her share; in a partnership it would be the amount each partner contributed to become a partner; in a sole proprietorship it is the proprietor's cash contribution to the office. **Retained earnings** represent the profit the business has made for the period in question. The profit (or loss) for the period is determined by reference to a second financial document known as the income statement, which will be discussed shortly.

EXAMPLE:

EQUITY

Capital	7,000.00
Retained Earnings	9,024.00

By putting the totals of all of the accounts described above together, the balance sheet can be created.

EXAMPLE:

ASSETS	=	LIABILITIES	+	EQUITY
29,685.00		13,661.00		16,024.00

In order to arrive at the totals that appear under each heading of the accounting equation, it is necessary to maintain separate accounts for each item, which are known as T-Accounts. **T-Accounts** simply indicate when an item is received or paid; they form a synopsis of the accounts maintained in the bookkeeping ledger.

The account is called a T-Account because it looks like the letter "T," the right side representing credits, the left side representing debits. For all asset accounts, as the money or property is acquired, its value appears on the debit (left) side of the T; once used, the value of the use appears on the credit (right) side of the T.

EXAMPLE:

	CHECKING ACCOUNT	
Funds Received	3,300	
Utilities Paid		136.00
Supplies Paid		25.00
Funds Received	250	

For liabilities the entries are reversed. Whenever an item becomes a payable, it appears on the right side of the account; when paid, it appears on the left side.

EXAMPLE:

	RENT PAYABLE	
Rent Due		3,500
Rent Paid	3,500	

At the end of the period all accounts are totaled, and the result appears as the balance sheet entry for the account. The total of these accounts is called a **spreadsheet;** all of the various accounts are spread over one (usually) large sheet of columned paper.

The Income Statement

The balance sheet alone does not tell the entire story of the business. In order to determine whether and why the business is operating at a profit or loss, a second document must be prepared known as the **income statement.** The income statement is a simple synopsis of all work billed during the period in question, less all expenses for the period, giving a subtotal of gross profit. From the gross profit the taxes due on this amount are calculated and deducted, and the resultant figure represents the net profit for the period. The net profit figure is posted on the balance sheet as retained earnings. This number indicates whether the owners of the business will receive a distribution above their salaries or, if there is a loss, will have to reevaluate billing and expenses.

EXAMPLE:

INCOME STATEMENT

Income (Receivables)	9,950.00
Expenses	1,886.00
GROSS PROFIT	8,064.00
Taxes	4,000.00
NET PROFIT	4,064.00

Following is a sample balance sheet and income statement for a service business taken from a public financial recording publication. By comparing these two statements a clear picture of the financial status of the company can be determined.

Exhibit 9: Balance Sheet and Income Statement

Consolidated Income Account, years ended Sept. 30 ($000):

	1992	[1] 1991	1990
Int & fees on loans	7,173	6,982	....
Interest on invests	1,840	1,286	....
Total interest inc	9,013	8,268	7,525
Interest expense	6,488	6,004	5,484
Net interest income	2,525	2,264	2,041
Prov for loan losses	489	324	396
Net int inc after			
prov for loan loss	2,036	1,940	1,645
Origination &			
application fees	....	....	106
Management fees	192	163	191
Other	30	47	70
Total other income	222	210	368
Salaries & empl bens	1,121	969	885
Other expenses	472	452	462
Tot gen & admin			
exp	1,593	1,421	1,346
Inc bef prov for			
income taxes	665	728	667
Prov for inc taxes	319	306	285
Net income	345	423	382
Prev retained earns	3,619	3,197	2,815
Retained earns	3,965	3,619	3,197
Common shares (000):			
Year-end	12	12	12

[1] Reclassified to conform with current presentation

Consolidated Balance Sheet, as of Sept. 30 ($000):

	1992	1991
Assets:		
Loans receiv, net of allow		
for loan loss	75,007	73,228
Less bank participations	dr9,937	dr11,923
Net loans receivable	65,070	61,305
Cash	214	269
Restricted investments	35,999	27,922
Accrued int receivable	1,075	777
Deferred tax benefits	745	585
Other assets	528	189
Total assets	103,632	91,046
Liabilities:		
Notes to pay members	11,500	12,500
Notes pay to State Com		
Retir Fund	75,000	65,000
Notes payable to banks	6,150	2,680
Notes pay to U.S. Small		
Bus Admin	450	600
Total notes payable	93,100	80,780
Accrued interest payable	574	577
Other liabilities	333	343
Total liabilities	94,007	81,701
Capital stock	[1] 1,165	[1] 1,174
Paid-in capital	4,494	4,553
Retained earnings	3,965	3,619
Total stkhldrs' equity	9,625	9,346
Total liabil & stk eq	103,632	91,046
Book value	$825.85	$796.21

[1] No par value; Auth shs: 500,000; Stated value: $100

One important distinction should be noted with respect to the difference in accounting statements for law offices and other service industries and general manufacturing concerns. A manufacturing concern's assets include all of its inventory or product. In order to increase income a manufacturing company can either increase the number of the item it produces, raise its prices, or both. For a law office, the major asset is the billable hours — the number of hours of work that can actually be charged to a client. The value of this asset does not appear on the balance sheet of the office. In order to increase this amount, either more staff must be hired, the current staff must work longer hours, or the office fees must go up (or a combination of all three). Therefore, hiring and firing decisions are based primarily on the balance sheet and income statement. A law office has no other inventory to sell but billable time.

Creating a Budget

Once the balance sheet is completed, the office can then create a budget for the business. A budget is a necessary ingredient in promoting the financial health of an enterprise. A law office, as a profit-making entity, must be able to plan its resources to ensure that its expenses will be met and a profit can be achieved. All of the information summarized in the balance sheet is used to prepare the budget.

The first element in preparing a budget is to determine all of the enterprise's costs for the period in question. Typically, budgets are created on a yearly basis. The most common items in a law office list of costs are:

1. Rent or mortgage payments on the office facility.
2. **General overhead,** which includes all utilities, office supplies, maintenance, cartage, and insurance.
3. **Administrative overhead,** which includes all taxes plus all fees and costs the office outlays for clients that will eventually be repaid.
4. Personnel, including salaries, fees, benefits, and employer taxes for employees, agents, and principals.

These costs indicate the annual outlay that the office must make in order to maintain operations. Additionally, the budget would include a projected amount to cover emergency situations and a suitable profit percentage; no one wants to stay in a business that makes no profit on its operations.

When the annual costs of the office have been calculated, the budget planners must analyze all income coming into the enterprise. For a law office the typical income is derived from the following sources:

1. **Capital contributions:** money or property paid into the office by persons who wish to buy an interest in the firm either as a partner, shareholder, or member.

2. Billing: all funds received from work performed. This item must
   be reduced by the actual **realization** of the funds; not all items
   billed will be paid in the year billed or ever.
3. Extraordinary income: money derived from investments the firm
   has acquired.

The figures needed to calculate these items of costs and income are derived from the balance sheet and income statement. Despite what the members of the office might wish, the balance sheet indicates all actual expenses
and receipts. From these numbers the office can determine whether it is
making a profit and, if so, if the profit is sufficient to maintain interest in the
office. The amount of profit a business makes in relation to its overall
income is called its **profit margin.** The budget is the first step in developing
a financial plan for the enterprise — a method to generate greater income
and profit in the coming period. The financial planner uses the actual numbers from the previous period to estimate the numbers for the coming period, thereby developing strategies to reduce expenses while increasing
income.

To increase revenues, the budget must be analyzed to determine the
office's actual **time to billing percentage.** This is the amount of hours the
staff actually works compared to the amount of hours that can be billed.
For instance, an attorney may spend 65 hours per week at the office, but
only 45 of those hours can be billed to the client; the other 20 hours are
spent in general office routine, waiting for books or computers, or just
thinking or taking work breaks. In order to increase billing, either the attorney must work more billable hours, additional staff must be hired
(which will increase costs), or the fees must be increased. The person in
charge of the financial affairs of the office must make the decision as to
which is the most appropriate course to take.

The other side of the income coin is the cost of operating the business.
If receivables cannot be increased, the profit margin can be affected by reducing costs. There are several methods that can be used to bring down
the expenses of the office. One method is known as **zero-based budgeting**
in which all personnel are required to justify each and every expenditure.
This method maintains a tight fiscal control on office expenses but may not
be looked on favorably by all personnel, and can reduce billable hours because time must be spent in writing expense justifications.

A second method of reducing costs is to change personnel by either
firing expensive employees and hiring less expensive replacements or
finding service personnel who charge less for similar services. This can result in dissatisfaction among employees and less effective services.

There is no one tactic that can create the "perfect" budget, but the
budget designed must reflect a realistic estimation of future earnings and
costs. The office must determine an appropriate rate of growth and plan
accordingly. The balance sheet indicates the actual financial history of the
business, which is the basis for forecasting the next period's budget. Both
items go hand in hand, and the result will be the creation of a cash-flow
budget.

Cash Flow and Accounts Receivable/Payable

A **cash-flow budget** specifies the point in time in which money comes in and money goes out of an enterprise. A creditor does not care that an office expects a large check to arrive next month if the money is owed today. A cash-flow budget anticipates when monetary distributions must be made, and when the cash must be on hand to meet these distributions.

To determine when money is coming in, the cash-flow budget must analyze the accounts receivable items on the balance sheet. The **accounts receivable** indicate all billing the firm has done for a given period. However, as indicated above, not all billing results in payment. Clients may dispute some or all of a bill or simply not pay. Checks received also may not clear on the day deposited. To determine when funds will be available for use by the office, first the billing must be analyzed to determine what percentage of total billing is paid in what period of time, and what percentage is never paid at all.

EXAMPLE:

Last year the office billed $100,000 each month. Of that $100,000, $65,000 was paid within 30 days, $20,000 was paid within 60 days, $5,000 was paid within 90 days, and $10,000 was never paid at all. Consequently, the office can estimate that of its total billing for any month 65 percent will be received within 30 days, 20 percent within 60 days, 5 percent within 90 days, and 10 percent will never be collected.

In addition to the actual receipt of payment, because most payments are made by check the office must also take into consideration the problems of **electronic funds transfers (EFT),** the amount of time the bank takes to let the depositor have use of the funds. Just because a check has been deposited does not mean the depositor can draw on the money. Each bank establishes its own period of time for clearing checks (subject to some government regulation) and maintains **transaction balances** for its customers (the amount of cash actually available from deposits and collection). At the end of each month the bank sends a statement calculating all deposits and the amount of funds actually available. The statement is called a **reconciliation** and may include charges for checks the office draws on deposits before the funds have cleared. These charges are a cost of using the funds before they are on hand, similar to a loan payment.

EXAMPLE:

The office deposited checks totaling $30,000 in a given month, and wrote checks on that amount totaling $27,000; however, by the end of the month only $26,000 of the checks deposited had cleared. Consequently, the office is charged a fee on $1,000 worth of its checks because those funds had not actually been cleared by the bank before the office wrote checks on the money.

Banks may also require depositors to maintain a **compensating balance,** a minimum amount that must be kept at all times in a checking account. Although these funds are in the account, they are not available to the office for use to pay its bills. Many offices also like to maintain a reserve of funds to cover emergencies, known as a **precautionary balance,** and may even keep a sum on hand to take advantage of extraordinary business opportunities, called a **speculative balance.** Neither of these amounts can be used to meet the ordinary outflow of the enterprise.

When the determination has been made as to when the money is received and available for use, the cash-flow budget must indicate when the office's bills must be paid — its **accounts payable.** Most **expenses** are monthly, such as rent, telephone, and utilities, and are fairly static, but some expenses are due on a quarterly or semiannual basis or fluctuate from period to period.

EXAMPLES:

1. The office maintains several insurance policies, both for liability and for health. Because the office uses one insurer, all of the premiums are set and payable four times each year: February 1, May 1, August 1, and November 1. The office must have the cash available on these dates to pay the premiums.

2. The office uses Westlaw and is billed monthly for actual use. The use varies but based on the office's historical use, it can be estimated that the charges will vary between $3,500 and $5,000 per month, due on the 15th of the month. The budget must anticipate this use and have funds available every month.

In order to maintain a happy balance between income and outflow, the office must practice strict **cash-flow management.** This involves managing all of the accounts receivable to get as much money up front and to eliminate or charge an additional fee to clients who do not pay or are recalcitrant in paying; maintaining the accounts payable by paying all bills on the last possible date, thereby retaining funds on hand as long as possible; and, finally, utilizing effective practice management by keeping strict internal controls on persons who have access to funds. In this fashion the office can maintain financial stability and not worry about its ability to meet its expenses.

One cautionary note. Remember that all client funds placed in a trust account belong to the client and not the office. In order to meet cash-flow problems, many attorneys are tempted to use these funds as a method of avoiding **shortfalls:** less cash on hand to meet currently due expenses. This is a violation of ethical responsibility; these funds are *never* considered part of a law office budget.

Inventory Control

The primary **inventory** in a law office is an intangible: the billable hours of its staff. This is not something that can be readily quantified and, unlike manufacturing operations, it is not an item that appears on the balance sheet of the office even though it is the major asset of the firm. However, law offices do purchase supplies that may be considered as part of its inventory, and as such a few words should be mentioned about the ordering process.

Typically, the personnel in a law office will requisition supplies from the office manager, who will make purchases based on these requests. Usually, the office uses a **purchase order form,** which is the documentary evidence of the purchase. When the item is ordered it is considered a payable account of the office, and when the item is received it is an asset. As supplies are dispensed and used, they should be deducted from the asset column of the balance sheet and included as an operating cost, or expense, of the office on the income statement. Maintaining a strict control on purchases and using supplies with restraint will result in a reduction of expenses and help with the cash flow of the enterprise.

Exhibit 10: Purchase Order Form

Purchase Order

Acme, Inc.
123 Front Street
City, State 00000

Purchaser:

Account Number:

Item Number:

Description:

Quantity:

Unit Price:
      Discount: 1% if ordering between 500 and 999 Units
              1.25% if ordering between 1000 and 2999 Units
              1.5% if ordering over 3000 Units

Merchandise Total Price:

Sales Tax (Tax Resale Number):

Delivery Charges:
      Express Delivery: Next Day Add:
                  One Week Add:
                  Special Shipper (Specify) Add:

Order Total:

Method of Payment:
      Discount: 2% for COD
              1.5% for 2-Week Payment
              1% for 30-Day Payment

Late Fee: 1% per month after 60 Days

Ship To:

Reading Financial Statements

The financial statements of a business give the clearest indication of how well an office is doing, a far better and more accurate indication than the braggadocio of its members or the firm's reputation in the community. Analyzing a financial record can provide greater insight into a business than all of the personal memoranda that the office generates.

There are two general methods of reading financial data. The first method is to analyze the information historically, looking at the financial statements of the office over a number of years. By comparing the assets and liabilities, the income and expenses, over several years one can evaluate the general direction in which the company is going. This method can also disclose how careful and accurate the company's financial plans and budgets have been, and can be used to project the future well-being of the enterprise.

The second method of reading financial statements is to use what are known as **ratios,** comparing specific items to each other from the same financial period. By using the ratios, comparisons not only can be made internally, but the firm can compare itself to other enterprises in the field.

Detailed financial analysis is beyond the scope of this text, but some mention of the most commonly used ratios should be made. The most used ratios fall into three broad categories: liquidity ratios, asset-management ratios, and profitability ratios.

Liquidity Ratio

Liquidity ratios indicate whether the company has more liabilities than assets; that is, is it near or at bankruptcy? The two liquidity ratios are:

CURRENT RATIO:

$$\frac{\text{Current Assets}}{\text{Current Liabilities}}$$

QUICK RATIO:

$$\frac{\text{Current Assets} - \text{Inventory} - \text{Marginal Receivables}}{\text{Current Liabilities}}$$

The **current ratio** indicates whether, at the moment, the office has more assets than liabilities. "Current" simply means within a short period of time — anywhere from a month to a year depending on the period analyzed. The **quick ratio** takes into account the fact that not all receivables (billing) will be collected, and so the assets must be reduced by the amount of uncollectible billings. Although this ratio indicates inventory, that would not apply to a law office.

EXAMPLE:

From the figures that appear in the examples earlier in this chapter, the liquidity ratios could be calculated from the balance sheet as follows:

$$\text{Current Ratio:} \quad \frac{17{,}295}{13{,}661} \quad = \quad 1.267$$

$$\text{Quick Ratio:} \quad \frac{16{,}655}{13{,}661} \quad = \quad 1.22$$

The difference between the current and quick ratios is the deduction of a portion of the receivables as uncollectible as well as the deduction of the office supplies, considering them as inventory. In both instances the office is in decent financial health.

Asset-Management Ratio

The **asset-management ratio** indicates the average period it takes the business to collect on its receivables. The shorter the period, the better the management of the business because it has more funds on hand. The ratio is:

AVERAGE COLLECTION PERIOD:

$$\frac{\text{Average Receivables}}{\text{Annual Fees}/365 \text{ days}}$$

EXAMPLE:

From the figures previously used:

$$\text{ACP:} \quad \frac{100{,}000}{12{,}000{,}000/365} = 3 \text{ days}$$

Based on this statistic, the office is collecting its receivables within three days, which is a very short period of time; it would be hard pressed to improve this number.

Profitability Ratio

The **profitablity ratio** indicates the percentage of total income representing profit as opposed to the mere covering of expenses. An office would want to be as profitable as possible. The profitability ratio is:

$$\text{Profitability:} \quad \frac{\text{Gross Profit}}{\text{Income}}$$

The lower the ratio, the more likely it is that the office will have to either increase billing or reduce expenses in order to achieve a desirable profit or rate of return for its members, partners, or shareholders. A business also can only expand if it has a sufficient profit to warrant and pay for the growth.

EXAMPLE:

From the figures previously given:

$$\text{Profitability:} \quad \frac{8{,}064}{9{,}950} = .81$$

Based on these figures, the office is showing a profit of over 80 percent; it is very profitable.

Simply creating the financial documents is not enough. All of the statements must be read and analyzed to determine what, if any, financial changes the office must introduce in order to grow and be profitable in the coming year.

Accounting and Ethics

The primary ethical problem encountered with respect to a law office's accounting system concerns the proper maintenance of client trust or escrow accounts. As stated above, Rule 1.15(b) of the Model Rules of Professional Conduct prohibits an attorney from commingling client funds with those of the law office. Strict control must be maintained at all times over the supervison of these accounts. The cases that appear below highlight the ethical considerations involved in law office accounting.

CHAPTER SUMMARY

Preparing and maintaining accurate financial records for a law office is a fundamental attribute of operating a successful practice. Each of the financial documents prepared presents a different and concise analysis of the health of the office and assists in determining the future of the enterprise. The paralegal plays an important role in the preparation of these documents.

The legal assistant will be required to input all pertinent data to maintain the basic books of the firm and the preparation of the balance sheet. These records must be kept either by hand or entered into one of the various computer programs many offices now use for this purpose. Although paralegals may not be called on to do the various calculations necessary to create the ledger or balance sheet, they will have to maintain complete records of all billing and expenses and prepare totals that can be input by the bookkeeper or accountant.

The figures given by the paralegal and used as the basis of the ledger and balance sheet will form the foundation of the office's budget and cash-flow projections. These statements will have a direct impact on the paralegal in terms of salary, overtime permitted, and whether he or she will be retained by the firm. The legal assistant will also be expected to keep a strict control on all supplies ordered and used.

The financial ratios that grow out of all the other accounting documents determine what path the law office will take in the future, a decision that has an immediate impact on all office personnel. Unless they are planning to go into office management, most legal assistants have only tangential contact with these financial statements; however, an understanding of how they are prepared and used can only assist paralegals in their role in the firm. Additionally, paralegals may be called on to assist the attorney in reading and interpreting financial documents for a client as part of a legal problem handled by the law office. A basic knowledge of accounting can only be a help to anyone involved in the legal field.

Key Terms

Accounting cycle: Recording, classifying, and summarizing financial information.
Accounting equation: Assets = Liabilities + Equity.
Accounting period: Specific period of time used to summarize financial data.
Accounts payable: Money owed.
Accounts receivable: Money due.
Administrative overhead: Expenses involved in operating a business.
Asset: Valuable property owned by a business.

Asset-management ratio: Method of determining whether property is being used productively; one form determines the average collection period for billing.

Balance sheet: Written summary of the accounting equation.

Bookkeeping: Method of maintaining financial records.

Bottom line: Profitability of the business.

Capital: Money or property.

Capital contribution: Money or property used to purchase an interest in a business.

Cash-flow budget: Document used to trace inflow and outflow of cash.

Cash-flow management: Method of operating a business by keeping a tight control on income and outflow.

Commingling: Mixing client funds with office funds.

Compensating balance: Minimum amount banks require a customer to keep in an account.

Credit: Method of reporting outflow of assets or increase in liabilities or equity.

Current assets: Assets with no more than one year of duration.

Current ratio: Equation used to measure liquidity.

Debit: Method of reporting inflow of assets or decrease in liabilities or equity.

Depreciation: Method of allocating as an expense property with a limited useful life.

Double-entry bookkeeping: Debiting and crediting an account.

Electronic funds transfer: Transferring funds by computer.

Equity: Ownership interest in a business.

Escrow account: Trust account.

Expenses: Cost of operating a business.

Fiduciary: Person held to a standard of care higher than ordinary care.

Fiscal year: Date at which yearly books of a business are closed.

Fixed assets: Property, plant, and equipment.

General overhead: Usual expenses involved in operating a business such as rent and utilities.

Gross loss: Monetary loss from the operation of a business.

Gross profit: Business profit calculated before deducting taxes due.

Income statement: Document showing all income, expenses, and taxes from operating a business during a given period.

Inflow: Money coming into a business.

Inventory: Business product.

Journal: Bookkeeping record of accounts prepared chronologically.

Ledger: Bookkeeping record of accounts by specific account.

Liabilities: Money owed.

Liquidity ratio: Equation used to determine whether assets exceed liabilities.

Net profit: Gross profit less taxes.

Outflow: Money going out of a business.

Payables: Accounts representing monies owed.

Posting: Placing a number in a ledger.
Precautionary balance: Money kept to meet emergency situations.
Profit margin: Percentage of profit in relation to income.
Profitability ratio: Equation used to determine the profit margin.
Purchase order form: Document used to order supplies, used to keep a tight control on expenses.
Quick ratio: Equation used to determine a business's liquidity.
Ratio: Equation used to read and interpret a financial statement.
Realization: Moment that funds become available.
Receivables: Account representing money owed to the business.
Reconciliation: Monthly document sent by a bank indicating actual cash on hand and checks written.
Retained earnings: Operational profit for a given period.
Shortfall: Term used to indicate a lack of funds to pay presently due debt.
Speculative balance: Money kept on hand to take advantage of unexpected business opportunities.
Spreadsheet: Columned paper used to write up a balance sheet.
T-Account: Method of documenting inflow and outflow of a particular account.
Time to billing percentage: Percentage of time spent that can actually be charged to a client.
Transaction balance: Amount of deposited funds actually available for use by the customer of a bank.
Trial balance: Intermediate calculation of account totals.
Trust account: Bank account used to maintain funds belonging to a client.
Useful life: Period of time a particular item may be used before it is worn out or becomes obsolete.
Zero-based budgeting: Requiring all personnel to justify expenses.

Cases for Analysis

The following two cases are presented in order to demonstrate problems that may occur when an attorney does not maintain proper trust accounts for his or her clients.

Kelly v. State Bar of California
808 P.2d 808, 280 Cal. Rptr. 298 (1991)

The Review Department of the State Bar Court (review department) has recommended that petitioner Patrick B. Kelly be suspended from the practice of law in California for three years, that execution of the suspension order be stayed, and that he be placed on probation for three years upon conditions that include actual suspension from the practice of law for one year.

The recommendation is based on the review department's findings that in one matter petitioner failed to deposit moneys received from a client into his trust account and commingled funds; and that in a second matter petitioner willfully failed to deliver to a client funds to which the client was entitled, and willfully misappropriated those funds.

Petitioner contends that the findings are not supported by the evidence, and that the recommended discipline is excessive. We conclude that the evidence supports the findings, but that the review department's recommendation of one-year actual suspension is excessive under the circumstances. The hearing panel's recommendation of a 120-day actual suspension is adequate to serve the purposes of professional discipline and is therefore the discipline we impose.

Background

Petitioner was admitted to the practice of law in California in June 1973. He has no prior record of discipline. The present disciplinary proceeding arose out of two separate incidents involving two clients.

1. The Northway Matter

In 1986, petitioner represented Northway, who was a defendant in a property damage action. As part of a settlement reached in June 1986, Northway agreed to pay plaintiff Peightel $2,000. Later that month, Northway gave petitioner a check for $2,000 to satisfy the settlement. Petitioner deposited the check in his general account rather than in his client trust account. He then made out a check for $2,000 payable to Peightel's counsel Schaefer and drawn on petitioner's client trust account. Schaefer deposited the check, but it was returned because of insufficient funds.

After Schaefer had contacted petitioner, petitioner gave him a check for $2,002.50 drawn on petitioner's general account. This check too was returned for insufficient funds. In mid-August 1986, petitioner gave Schaefer a cashier's check for $2,002.50. Schaefer filed a complaint with the State Bar.

When these transactions occurred, petitioner was in the process of moving his office from Vista to Escondido and changing bank branches. Also, petitioner's secretary of six years, who handled his banking, left his employ. As an apparent result of his secretary's departure, petitioner changed the method of handling his accounts; payment was stopped on certain checks petitioner had deposited in his trust account; and the Internal Revenue Service levied on petitioner's general account.

2. The Smyth Matter

Petitioner had represented Smyth in various business matters for a number of years. In 1986, Smyth loaned money to the owner of an airplane, the owner defaulted, and Smyth became the owner of the airplane. Smyth and petitioner agreed that petitioner would sell the plane and that petitioner would receive 50 percent of the sale price as his compensation.

In August 1986, petitioner sold the plane for $3,000. With the proceeds, petitioner satisfied a $1,500 lien on the plane. Petitioner did not deposit the remaining $1,500 in his client trust account. Three days after the sale, petitioner gave Smyth a check for $1,500 drawn on his client trust account; the sum included $750 for the plane sale proceeds and additional money that petitioner owed Smyth from transactions not related to this case. The check was returned because of insufficient funds. The account on which the check was drawn had been closed before the check was written.

In mid-March 1987, petitioner gave Smyth a second check for $1,500. The check was drawn on petitioner's general account and was postdated to the end of the month. Smyth deposited the cheek before the end of the month; it was returned for insufficient funds. There is a conflict in the evidence as to whether petitioner requested that Smyth not deposit this check before March 31, 1987. Also, according to petitioner, Smyth owed him attorney fees and petitioner believed he was entitled to offset those unpaid fees against the amounts he owed Smyth.

Smyth complained to the State Bar. Smyth and petitioner then conferred. In August 1988, petitioner paid Smyth $1,500 by cashier's check, and Smyth signed a letter to the State Bar composed by petitioner stating that the matter had been resolved satisfactorily.

3. Proceedings Before Hearing Panel and Review Department

The hearing panel, consisting of a single referee, found that in the Northway matter petitioner had failed to deposit the settlements funds received from Northway in his client trust account, allowed the funds to be commingled with other funds, and did not promptly pay the funds received, in violation of Business and Professions Code sections 6068, subdivision (a), 6103, and 6106 and former rules 8-101(A) and 8-101(B)(4) of the Rules of Professional Conduct. The hearing panel also found that petitioner did not misappropriate any funds.

In the Smyth matter, the hearing panel found that petitioner had failed to promptly pay Smyth the funds due Smyth, in violation of former rule 8-101(B)(4) of the Rules of Professional Conduct. The hearing panel also found that petitioner did not willfully misappropriate any funds.

In mitigation, the hearing panel found that petitioner had no prior discipline in 16 years of law practice. The hearing panel also noted that in 1986 and 1987 petitioner was in the process of a divorce and was subject to unusual emotional strain, but it found that the evidence did not establish "personal problems" or "severe psychological difficulties" as mitigating factors. The hearing panel recommended that petitioner be suspended from law practice for two years, with execution of the suspension stayed on the condition that he be placed on probation for two years and actually suspended for four months.

The review department, by a vote of 11 to 1, modified the findings and conclusions of the hearing panel. In the Northway matter, the review department adopted the findings and conclusions of the hearing panel, with one exception. It determined that petitioner had not committed an act of moral turpitude, dishonesty or corruption and thus had not violated Business and Professions Code section 6106.

In the Smyth matter, the review department replaced the hearing panel's finding that petitioner had violated only former rule 8-101(B)(4) of the Rules of Professional Conduct (by failing to promptly pay to Smyth the funds Smyth was entitled to receive) with its own finding that he had willfully failed to promptly pay the funds due Smyth and that he had willfully misappropriated $750, in violation of Business and Professions Code sections 6068, subdivision (a), 6103, 6106 and former rule 8-101(B)(4) of the Rules of Professional Conduct.

The review department recommended that petitioner be suspended from the practice of law for three years, with the suspension stayed on conditions that included three years of probation and one-year actual suspension.

Discussion

As noted earlier, petitioner raises two issues. He maintains that the evidence does not support the findings of the hearing panel and that the discipline recommended by the review department is excessive.

1. Sufficiency of Evidence [Omitted]

2. Discipline

We accord great weight to the disciplinary recommendation of the review department. (Hartford v. State Bar (1990) 50 Cal. 3d 1139, 1154, 270 Cal. Rptr. 12, 791 P.2d 598.) Petitioner bears the burden of demonstrating that the recommended discipline is erroneous or unlawful. (In re Abbott (1977) 19 Cal. 3d 249, 253, 137 Cal. Rptr. 195, 561 P.2d 285.) But we exercise our independent judgment in deciding appropriate discipline (Howard v. State Bar (1990) 51 Cal. 3d 215, 220, 270 Cal. Rptr. 856, 793 P.2d 62), considering all relevant aggravating and mitigating circumstances (Waysman v. State Bar (1986) 41 Cal. 3d 452, 457, 224 Cal. Rptr. 101, 714 P.2d 1239).

In determining what discipline to impose here we consider these factors: In the Northway matter, petitioner failed to deposit in his trust account funds received from the client, he commingled these funds with other funds, and he did not promptly pay the funds. In the Smyth matter, petitioner willfully failed to promptly pay the funds due Smyth, and he willfully misappropriated $750.

Standard 2.2(b) of the Standards for Attorney Sanctions for Professional Misconduct (Rules Proc. of State Bar, div. V, Stds. for Atty. Sanctions for Prof. Misconduct) (all further references to standards are to these provisions) states that commingling of entrusted funds, or other offenses involving client funds not amounting to willful misappropriation, shall result in at least three months' actual suspension. Standard 2.2(a) provides that disbarment is the usual discipline for an attorney who has willfully misappropriated entrusted funds, and that a lesser discipline shall be imposed only if the amount misappropriated is insignificantly small or "the most compelling mitigating circumstances clearly predominate," in which case the attorney shall be actually suspended for one year. We have stressed, however, that we do not follow the standards in rigid fashion (Howard v. State Bar, supra, 51 Cal. 3d at p.221, 270 Cal. Rptr. 856, 793 P.2d 62), and have observed that standard 2.2(a), insofar as it requires a minimum of one year of actual suspension, is "not faithful to the teachings of this court's decisions." (Edwards v. State Bar (1990) 52 Cal. 3d 28, 38, 276 Cal. Rptr. 153, 801 P.2d 396.)

The most serious conclusion that can be drawn from petitioner's misconduct is that he willfully misappropriated $750 belonging to Smyth. As used in attorney discipline cases, the term willful misappropriation covers "a broad range of conduct varying significantly in the degree of culpability." (Edwards v. State Bar, supra, 52 Cal. 3d at p.38, 276 Cal. Rptr. 153, 801 P.2d 396.)

In this case, petitioner's willful misappropriation of client funds was not accompanied by acts of deceit. Although the record is unclear on this point, the circumstances surrounding the Smyth matter indicate that petitioner's failure to promptly remit the funds to Smyth, though inexcusable, was probably the result of petitioner's negligent banking practices and a misunderstanding of his duties rather than an intent to harm. This conclusion is supported by the fact that the hearing referee, who heard the evidence and evaluated the credibility of the witnesses, said at the misconduct hearing there was no evidence that petitioner had willfully misappropriated and converted to his own use any entrusted funds. Although the referee may not have been aware that under our decisions willful misappropriation may be found in the absence of deliberate wrongdoing (Palomo v. State Bar (1984) 36 Cal. 3d 785, 795, 205 Cal. Rptr. 834, 685 P.2d 1185), this determination underscores the absence of any evidence of fraudulent intent.

The absence of harm to the attorney's clients or others resulting from the misconduct may be a significant mitigating factor in attorney discipline cases. (Std. 1.2(e)(iii).) Here, in the Northway matter, both the hearing panel and the review department concluded that no one suffered any monetary loss as a result of petitioner's conduct. We disagree. Petitioner's failure to promptly pay to plaintiff Peightel the funds received from petitioner's client, defendant Northway, deprived Peightel of the use of $2,000 for approximately six weeks. This was a monetary loss, albeit not a particularly grievous one.

With respect to Smyth, the hearing panel found that he sustained no monetary loss as a result of petitioner's misconduct; the review department did not adopt this finding. We disagree with the hearing panel: Smyth was deprived of $750 for approximately two years. This monetary injury is genuine, although not severe.

In the Northway matter, petitioner's delivery of a cashier's check on notification that his second check had been returned for insufficient funds, before any complaint to the State Bar or knowledge that a complaint would be made, indicates the absence of intent to misappropriate. In the Smyth matter, the hearing panel specifically found that there was a dispute between Smyth and petitioner regarding whether petitioner was entitled to offset the amount due Smyth for the proceeds of the plane sale with other amounts assertedly due to petitioner for attorney fees. Although the lack of wrongful intent does not excuse petitioner's misconduct, it is an important consideration in determining what discipline to impose. (See Edwards v. State Bar, supra, 52 Cal. 3d at p.38, 276 Cal. Rptr. 153, 801 P.2d 396.)

Before the misconduct petitioner had practiced for 13 years in this state without any disciplinary record. We have previously found an unblemished record for a similar period to be "an important mitigating circumstance." (Schneider v. State Bar, 43 Cal. 3d at pp.798-799, 239 Cal. Rptr. 111, 739 P.2d 1279; accord Waysman v. State Bar, supra, 41 Cal. 3d at p.457, 224 Cal. Rptr. 101, 714 P.2d 1239.)

Petitioner's misconduct is serious and inexcusable. Therefore, a period of actual suspension is necessary to serve the purposes of professional discipline, including preservation of public confidence in the legal profession. But in light of the mitigating circumstances discussed previously, including petitioner's 13 years of practice without discipline, the absence of serious injury to petitioner's clients or other parties, and the lack of convincing evidence of wrongful intent, the one-year period of actual suspension recommended by the review department is excessive. A 120-day actual suspension, as recommended by the hearing panel, is adequate to protect the public.

Disposition

We order that petitioner Patrick B. Kelly be suspended from the practice of law for three years from the date this opinion is final but that execution of the suspension order be stayed and that he be placed on probation for three years on all the conditions of probation adopted by the review department at its October 30, 1989, meeting, except that petitioner shall be actually suspended from the practice of law for only the first 120 days of the probationary period.

It is further ordered that petitioner Patrick B. Kelly comply with the requirements of rule 955 of the California Rules of Court, that he perform the acts specified in subdivisions (a) and (c) of that rule within 30 and 40 days, respectively, after the effective date of this order (under Bus. & Prof. Code, §6126, subd. (c), failure to comply with rule 955 of the California Rules of Court may result in imprisonment) and that he take and pass the Professional Responsibility Examination given by the National Conference of Bar Examiners within one year of the effective date of this order.

This order is effective upon finality of this decision in this court. (See Cal. Rules of Court, rule 953(a).)

In re Disciplinary Action Against Lochow
469 N.W.2d 91 (Minn. 1991)

PER CURIAM.

This case comes before us after the director of the Lawyers Professional Responsibility Board filed a petition for disciplinary proceedings against respondent. . . .

Respondent has been licensed to practice law in Minnesota since 1982. After graduating from Jamestown College in 1968 and serving in the military for 3 years, respondent attended law school at the University of North Dakota where he graduated in 1974. He has been licensed to practice in North Dakota since July 1974. After working for various governmental agencies, respondent became a partner with William Gray, forming Gray & Lochow. They were partners from 1979 until 1982, when Gray began working for a life insurance company. Respondent is currently a sole practitioner in Fargo, North Dakota.

The problems arose out of a probate action resulting from the death of Minnesota resident Robert H. Peterson on January 11, 1982, who died in a plane crash. The decedent's wife, Susan Peterson (hereinafter referred to as Peterson), retained Gray & Lochow to probate the estate and resolve other related litigation in Minnesota. Gray & Lochow had done work for the Petersons prior to Mr. Peterson's death and had contact with Susan Peterson in January and February 1982. Susan Peterson was appointed personal representative February 12, 1982.

First Count: Peterson Estate Fund Violations

On February 8, 1982, Gray & Lochow requested and received $75,000 from Peterson. Respondent deposited the $75,000 in the firm's trust account at Fargo National Bank, then returned $10,000 to Peterson to open an estate account. There is some dispute as to how the remaining $65,000 was to be used. Respondent claims that his understanding with Gray was that the $65,000 was to be used to pay expected attorney fees; however, respondent admits that he never discussed or confirmed this with Peterson. Nothing was memorialized in writing.

Two other transactions occurred on February 8, 1982. Respondent transferred $7,500 from the trust account to the Gray & Lochow business account. This was done without Peterson's knowledge or consent. Also on this date, Gray withdrew $2,500 from the trust account for his own use and then transferred the remaining $55,000 to a Merrill Lynch cash management account (CMA), all without Peterson's knowledge or consent. These latter transactions by Gray were made also without respondent's consent; however, when he did learn of the transactions, he did not act to reverse them.

The Merrill Lynch CMA was not a properly administered trust account. The referee found, however, that respondent believed that the CMA was a trust account at the time it was opened. The first monthly statement had a "trust account" designation on it although this was dropped after Merrill Lynch determined that it could not be used as a trust account. The CMA could be, and was, used to pay, among other things, credit card charges and checks issued by the account holders. From February 1982 through December 1983, respondent and Gray withdrew $25,700 on checks made out to Gray & Lochow from the CMA with respondent's knowledge and consent. During this time period, respondent individually withdrew $2,250 from the CMA.

In addition to the $2,500 that Gray withdrew in February 1982, from March 1982 through June 1983, Gray individually withdrew a total of $13,000 from the CMA through credit card charges or cash withdrawals. According to the findings of the referee, respondent did not know of Gray's transfers and credit card charges until they appeared on the monthly statement for the CMA. He did nothing to report these withdrawals to Peterson.

On April 28, 1982, respondent requested a $7,500 retainer from Peterson, which she sent and which respondent deposited in the Gray & Lochow trust account. On December 31, 1982, $21,250 was transferred from the CMA to the Gray & Lochow trust account. On November 1, 1983, respondent requested an additional $7,500 retainer from Peterson. This time, however, she did not send respondent the funds, but authorized him to withdraw the $7,500 from the trust account. From January 1, 1983, through December 1985, respondent periodically withdrew the remaining $21,250 from the trust account, including the interest earned. Except for the authorization from Peterson for $7,500 in November 1983, all transfers and withdrawals were made without Peterson's explicit knowledge or consent.

The referee found that, based on respondent's understanding that the Peterson funds were to be used for payment of legal fees (an understanding which Gray communicated to respondent but which respondent did not confirm with Peterson), the periodic withdrawals were intended as payment for services which had been or would be rendered. Respondent admits that the procedures utilized in withdrawing funds were inappropriate because: (1) he did not send periodic billings to Peterson to account for the funds; (2) he did not advise her of withdrawals as they occurred; and (3) he failed to preserve appropriate records to substantiate the withdrawals, including a record of services performed, the time devoted thereto, and the reasonable value thereof. Accordingly, respondent admits that the withdrawals from the Peterson funds violated DR 9-102(A)(2), Minn. Code Prof. Resp. (1985) and Minn. R. Prof. Conduct 1.15(a)(2). He also admits that the CMA was not a properly administered trust fund and violated DR 9-103, Minn. Code of Prof. Resp. Furthermore, respondent's failure to provide periodic accounting to Peterson for claimed fees violated DR 9-102(B)(3), Minn. Code of Prof. Resp. and Minn. R. Prof. Conduct 1.15(b)(3). Finally, the withdrawals by means other than check from the CMA and trust account violated Lawyers Professional Board Opinion No. 11.

Second Count: Misrepresentations to the Court
and Unreasonable Fees

After respondent filed a Final Account and Amended Final Account listing attorney fees, and after hearing on the matter, the district court approved the accounting and the probate estate was closed. In June 1988, after securing new counsel, Peterson filed an order to show cause on the appropriateness of the fees. Respondent testified at the hearing to show cause before the district court that $72,500 was charged as attorney fees; that he had maintained records of his withdrawals from the trust accounts; that the fee charged was directly related to the number of hours spent on the estate; and that he had the exact numbers at his office. Respondent also stated at the hearing to show cause that he would provide the court with a record of disbursements from the trust.

Respondent later filed an affidavit and accounting with the court. He did not provide the court with the number of hours spent on the estate. As the referee found, and respondent concedes, the accounting with the court was false and misleading:

> The accounting did not show that withdrawals were made by Visa charges against the CMA. The accounting did not show that some disbursements were made to respondent or Gray individually, instead representing that all withdrawals from trust were to the law firm business account. The accounting also did not show transfer of funds from the trust account to the CMA account or to the Northwest Bank savings account although respondent testified he did not believe this omission was false or misleading.

Respondent concedes that these misrepresentations to the court violated Minn. R. Prof. Conduct 3.3(a)(1), (4), 8.4(d).

After the hearing to show cause, the court held that the attorney fees of $72,500 were excessive and unreasonable. The court ordered respondent to refund $36,250 to Peterson. In the court's findings of fact and conclusions of law, it found that the fees were neither justified by the time and labor spent on the project nor warranted by the experience and expertise of respondent. The court found that the fees were in excess of that which is customarily charged for such services. After the order, respondent and Peterson, who was represented by independent counsel, executed a settlement whereby the order was compromised requiring a refund by respondent to Peterson of $15,000 in exchange for full release of all claims. Respondent concedes, at least to the extent of the $15,000 settlement, that the fees were excessive and unreasonable in violation of Minn. R. Prof. Conduct 1.5.

Third Count: Neglect of Estate Matters [Omitted]

Fourth Count: Misrepresentations to the Board
[Omitted]

Trust Account Improprieties and Excessive Fees

Respondent points to the referee's finding that there was no misap-propriation of funds:

> However, because respondent had a claim of right to the funds, i.e., fees earned or to be earned, technical misappropriation is denied; the Direc-tor's Office concedes such allegation is not proved; and no finding of mis-appropriation of client funds is made.

Respondent also states, citing ABA standards, that, where client funds are separately maintained, but sloppy bookkeeping makes it difficult to deter-mine the state of the client trust account, admonition is appropriate. Stan-dards for Imposing Lawyer Sanctions commentary to standard 4.14 (1986). Furthermore, although respondent concedes that some sanction for the im-proprieties is appropriate, he notes that, even where inadequate trust pro-cedures result in misappropriation, suspension did not always follow. In re Fling, 316 N.W.2d 556, 558 (Minn. 1982) (attorney did not intentionally convert funds, but misappropriation was not excused because of misman-agement; attorney required to pay retribution and allow supervision of trust account by another attorney). The director responds, citing standard 4.12, that failure to maintain a proper trust account is a serious violation:

> Suspension is generally appropriate when a lawyer knows or should know that he is dealing improperly with client property and causes injury or potential injury to a client.

Standards for Imposing Lawyer Sanctions standard 4.12. Furthermore, the director maintains that the fees taken from the accounts amount to a de-pletion of client trust funds without justification. While the referee did not find misappropriation, the director notes that the withdrawals are suspect and reflect on respondent's honesty. The director submitted exhibits show-ing that respondent's file inventory does not reflect the hours necessary to account for the fees.

With respect to the withdrawals by respondent and Gray and the fail-ure to hold the funds in a proper trust account, respondent concedes that the procedures were inappropriate. However, respondent contends that the current status of Minnesota law as to the appropriate placement of funds used essentially for services rendered makes the 18-month suspen-sion too severe. Respondent notes that a minority of jurisdictions allows advances for future services to be put into the attorney's business account. As authority for this proposition, respondent cites ABA/BNA Lawyers' Manual on Professional Responsibility 45:101:

Funds belonging only in part or potentially to the lawyer, such as advance fees ... usually must be deposited in clients' trust accounts, and may be withdrawn only when there is an accounting and severance of interests or when advanced fees are actually earned by the lawyer. A minority view permits lawyers to deposit advanced fees in their personal accounts and then refund any unearned portion at the end of the representation.

In a recent edition of the Minnesota Bench & Bar, the director stated:

> If the fee is an *advance for future services,* the majority view is that it must be deposited in the trust account and withdrawn only as earned. In Minnesota, the Director's Office has taken the majority view on fees for future services. This view has also been applied in at least two lawyer discipline decisions of the Minnesota Supreme Court. In re Green, unpublished order (Minn., March 6, 1984); In re Getty, 452 N.W.2d 694 (Minn. 1990).

Wernz, Ethics Opinions, Bench & B. Minn., May-June, 1990, at 18. Respondent contends that *Green* is no authority because it is unpublished. Furthermore, he argues that language in *Getty*, by implication, supports his view that the Peterson funds, as services to be earned, need not be put in a trust account. In *Getty*, the attorney offered to represent a client for a flat fee of $10,000. A dispute arose between Getty and the client, and Getty offered to refund a portion of the funds. This court stated that there was no evidence that Getty earned the right to the $10,000 retainer, either before or after his representation. Id. at 698. Respondent relies on this court's statement that the attorney admitted that he did not place the $10,000 in trust "when a dispute arose concerning the funds." Id. Respondent here contends that this language implies that the funds do not have to be placed in trust until a dispute arises. We disagree.

As the director notes, it has long been the view in Minnesota that advance payments for future services are client funds until earned:

> Retainers are a source of confusion in many cases. Retainers which are charged to ensure the lawyer's availability for the case may, if reasonable, be non-refundable and earned at the time they are collected. Other retainers may be advances by the client to be applied to future costs and services. Such retainers are not earned at the time they are collected and should be placed in the trust account. Withdrawals should be made only as services are performed and costs incurred in behalf of the client. In all events, the exact nature of the retainer should be made clear to the client at the time the retainer is paid.

Hoover, Many Ethics Complaints Are Completely Avoidable, Bench & B. Minn., Feb. 1982, at 21. Minnesota has been at the forefront of trust account recordkeeping and compliance. In what the ABA/BNA Manual calls the "Minnesota Model," since 1976, Minnesota has spelled out the requirements of trust accounting and recordkeeping with special emphasis on keeping the client apprised of the use and location of such funds. See Opinion No. 9, Bench & B. Minn., May-June 1976, at 58-59.

It appears to this court, however, that the question of the use of the $72,500 was largely a dispute over fees. The misconduct consisted of failing to advise the client properly when withdrawals of money for attorney fees and costs were being made and to explain, justify and give accountings thereof. The referee found that respondent believed that the money placed in the Merrill Lynch account was in trust, and the director concedes that there has been no misappropriation of funds. Moreover, the amount of attorney fees was ultimately compromised after the dispute became apparent.

We do feel an obligation to advise the bar that this court is getting increasingly alarmed at the numerous cases of trust account violations by lawyers of this state. The number of instances of notorious cases should have by now alerted lawyers to the seriousness of this problem. We thus can no longer treat lightly any abuse of trust accounts. Moreover, these violations are becoming increasingly costly to every lawyer in this state. Therefore, we feel compelled to advise the bar that misuse of trust accounts in the future will (1) almost invariably result in lengthy suspension at the very least and disbarment at worst and (2) that retainer fees not immediately placed in a trust account will be looked upon with suspicion. We are fully aware that there may be cases when the client's desire to have a particular attorney represent him or her will necessitate an immediate commitment. That attorney will possibly have to forego representation of other clients and might lose other business while the attorney commits him- or herself to the client now seeking representation. Such a retainer fee, if reasonable, may be immediately earned. However, the purpose of the retainer fee and the consent of the client for the payment and use thereof must be reduced to writing and approved by the client. Furthermore, attorney fees for payment of services to be performed in the future must be placed in a trust account and removed only by giving the client notice in writing of the time, amount, and purpose of the withdrawal, together with a complete accounting thereof. . . .

Accordingly, it is ordered by this court:

1. That, upon filing of this order, respondent is immediately indefinitely suspended from the practice of law in the State of Minnesota. He shall not be eligible to petition for reinstatement for a period of at least 6 months.

2. Respondent shall pay $750 in costs and $2,000 in disbursements pursuant to the agreement of the parties made in this proceeding and Rule 24, Rules on Lawyers Professional Responsibility.

EXERCISES

1. Create a personal budget for yourself indicating all income and expenses.
2. Create a cash-flow budget for yourself based on your personal budget.

3. Go to the library and obtain a copy of a public corporation's financial statements and use its figures to prepare a ratio analysis of the company.
4. How would you indicate the value of the services of the attorneys and support staff in an evaluation of a law office's financial status?
5. Obtain a printout of a computer spreadsheet program and analyze its categories of accounts for appropriateness to a law office.
6. Discuss the ethical considerations in managing a trust account for clients.
7. Indicate how understanding a client's financial records would help in representing that client effectively.
8. Discuss the importance of an office's cash flow with respect to billing procedures.
9. Discuss the different areas of law that may require the use and understanding of balance sheets, income statements, and budgets.
10. What is your opinion of the court's reasoning in In re Disciplinary Action Against Lochow?

SITUATIONAL ANALYSIS

An attorney deposited settlement funds entrusted to her by her client into an account that she was using as a firm operating account. Rather than pay the opposing party, she wrote several checks on the account to pay firm operating expenses. When opposing counsel did not receive payment, he filed a motion to reopen the underlying civil case. Again, settlement was reached at an amount exceeding the first settlement by $500. The attorney misrepresented to opposing counsel that the settlement funds were in her escrow account, although they were not. To preserve the settlement, the attorney tendered a check drawn on her escrow account; upon receipt, opposing counsel again dismissed the civil complaint. The check was later returned for insufficient funds.

Discuss the ethical and legal problems of the above situation.

6 Marketing the Law Office

One of the best marketing and communication tools I have seen developed as a means of disseminating accurate information in personal injury/mass tort litigation is the newsletter. A regular, accurate, attractively designed, and professionally written newsletter goes a long way towards publishing fact and dispelling rumor and keeping the client's anxiety in check. Clients particularly love to read of the firm's big wins!

Leslie Lilienfeld DeHoust
Marketing Consultant
Guttenberg, New Jersey

CHAPTER OVERVIEW

In order to generate business and income it is not enough that a law office be well structured organizationally and financially. If no one knows that the firm exists, the office will soon be out of business.

As a natural outgrowth of creating an office image, the enterprise must make that image known. **Marketing** is the method whereby an organization creates new business by ensuring that the largest community possible is aware of and values its name and product. For a law office this means letting the public know who it is and what services it provides.

The basic concept of marketing is **name recognition.** As discussed previously, there are a multitude of lawyers and law offices in any geographic area, and a law office must be able to distinguish itself from its competitors if it wishes to stay in business and continue to grow. However, unlike a general business enterprise, a law office has some ethical considerations that must be weighed in developing a particular market strategy. Both the American Bar Association and state bar associations place certain prohibitions on an attorney's ability to market and advertise his or her services.

EXAMPLE:

A law office produces a television commercial in which the senior partner states that the office "guarantees positive results for all of its clients." Such guarantees are not only misleading but are also violations of several ethical considerations because in the law nothing is ever "guaranteed."

When it comes to marketing the law office, everyone in the office must be involved. As discussed in Chapter 3, every member of the legal team plays an important part in projecting the image of the office, and it is this image that is the basis of marketing the firm. Each member of the legal team is a spokesperson for the office; if the public likes the spokesperson, it is more likely to utilize the services of the office. This form of salesmanship builds awareness of the office name.

EXAMPLE:

A paralegal from the same law office is at a large party. The paralegal is well-dressed, well-spoken, and well-educated. When other partygoers become interested and ask the paralegal where she works, she has acted as a marketing agent for the office.

For a law office, marketing must answer two basic questions: (1) is it effective, that is, has the public become aware of the office's name and services? (2) is it ethical, not violating any bar association prohibition? If these two questions can be answered in the affirmative, the law office has created an appropriate marketing strategy.

Basic Marketing Concepts

The primary objective of any marketing strategy is to get the office's name known. The public must be made aware of the specific services the office provides and of the expertise of each member of the legal team. To accomplish this, the strategy must create a positive image of the office in the minds of the public and must create goodwill so that clients, both current and potential, desire to retain the services of the office.

There are three basic methods that most law offices use to get their names before the public. The first method is by using **letterhead** stationery and business cards bearing the name, address, and telephone number of the office. See Exhibit 11. Each time the stationery is used or the card handed out, the office's name is subconsciously planted in the mind of the reader. The style of the printing and the quality of the paper used also aid in creating a specific image for the office. People are impressed by quality, and the better the stationery, the greater the positive effect.

The second method used by most firms of getting the office's name before the public is the placement of an ad in the business pages of the telephone directory. Many people suddenly faced with a legal problem will look in a telephone directory to find an attorney. See Exhibit 12.

The third method used by most firms to create name recognition is to be listed in a directory of lawyers known as **Martindale-Hubbell.** Martindale-Hubbell is a publication used primarily by professionals and lawyers to find other lawyers in different cities or with different specialties, and is also used by some segments of the general public. See Exhibit 13.

These three methods are relatively modest, traditional methods of marketing a law office. However, because of increasingly growing competition, many law offices have adopted more aggressive approaches to market the firm. Generally, a law office targets two specific groups in marketing its services: existing clients and potential clients. Discussed below are several methods that an office may employ to market each group.

Marketing Existing Clients

Newsletters and Brochures.   Many law offices regularly print and mail newsletters and brochures to existing clients. This published material indicates new personnel who have joined the office, describing their areas of expertise and backgrounds; it highlights particular services of members of the office and may include reprints of articles written by the lawyers in the office for various learned publications. These newsletters and brochures create contact with the clients and assure them that the firm is interested in keeping them informed about changes in the office. Typically, a law office will send out a newsletter or brochure once or twice a year.

Host Functions.   Several times a year, especially during the December holidays, many offices host parties for their clients. Seeing the legal team in a quasi-social setting creates a positive image for the office and makes the client feel more relaxed around the legal team. Parties also create the impression of a friendly, rather than stuffy, business relationship between the office and the client.

In addition to yearly social events, many offices encourage members of the legal team to invite clients for lunch or dinner to discuss legal matters rather than always communicating with clients at office meetings or over the telephone. Once again, this creates a positive personal image of the office in the mind of a client.

Exhibit 11: Sample Letterhead and Business Card

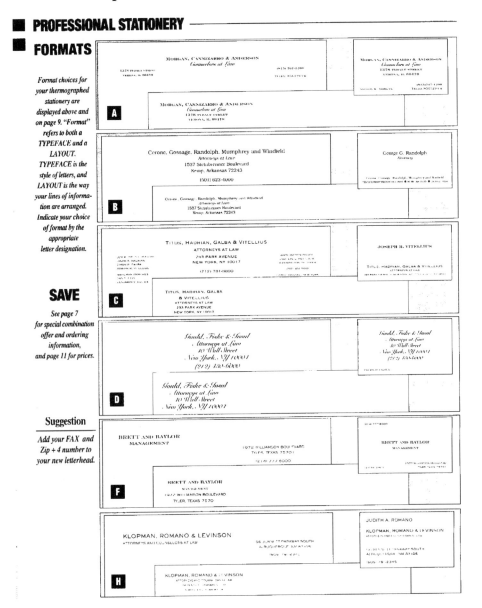

Reprint from Blumberg-Excelsior, 1-800-Lawmart.

Exhibit 11: *(continued)*

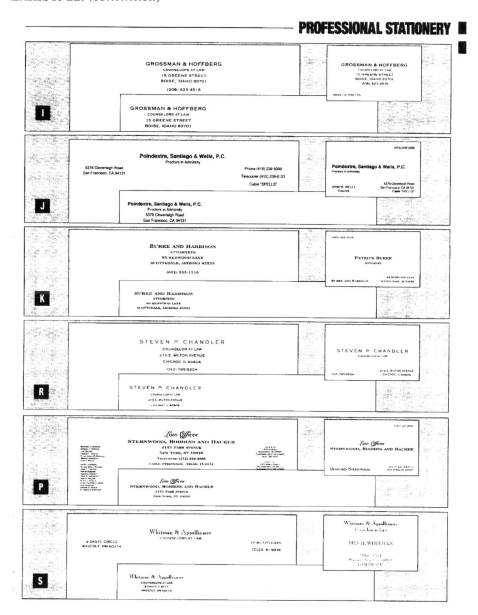

Exhibit 12: Ad from the Yellow Pages

Exhibit 13: Sample Page from Martindale-Hubbell

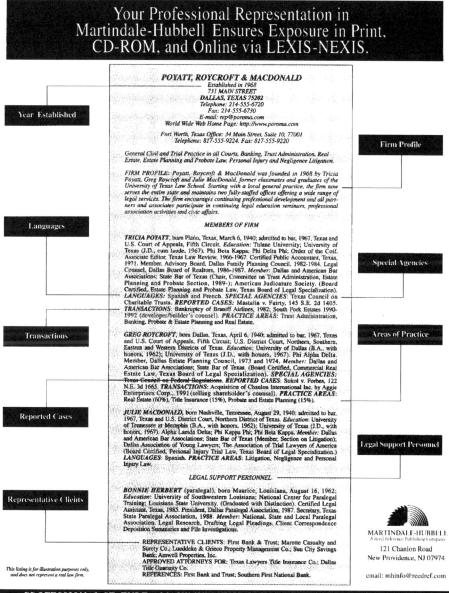

Client Reviews. In order to understand the nonlegal needs of their clients, law offices ask clients to fill out questionnaires or evaluation forms, encouraging their suggestions for changes and improvements in the office. By using these evaluation forms, the office can discover ways to improve its image and services, and the clients feel like active participants in the work of the legal team.

Cross-servicing. Cross-servicing is encouraging clients to utilize other services of the office in different legal areas. The office lets the client know of the variety of services it can provide and gently encourages the client to make use of the full spectrum of office services available. This can be viewed as a direct sales approach to marketing the office.

EXAMPLE:

A client hires a law office for representation in a securities law matter. After the successful conclusion of the problem, the office lets the client know that it also specializes in estate and real property matters. The client is asked whether his will needs revising. This method is not necessarily subtle but is generally effective.

Marketing New Clients

Direct Mail. Just as it does with existing clients, the law office can send out newsletters and brochures to the general public. The office can send out a general mailing to all persons living in a particular geographic area or may purchase names and addresses of persons from direct mail marketing operations. The office can even send out a simple flier highlighting its services and personnel to the public if it does not want to go to the expense of mailing bulky newsletters and brochures.

Publications. Attorneys often write articles on specific areas of law that are published not only in legal journals but also in newsletters and magazines geared for special interest groups. When subscribers to the publications read the article, they are made aware of the name of the attorney-author and that his or her law office has at least one area of expertise in which the reader is likely to have some interest. This can be a particularly effective way of marketing the firm.

EXAMPLE:

A partner in the law office writes an article on the effect of changes in the law on estate taxes. The article is published in a magazine aimed at retired persons. When the magazine subscribers read the article, they may feel the need to redo their wills based on the new law, and the author's name is already associated in their minds with effectuating these changes.

Open Houses. Law offices may host receptions that are open not only to existing clients but to anyone who wishes to attend. As with functions for existing clients, this has proven to be an effective method of marketing a firm and attracting new business.

Seminars. Every time a member of the office attends or speaks at a seminar he or she is marketing the law office. Lists of persons attending the seminar can be obtained, and the office can send follow-up letters to all seminar participants. This is a more specific method of doing a public mailing, and targets people who have seen and heard members of the office and presumably already have an interest in the particular area of law covered by the seminar.

The Rainmaker. Rainmaker is the term given to the member of the office whose primary function is to attract new business. This person, generally a partner in the firm, can be viewed as a "meeter and greeter," and has the type of personality that automatically attracts people. Outgoing and gregarious, rainmakers are usually sent to seminars and meetings, and have personal lives that place them in contact with large groups of people. The office rainmaker is the primary spokesperson for marketing the office.

Regardless of which method is used — and many more exist than have been mentioned here — it is important to understand that the best and most effective marketing tool that a law office has is a satisfied client. If a client feels well-treated and cared for, and that the office has presented a competent and confident image, he or she is very likely to recommend the office to friends and colleagues. Most new accounts are generated by word of mouth, which is why it is important to remember that a law office is a service industry, and that every member of the legal team represents the office whenever he or she provides a service to the client. The client's interests and needs should always be kept foremost in the minds and attitudes of the legal team.

Strategic Planning

In addition to its primary purpose of generating name recognition and business, marketing also helps the office to create an appropriate plan for future development. **Strategic planning,** the commitment to planning for the future of the organization, involves knowing where the office is and where it wishes to go. This planning may involve adding personnel to develop different or expanded areas of expertise, acquiring newer or larger office space, and developing a financial plan to increase income. All of these plans are developed by having an appropriate marketing strategy. For instance, if the office wishes to expand, adding more staff and increasing its physical size, marketing can generate additional clients, thereby justifying and paying for the growth. If the office wants to specialize or develop a particular area of expertise, effective marketing can target a client base that would be in need of these different services. And, of course, if the office wants simply to increase income, a good marketing strategy can help attract additional business.

Strategic planning, in conjunction with coordinated marketing, can help a law office develop in four main areas:

1. Compensation and Billing.   By expanding the client base, the office can increase the compensation paid to the members of the legal team because of the additional revenue and can create an effective method of billing.

2. Growth.   Expansion of office facilities and staff can be justified by developing a plan that will generate increased business.

3. Marketing.   By creating a strategic plan and targeting specific areas of change for the law office, a better marketing strategy can be developed that will help effectuate the desired changes.

4. Management.   Having a plan that indicates where the office is going can streamline the management of the enterprise, helping to put effort into the desired areas of change and reducing effort in areas that will be downscaled or eliminated.

Strategic planning helps determine the best path for the office to take, and marketing helps speed up the movement along that path.

Advertising

Newsletters, brochures, listings in the yellow pages, and professional publications are all methods of **advertising** the law office, as are television and radio commercials. Historically, attorneys and law offices were prohibited from advertising their services; however, several decades ago the courts decided that attorneys could advertise, and the American Bar Association (ABA) promulgated guidelines for attorneys to follow.

Pursuant to Model Rule of Professional Conduct 7.2, the ABA has affirmatively stated that attorneys may advertise; however, several caveats are attached to the rule. First of all, all advertisements, meaning all printed material plus anything that can be reduced to a tangible physical object such as tape, must be retained by the advertising attorney for a period of at least two years in case of a problem arising with respect to the ethics or legality of what was stated in the advertisement. Second, the advertisement must indicate the name of at least one attorney who will be legally responsible for whatever statements appear in the copy. And, third, an attorney may not compensate someone for merely recommending the attorney's services. This might be considered fee splitting, which is strictly prohibited.

For a detailed discussion of the problems incident to attorneys and advertising, see the cases appearing at the end of this chapter.

Marketing and Ethics

In addition to the specific advertising rules stated above, the American Bar Association has also promulgated specific ethical standards that must be adhered to in any marketing strategy utilized by a law office.

Model Rule of Professional Conduct 7.1 states that an attorney may not make any false or misleading statements in any aspect of marketing. The rule is designed to protect the public from being lured to use the services of a particular office based on fraudulent, false, or misrepresentative statements.

 EXAMPLE:

A law office states in its notice in the yellow pages that it has over 20 years' experience in contract negotiations. In fact, the office has never participated in contract negotiations, except to a very limited extent, and is hoping that this ad will generate a different client base. The ad violates Rule 7.1.

Rule 7.3 states that an attorney may make no direct solicitation of a client. In common parlance, an attorney may not "ambulance chase," that is, arrive at the scene of an accident with business cards in hand, asking to represent the victim. There is a distinction between making a person aware of or offering legal services, and asking a person directly if the attorney may represent him.

 EXAMPLE:

A corporate raider makes a tender offer for shares of stock in a corporation. An attorney telephones and writes to all the shareholders of the company telling them that she can get them more than is presently being offered for the stock, but only if they retain her services. This is direct solicitation of clients and is prohibited.

Model Rule 7.4 prohibits attorneys from declaring that they are specialists in particular areas of law. All lawyers are expected to be competent in all legal matters, and whereas they may indicate areas of experience, they cannot declare themselves to be specialists.

Most lawyers do develop expertise in certain areas of law because of the legal problems presented by their clients, and may get to be known in a community as having experience in a particular legal field. However, the attorney may only indicate areas of experience and cannot affirmatively claim to be a "specialist."

It is important to note that all of the ethical considerations that apply to the attorneys in a law office apply equally to the paralegals working as members of the legal team. The attorney is ultimately responsible for the ethics of the office, and so every member of the office is held, legally and morally, to the same ethical standard as the lawyer.

CHAPTER SUMMARY

Marketing is the method whereby a law office makes its name known and projects a favorable image to the general public. The reputation that the office has earned and the expertise of its legal team must be communicated to the public if the office hopes to attract clients and generate income.

Each member of the legal team plays an important role in the marketing of the office because each acts as a representative for the firm, both in the office and out in public. All members of the staff must be made aware of their important marketing function.

In addition to general marketing concepts and strategies, a law office must also pay attention to specific ethical prohibitions that exist with respect to marketing its services. Lawyers, as officers of the court, are expected to act in a manner that will earn the trust of the general public, and to accomplish this they are held to a higher standard of ethical care than the general population. All members of an attorney's office, as representatives of the attorney and the firm, are expected to adhere to the same ethical standards as the attorney.

Marketing is salesmanship, and the best product or service will generate no business if the public is unaware of its existence. If a law office does not advertise its services, it will soon be out of business.

Key Terms

Advertising: All methods of marketing designed to bring the name of the office before the public's consciousness.
Cross-servicing: Making current clients aware of additional services the office provides.
Letterhead: Stationery with the name and address of the office embossed on the top.
Marketing: Method of generating new business by making an office's services known to the public.
Martindale-Hubbell: Directory of lawyers and law firms.
Name recognition: Making the public aware of the office's name and image.
Rainmaker: Member of the office whose primary function is to develop client contacts.
Strategic planning: Targeting the future of the office in terms of growth.

Cases for Analysis

In re R.M.J. and Peel v. Attorney Disciplinary Commission of Illinois detail several of the problems incident to marketing and advertising legal services.

In re R.M.J.
455 U.S. 191 (1982)

Justice POWELL delivered the opinion of the Court.

The Court's decision in Bates v. State Bar of Arizona, 433 U.S. 350 (1977), required a re-examination of long-held perceptions as to "advertising" by lawyers. This appeal presents the question whether certain aspects of the revised ethical rules of the Supreme Court of Missouri regulating lawyer advertising conform to the requirements of *Bates.*

I

As with many of the States, until the decision in *Bates,* Missouri placed an absolute prohibition on advertising by lawyers. After the Court's invalidation of just such a prohibition in *Bates,* the Committee on Professional Ethics and Responsibility of the Supreme Court of Missouri revised that court's Rule 4 regulating lawyer advertising. The Committee sought to "strike a midpoint between prohibition and unlimited advertising," and the revised regulation of advertising, adopted with slight modification by the State Supreme Court, represents a compromise. Lawyer advertising is permitted, but it is restricted to certain categories of information, and in some instances, to certain specified language.

Thus, part B of DR 2-101 of the Rule states that a lawyer may "publish . . . in newspapers, periodicals and the yellow pages of telephone directories" 10 categories of information: name, address and telephone number; areas of practice; date and place of birth; schools attended; foreign language ability; office hours; fee for an initial consultation; availability of a schedule of fees; credit arrangements; and the fixed fee to be charged for certain specified "routine" legal services. Although the Rule does not state explicitly that these 10 categories of information or the 3 indicated forms of printed advertisement are the only information and the only means of advertising that will be permitted, that is the interpretation given the Rule by the State Supreme Court and the Advisory Committee charged with its enforcement.

In addition to these guidelines, and under authority of the Rule, the Advisory Committee has issued an addendum to the Rule providing that if the lawyer chooses to list areas of practice in his advertisement, he must do so in one of two prescribed ways. He may list one of three general descriptive terms specified in the Rule — "General Civil Practice," "General Criminal Practice," or "General Civil and Criminal Practice." Alternatively, he may use one or more of a list of 23 areas of practice, including, for example,

"Tort Law," "Family Law," and "Probate and Trust Law." He may not list both a general term and specific subheadings, nor may he deviate from the precise wording stated in the Rule. He may not indicate that his practice is "limited" to the listed areas and he must include a particular disclaimer of certification of expertise following any listing of specific areas of practice.

Finally, one further aspect of the Rule is relevant in this case. DR 2-102 of Rule 4 regulates the use of professional announcement cards. It permits a lawyer or firm to mail a dignified "brief professional announcement card stating new or changed associates or addresses, change of firm name, or similar matters." The Rule, however, does not permit a general mailing; the announcement cards may be sent only to "lawyers, clients, former clients, personal friends, and relatives." Mo. Rev. Stat., Sup. Ct. Rule 4, DR 2-102(A)(2) (1978) (Index Vol.).

II

Appellant graduated from law school in 1973 and was admitted to the Missouri and Illinois Bars in the same year. After a short stint with the Securities and Exchange Commission in Washington, D.C., appellant moved to St. Louis, Mo., in April 1977, and began practice as a sole practitioner. As a means of announcing the opening of his office, he mailed professional announcement cards to a selected list of addressees. In order to reach a wider audience, he placed several advertisements in local newspapers and in the yellow pages of the local telephone directory.

The advertisements at issue in this litigation appeared in January, February, and August 1978, and included information that was not expressly permitted by Rule 4. They included the information that appellant was licensed in Missouri and Illinois. They contained, in large capital letters, a statement that appellant was "Admitted to Practice Before THE UNITED STATES SUPREME COURT." And they included a listing of areas of practice that deviated from the language prescribed by the Advisory Committee — e.g., "personal injury" and "real estate" instead of "tort law" and "property law" — and that included several areas of law without analogue in the list of areas prepared by the Advisory Committee — e.g., "contract," "zoning & land use," "communication," "pension & profit sharing plans." In addition, and with the exception of the advertisement appearing in August 1978, appellant failed to include the required disclaimer of certification of expertise after the listing of areas of practice.

On November 19, 1979, the Advisory Committee filed an information in the Supreme Court of Missouri charging appellant with unprofessional conduct. The information charged appellant with publishing three advertisements that listed areas of law not approved by the Advisory Committee, that listed the courts in which appellant was admitted to practice, and, in the case of two of the advertisements, that failed to include the required disclaimer of certification. The information also charged appellant with sending announcement cards to "persons other than lawyers, clients, former clients, personal friends, and relatives" in violation of DR 2-102(A)(2).

In response, appellant argued that, with the exception of the disclaimer requirement, each of these restrictions upon advertising was unconstitutional under the First and Fourteenth Amendments.

In a disbarment proceeding, the Supreme Court of Missouri upheld
the constitutionality of DR 2-101 of Rule 4 and issued a private reprimand.
609 S.W.2d 411 (1981). But the court did not explain the reasons for its decision, nor did it state whether it found appellant to have violated each of
the charges lodged against him or only some of them. Indeed, the court
only purported to uphold the constitutionality of DR 2-101; it did not mention the propriety of DR 2-102, which governs the use of announcement
cards.

Writing in separate dissenting opinions, Chief Justice Bardgett and
Judge Seiler argued that the information should be dismissed. The dissenters suggested that the State did not have a significant interest either in
requiring the use of certain, specified words to describe areas of practice or
in prohibiting a lawyer from informing the public as to the States and
courts in which he was licensed to practice. Nor would the dissenters have
found the mailing of this sort of information to be unethical.

III

In Bates v. State of Arizona, 433 U.S. 350 (1977), the Court considered
whether the extension of First Amendment protection to commercial
speech announced in Virginia Pharmacy Board v. Virginia Citizens Consumer Council, 425 U.S. 748 (1976), applied to the regulation of advertising
by lawyers. The *Bates* Court held that indeed lawyer advertising was a
form of commercial speech, protected by the First Amendment, and that
"advertising by attorneys may not be subjected to blanket suppression."
433 U.S., at 383.

More specifically, the *Bates* Court held that lawyers must be permitted
to advertise the fees they charge for certain "routine" legal services. The
Court concluded that this sort of price advertising was not "inherently"
misleading, and therefore could not be prohibited on that basis. The Court
also rejected a number of other justifications for broad restrictions upon
advertising including the potential adverse effect of advertising on professionalism, on the administration of justice, and on the cost and quality of
legal services, as well as the difficulties of enforcing standards short of
an outright prohibition. None of these interests was found to be sufficiently strong or sufficiently affected by lawyer advertising to justify a prohibition.

But the decision in *Bates* nevertheless was a narrow one. The Court
emphasized that advertising by lawyers still could be regulated. False, deceptive, or misleading advertising remains subject to restraint, and the
Court recognized that advertising by the professions poses special risks of
deception — "because the public lacks sophistication concerning legal services, misstatements that might be overlooked or deemed unimportant in
other advertising may be found quite inappropriate in legal advertising."

Ibid. (footnote omitted). The Court suggested that claims as to quality or in-person solicitation might be so likely to mislead as to warrant restriction. And the Court noted that a warning or disclaimer might be appropriately required, even in the context of advertising as to price, in order to dissipate the possibility of consumer confusion or deception. "[T]he bar retains the power to correct omissions that have the effect of presenting an inaccurate picture, [although] the preferred remedy is more disclosure, rather than less." Id., at 375.

In short, although the Court in *Bates* was not persuaded that price advertising for "routine" services was necessarily or inherently misleading, and although the Court was not receptive to other justifications for restricting such advertising, it did not by any means foreclose restrictions on potentially or demonstrably misleading advertising. Indeed, the Court recognized the special possibilities for deception presented by advertising for professional services. The public's comparative lack of knowledge, the limited ability of the professions to police themselves, and the absence of any standardization in the "product" renders advertising for professional services especially susceptible to abuses that the States have a legitimate interest in controlling.

Thus, the Court has made clear in *Bates* and subsequent cases that regulation — and imposition of discipline — are permissible where the particular advertising is inherently likely to deceive or where the record indicates that a particular form or method of advertising has in fact been deceptive. In Ohralik v. Ohio State Bar Assn., 436 U.S. 447, 462 (1978), the Court held that the possibility of "fraud, undue influence, intimidation, overreaching, and other forms of 'vexatious conduct'" was so likely in the context of in-person solicitation, that such solicitation could be prohibited. And in Friedman v. Rogers, 440 U.S. 1 (1979), we held that Texas could prohibit the use of trade names by optometrists, particularly in view of the considerable history in Texas of deception and abuse worked upon the consuming public through the use of trade names.

Commercial speech doctrine, in the context of advertising for professional services, may be summarized generally as follows: Truthful advertising related to lawful activities is entitled to the protections of the First Amendment. But when the particular content or method of the advertising suggests that it is inherently misleading or when experience has proved that in fact such advertising is subject to abuse, the States may impose appropriate restrictions. Misleading advertising may be prohibited entirely. But the States may not place an absolute prohibition on certain types of potentially misleading information, e.g., a listing of areas of practice, if the information also may be presented in a way that is not deceptive. Thus, the Court in *Bates* suggested that the remedy in the first instance is not necessarily a prohibition but preferably a requirement of disclaimers or explanation. 433 U.S., at 375. Although the potential for deception and confusion is particularly strong in the context of advertising professional services, restrictions upon such advertising may be no broader than reasonably necessary to prevent the deception.

Even when a communication is not misleading, the State retains some authority to regulate. But the State must assert a substantial interest and the interference with speech must be in proportion to the interest served. Central Hudson Gas & Electric Corp. v. Public Service Commn., 447 U.S. 557, 563-564 (1980). Restrictions must be narrowly drawn, and the State lawfully may regulate only to the extent regulation furthers the State's substantial interest. Thus, in *Bates*, the Court found that the potentially adverse effect of advertising on professionalism and the quality of legal services was not sufficiently related to a substantial state interest to justify so great an interference with speech. 433 U.S., at 368-372, 375-377.

IV

We now turn to apply these generalizations to the circumstances of this case.

The information lodged against appellant charged him with four separate kinds of violation of Rule 4: listing the areas of his practice in language or in terms other than that provided by the Rule, failing to include a disclaimer, listing the courts and States in which he had been admitted to practice, and mailing announcement cards to persons other than "lawyers, clients, former clients, personal friends, and relatives." Appellant makes no challenge to the constitutionality of the disclaimer requirement, and we pass on to the remaining three infractions.

Appellant was reprimanded for deviating from the precise listing of areas of practice included in the Advisory Committee addendum to Rule 4. The Advisory Committee does not argue that appellant's listing was misleading. The use of the words "real estate" instead of "property" could scarcely mislead the public. Similarly, the listing of areas such as "contracts" or "securities," that are not found on the Advisory Committee's list in any form, presents no apparent danger of deception. Indeed, as Chief Justice Bardgett explained in dissent, in certain respects appellant's listing is more informative than that provided in the addendum. Because the listing published by the appellant has not been shown to be misleading, and because the Advisory Committee suggests no substantial interest promoted by the restriction, we conclude that this portion of Rule 4 is an invalid restriction upon speech as applied to appellant's advertisements.

Nor has the Advisory Committee identified any substantial interest in a rule that prohibits a lawyer from identifying the jurisdictions in which he is licensed to practice. Such information is not misleading on its face. Appellant was licensed to practice in both Illinois and Missouri. This is factual and highly relevant information particularly in light of the geography of the region in which appellant practiced.

Somewhat more troubling is appellant's listing, in large capital letters, that he was a member of the Bar of the Supreme Court of the United States. The emphasis of this relatively uninformative fact is at least bad taste. Indeed, such a statement could be misleading to the general public unfamiliar with the requirements of admission to the Bar of this Court. Yet there is no finding to this effect by the Missouri Supreme Court. There is nothing in the record to indicate that the inclusion of this information was misleading. Nor does the Rule specifically identify this information as potentially misleading or, for example, place a limitation on type size or require a statement explaining the nature of the Supreme Court Bar.

Finally, appellant was charged with mailing cards announcing the opening of his office to persons other than "lawyers, clients, former clients, personal friends and relatives." Mailings and handbills may be more difficult to supervise than newspapers. But again we deal with a silent record. There is no indication that an inability to supervise is the reason the State restricts the potential audience of announcement cards. Nor is it clear that an absolute prohibition is the only solution. For example, by requiring a filing with the Advisory Committee of a copy of all general mailings, the State may be able to exercise reasonable supervision over such mailings. There is no indication in the record of a failed effort to proceed along such a less restrictive path. See Central Hudson Gas & Electric Corp. v. Public Service Commn., 447 U.S., at 566 ("we must determine whether the regulation . . . is not more extensive than is necessary to serve" the governmental interest asserted).

In sum, none of the three restrictions in the Rule upon appellant's First Amendment rights can be sustained in the circumstances of this case. There is no finding that appellant's speech was misleading. Nor can we say that it was inherently misleading, or that restrictions short of an absolute prohibition would not have sufficed to cure any possible deception. We emphasize, as we have throughout the opinion, that the States retain the authority to regulate advertising that is inherently misleading or that has proved to be misleading in practice. There may be other substantial state interests as well that will support carefully drawn restrictions. But although the States may regulate commercial speech, the First and Fourteenth Amendments require that they do so with care and in a manner no more extensive than reasonably necessary to further substantial interests. The absolute prohibition on appellant's speech, in the absence of a finding that his speech was misleading, does not meet these requirements.

Accordingly, the judgment of the Supreme Court of Missouri is Reversed.

[The appendix to the opinion has been omitted.]

Peel v. Attorney Disciplinary Commission of Illinois
496 U.S. 91 (1990)

Justice STEVENS announced the judgment of the Court and delivered an opinion, in which Justice BRENNAN, Justice BLACKMUN, and Justice KENNEDY join.

The Illinois Supreme Court publicly censured petitioner because his letterhead states that he is certified as a civil trial specialist by the National

Board of Trial Advocacy. We granted certiorari to consider whether the statement on his letterhead is protected by the First Amendment. 492 U.S. 917 (1989).

I

This case comes to us against a background of growing interest in lawyer certification programs. In the 1973 Sonnett Memorial Lecture, then Chief Justice Warren E. Burger advanced the proposition that specialized training and certification of trial advocates is essential to the American system of justice. That proposition was endorsed by a number of groups of lawyers who were instrumental in establishing the National Board of Trial Advocacy (NBTA) in 1977.

Since then, NBTA has developed a set of standards and procedures for periodic certification of lawyers with experience and competence in trial work. Those standards, which have been approved by a board of judges, scholars, and practitioners, are objective and demanding. They require specified experience as lead counsel in both jury and nonjury trials, participation in approved programs of continuing legal education, a demonstration of writing skills, and the successful completion of a day-long examination. Certification expires in five years unless the lawyer again demonstrates his or her continuing qualification.

NBTA certification has been described as a "highly-structured" and "arduous process that employs a wide range of assessment methods." Task Force on Lawyer Competence, Report With Findings and Recommendations to the Conference of Chief Justices, Publication No. NCSC-021, pp. 33-34 (May 26, 1982). After reviewing NBTA's procedures, the Supreme Court of Minnesota found that "NBTA applies a rigorous and exacting set of standards and examinations on a national scale before certifying a lawyer as a trial specialist." In re Johnson, 341 N.W.2d 282, 283 (1983). The Alabama Supreme Court similarly concluded that "a certification of specialty by NBTA would indicate a level of expertise with regard to trial advocacy in excess of the level of expertise required for admission to the bar generally." Ex parte Howell, 487 So. 2d 848, 851 (1986).

II

Petitioner practices law in Edwardsville, Illinois. He was licensed to practice in Illinois in 1968, in Arizona in 1979, and in Missouri in 1981. He has served as president of the Madison County Bar Association and has been active in both national and state bar association work. He has tried to verdict over 100 jury trials and over 300 nonjury trials, and has participated in hundreds of other litigated matters that were settled. NBTA issued petitioner a "Certificate in Civil Trial Advocacy" in 1981, renewed it in 1986, and listed him in its 1985 Directory of "Certified Specialists and Board Members."

Since 1983 petitioner's professional letterhead has contained a statement referring to his NBTA certification and to the three States in which he is licensed. It appears as follows:

Gary E. Peel
  Certified Civil Trial Specialist
  By the National Board of Trial Advocacy
Licensed: Illinois, Missouri, Arizona.

In 1987, the Administrator of the Attorney Registration and Disciplinary Commission of Illinois (Commission) filed a complaint alleging that petitioner, by use of this letterhead, was publicly holding himself out as a certified legal specialist in violation of Rule 2-105(a)(3) of the Illinois Code of Professional Responsibility. That Rule provides:

A lawyer or law firm may specify or designate any area or field of law in which he or its partners concentrates or limits his or its practice. Except as set forth in Rule 2-105(a), no lawyer may hold himself out as "certified" or a "specialist."

The complaint also alleged violations of Rule 2-101(b), which requires that a lawyer's public "communication shall contain all information necessary to make the communication not misleading and shall not contain any false or misleading statement or otherwise operate to deceive," and of Rule 1-102(a)(1), which generally subjects a lawyer to discipline for violation of any Rule of the Code of Professional Responsibility. Disciplinary Rules 2-101(b), 1-102(a)(1) (1988).

After a hearing, the Commission recommended censure for a violation of Rule 2-105(a)(3). It rejected petitioner's First Amendment claim that a reference to a lawyer's certification as a specialist was a form of commercial speech that could not be "'subjected to blanket suppression.'" Report of the Hearing Panel, App. C to Pet. for Cert. 19a. Although the Commission's "Findings of Facts" did not contain any statement as to whether petitioner's representation was deceptive, its "Conclusion of Law" ended with the brief statement that petitioner,

by holding himself out, on his letterhead as "Gary E. Peel, Certified Civil Trial Specialist — By the National Board of Trial Advocacy," is in direct violation of the above cited Rule [2-105(a)(3)].

We hold it is "misleading" as our Supreme Court has never recognized or approved any certification process.

Id., at 20a.

The Illinois Supreme Court adopted the Commission's recommendation for censure. It held that the First Amendment did not protect petitioner's letterhead because the letterhead was misleading in three ways. First, the State Supreme Court concluded that the juxtaposition of the reference to petitioner as "certified" by NBTA and the reference to him as "licensed" by Illinois, Missouri, and Arizona "could" mislead the general public into a belief that petitioner's authority to practice in the field of trial advocacy was derived solely from NBTA certification. It thus found that the statements on the letterhead impinged on the court's exclusive authority to license its attorneys because they failed to distinguish voluntary certification by an unofficial group from licensure by an official organization. In re Peel, 126 Ill. 2d 397, 405-406, 534 N.E. 980, 983-984 (1989).

Second, the court characterized the claim of NBTA certification as "misleading because it tacitly attests to the qualifications of [petitioner] as a civil trial advocate." Id., at 406, 534 N.E.2d, at 984. The court noted confusion in the parties' descriptions of NBTA's requirements, but did not consider whether NBTA certification constituted reliable, verifiable evidence of petitioner's experience as a civil trial advocate. Rather, the court reasoned that the statement was tantamount to an implied claim of superiority of the quality of petitioner's legal services and therefore warranted restriction under our decision in In re R.M.J., 455 U.S. 191 (1982). 126 Ill. 2d, at 406, 534 N.E.2d, at 984.

Finally, the court reasoned that use of the term "specialist" was misleading because it incorrectly implied that Illinois had formally authorized certification of specialists in trial advocacy. The court concluded that the conjunction of the reference to being a specialist with the reference to being licensed implied that the former was the product of the latter. Id., at 410, 534 N.E.2d, at 986. Concluding that the letterhead was inherently misleading for these reasons, the court upheld the blanket prohibition of Rule 2-105(a) under the First Amendment.

III

The Illinois Supreme Court considered petitioner's letterhead as a form of commercial speech governed by the "constitutional limitations on the regulation of lawyer advertising." 126 Ill. 2d, at 402, 534 N.E.2d, at 982. The only use of the letterhead in the record is in petitioner's correspondence with the Commission itself. Petitioner contends that, absent evidence of any use of the letterhead to propose commercial transactions with potential clients, the statement should be accorded the full protections of noncommercial speech. However, he also acknowledges that "this case can and should be decided on the narrower ground that even if it is commercial speech it cannot be categorically prohibited." Tr. of Oral Arg. 9. We agree that the question to be decided is whether a lawyer has a constitutional right, under the standards applicable to commercial speech, to advertise his or her certification as a trial specialist by NBTA.

In Bates v. State Bar of Arizona, 433 U.S. 350 (1977), this Court decided that advertising by lawyers was a form of commercial speech entitled to protection by the First Amendment. Justice Powell summarized the standards applicable to such claims for the unanimous Court in In re R.M.J., 455 U.S., at 203:

> Truthful advertising related to lawful activities is entitled to the protections of the First Amendment. But when the particular content or method of the advertising suggests that it is inherently misleading or

when experience has proved that in fact such advertising is subject to abuse, the States may impose appropriate restrictions. Misleading advertising may be prohibited entirely. *But the States may not place an absolute prohibition on certain types of potentially misleading information,* e.g., *a listing of areas of practice, if the information also may be presented in a way that is not deceptive. . . .*

   Even when a communication is not misleading, the State retains some authority to regulate. But the State must assert a substantial interest and the interference with speech must be in proportion to the interest served.

(Emphasis added.) In this case we must consider whether petitioner's statement was misleading and, even if it was not, whether the potentially misleading character of such statements creates a state interest sufficiently substantial to justify a categorical ban on their use.

   The facts stated on petitioner's letterhead are true and verifiable. It is undisputed that NBTA has certified petitioner as a civil trial specialist and that three States have licensed him to practice law. There is no contention that any potential client or person was actually misled or deceived by petitioner's stationery. Neither the Commission nor the State Supreme Court made any factual finding of actual deception or misunderstanding, but rather concluded, as a matter of law, that petitioner's claims of being "certified" as a "specialist" were necessarily misleading absent an official state certification program. Notably, although petitioner was originally charged with a violation of Disciplinary Rule 2-101(b), which aims at misleading statements by an attorney, his letterhead was not found to violate this rule.

   In evaluating petitioner's claim of certification, the Illinois Supreme Court focused not on its facial accuracy, but on its implied claim "as to the quality of [petitioner's] legal services," and concluded that such a qualitative claim "'might be so likely to mislead as to warrant restriction.'" 126 Ill. 2d, at 406, 534 N.E.2d, at 984 (quoting In re R.M.J., 455 U.S., at 201). This analysis confuses the distinction between statements of opinion or quality and statements of objective facts that may support an inference of quality. A lawyer's certification by NBTA is a verifiable fact, as are the predicate requirements for that certification. Measures of trial experience and hours of continuing education, like information about what schools the lawyer attended or his or her bar activities, are facts about a lawyer's training and practice. A claim of certification is not an unverifiable opinion of the ultimate quality of a lawyer's work or a promise of success, cf. In re R.M.J., 455 U.S., at 201, n.14, but is simply a fact, albeit one with multiple predicates, from which a consumer may or may not draw an inference of the likely quality of an attorney's work in a given area of practice.

   We must assume that some consumers will infer from petitioner's statement that his qualifications in the area of civil trial advocacy exceed the general qualifications for admission to a state bar. Thus if the certification had been issued by an organization that had made no inquiry into petitioner's fitness, or by one that issued certificates indiscriminately for a price, the statement, even if true, could be misleading. In this case, there is no evidence that a claim of NBTA certification suggests any greater degree of professional qualification than reasonably may be inferred from an evaluation of its rigorous requirements. Much like a trademark, the strength of a certification is measured by the quality of the organization for which it stands. The Illinois Supreme Court merely notes some confusion in the parties' explanation of one of those requirements. We find NBTA standards objectively clear, and, in any event, do not see why the degree of uncertainty identified by the State Supreme Court would make the letterhead inherently misleading to a consumer. A number of other States have their own certification plans and expressly authorize references to specialists and certification, but there is no evidence that the consumers in any of these States are misled if they do not inform themselves of the precise standards under which claims of certification are allowed.

Nor can we agree with the Illinois Supreme Court's somewhat contradictory fears that juxtaposition of the references to being "certified" as a "specialist" with the identification of the three States in which petitioner is "licensed" conveys, on the one hand, the impression that NBTA had the authority to grant those licenses and, on the other, that the NBTA certification was the product of official state action. The separate character of the two references is plain from their texts: one statement begins with the verb "[c]ertified" and identifies the source as the *National* Board of Trial Advocacy," while the second statement begins with the verb "[l]icensed" and identifies *States* as the source of licensure. The references are further distinguished by the fact that one is indented below petitioner's name while the other uses the same margin as his name. See supra. There has been no finding that any person has associated certification with governmental action — state or federal — and there is no basis for belief that petitioner's representation generally would be so construed.

We are satisfied that the consuming public understands that licenses — to drive cars, to operate radio stations, to sell liquor — are issued by governmental authorities and that a host of certificates — to commend job performance, to convey an educational degree, to commemorate a solo flight or a hole in one — are issued by private organizations. The dictionary definition of "certificate," from which the Illinois Supreme Court quoted only excerpts, comports with this common understanding:

> [A] document issued by a *school,* a state agency, *or a professional organization* certifying that one has satisfactorily *completed a course of studies, has passed a qualifying examination, or has* attained professional standing in a given field and may officially practice or hold a position in that field.

Webster's Third New International Dictionary 367 (1986 ed.) (emphasis added to portions omitted from 126 Ill. 2d, at 405, 534 N.E.2d, at 984).

The court relied on a similarly cramped definition of "specialist," turning from Webster's — which contains no suggestion of state approval of "specialists" — to the American Bar Association's Comment to Model Rule 7.4, which prohibits a lawyer from stating or implying that he is a "specialist" except for designations of patent, admiralty, or state-designated specialties. The Comment to the Rule concludes that the terms "specialist" and "specialty" "have acquired a secondary meaning implying formal recognition as a specialist and, therefore, use of these terms is misleading" in States that have no formal certification procedures. ABA Model Rule of Professional Conduct 7.4 and Comment (1989). We appreciate the difficulties that evolving standards for attorney certification present to national organizations like the ABA. However, it seems unlikely that petitioner's statement about his certification as a "specialist" by an identified national organization necessarily would be confused with formal state recognition. The Federal Trade Commission, which has a long history of reviewing claims of deceptive advertising, fortifies this conclusion with its observation that "one can readily think of numerous other claims of specialty — from 'air conditioning specialist' in the realm of home repairs to 'foreign car specialist' in the realm of automotive repairs — that cast doubt on the notion that the public would automatically mistake a claim of specialization for a claim of formal recognition by the State." Brief for Federal Trade Commission as Amicus Curiae 24.

We reject the paternalistic assumption that the recipients of petitioner's letterhead are no more discriminating than the audience for children's television. Cf. Bolger v. Youngs Drug Products Corp., 463 U.S. 60, 74 (1983). The two state courts that have evaluated lawyers' advertisements of their certifications as civil trial specialists by NBTA have concluded that the statements were not misleading or deceptive on their face, and that, under our recent decisions, they were protected by the First Amendment. Ex parte Howell, 487 So. 2d 848 (Ala. 1986); In re Johnson, 341 N.W.2d 282 (Minn. 1983). Given the complete absence of any evidence of deception in the present case, we must reject the contention that petitioner's letterhead is actually misleading.

IV

Even if petitioner's letterhead is not actually misleading, the Commission defends Illinois' categorical prohibition against lawyers' claims of being "certified" or a "specialist" on the assertion that these statements are potentially misleading. In the Commission's view, the State's interest in avoiding any possibility of misleading some consumers with such communications is so substantial that it outweighs the cost of providing other consumers with relevant information about lawyers who are certified as specialists. See Central Hudson Gas & Electric Corp. v. Public Service Commn. of New York, 477 U.S. 557, 566 (1980).

We may assume that statements of "certification" as a "specialist," even though truthful, may not be understood fully by some readers. However, such statements pose no greater potential of misleading consumers than advertising admission to "Practice before: The United States Supreme Court," In re R.M.J., 455 U.S. 191 (1982), of exploiting the audience of a targeted letter, Shapero v. Kentucky Bar Assn., 486 U.S. 466 (1988), or of confusing a reader with an accurate illustration, Zauderer v. Office of Disciplinary Counsel of Supreme Court of Ohio, 471 U.S. 626 (1985). In this case, as in those, we conclude that the particular state rule restricting lawyers' advertising is "'broader than reasonably necessary to prevent the' perceived evil." *Shapero*, 486 U.S., at 472, (quoting In re R.M.J., 455 U.S. at 203). Cf. Ohralik v. Ohio State Bar Assn., 436 U.S. 447 (1978) (restricting in-person solicitation). The need for a complete prophylactic against any claim of specialty is undermined by the fact that use of titles such as "Registered Patent Attorney" and "Proctor in Admiralty," which are permitted under Rule 2-105(a)'s exceptions, produces the same risk of deception.

Lacking empirical evidence to support its claim of deception, the Commission relies heavily on the inherent authority of the Illinois Supreme Court to supervise its own bar. Justice O'Connor's dissent urges that "we should be more deferential" to the State, asserting without explanation that "the Supreme Court of Illinois is in a far better position than is this Court to determine which statements are misleading or likely to mislead." Whether the inherent character of a statement places it beyond the protection of the First Amendment is a question of law over which Members of this Court should exercise de novo review. Cf. Bose Corp. v. Consumers Union of United States, Inc., 466 U.S. 485, 498-511 (1984). That the judgment below is by a State Supreme Court exercising review over the actions of its State Bar Commission does not insulate it from our review for constitutional infirmity. See, e.g., Baird v. State Bar of Arizona, 401 U.S. 1 (1971). The Commission's authority is necessarily constrained by the First Amendment to the Federal Constitution, and specifically by the principle that disclosure of truthful, relevant information is more likely to make a positive contribution to decisionmaking than is concealment of such information. Virginia Pharmacy Bd. v. Virginia Citizens Consumer Council, Inc., 425 U.S. 748, 770 (1976); Central Hudson Gas & Electric Corp., 447 U.S., at 562. Even if we assume that petitioner's letterhead may be potentially misleading to some consumers, that potential does not satisfy the State's heavy burden of justifying a categorical prohibition against the dissemination of accurate factual information to the public. In re. R.M.J., 455 U.S. at 203.

The presumption favoring disclosure over concealment is fortified in this case by the separate presumption that members of a respected profession are unlikely to engage in practices that deceive their clients and potential clients. As we noted in Bates v. State Bar of Arizona, 433 U.S., at 379:

> It is at least somewhat incongruous for the opponents of advertising to extol the virtues and altruism of the legal profession at one point, and, at another, to assert that its members will seize the opportunity to mislead and distort.

We do not ignore the possibility that some unscrupulous attorneys may hold themselves out as certified specialists when there is no qualified organization to stand behind that certification. A lawyer's truthful statement that "XYZ Board" has "certified" him as a "specialist in admiralty law" would not necessarily be entitled to First Amendment protection if the certification were a sham. States can require an attorney who advertises "XYZ certification" to demonstrate that such certification is available to all lawyers who meet objective and consistently applied standards relevant to

practice in a particular area of the law. There has been no showing —
indeed no suggestion — that the burden of distinguishing between certifying boards that are bona fide and those that are bogus would be
significant, or that bar associations and official disciplinary committees
cannot police deceptive practices effectively. Cf. *Shapero,* 486 U.S. at 477
("The record before us furnishes no evidence that scrutiny of targeted solicitation letters will be appreciably more burdensome or less reliable than
scrutiny of advertisements").

"If the naiveté of the public will cause advertising by attorneys to be
misleading, then it is the bar's role to assure that the populace is sufficiently
informed as to enable it to place advertising in its proper perspective."
Bates, 433 U.S., at 375. To the extent that potentially misleading statements
of private certification or specialization could confuse consumers, a State
might consider screening certifying organizations or requiring a disclaimer
about the certifying organization or the standards of a specialty. In re
R.M.J., 455 U.S. at 201-203. A State may not, however, completely ban statements that are not actually or inherently misleading, such as certification as
a specialist by bona fide organizations such as NBTA. Cf. In re Johnson, 341
N.W.2d, at 283 (striking down the Disciplinary Rule that prevented statements of being "'a specialist unless and until the Minnesota Supreme Court
adopts or authorizes rules or regulations permitting him to do so'"). Information about certification and specialties facilitates the consumer's access
to legal services and thus better serves the administration of justice.

Petitioner's letterhead was neither actually nor inherently misleading. There is no dispute about the bona fides and the relevance of NBTA
certification. The Commission's concern about the possibility of deception
in hypothetical cases is not sufficient to rebut the constitutional presumption favoring disclosure over concealment. Disclosure of information such
as that on petitioner's letterhead both serves the public interest and encourages the development and utilization of meritorious certification programs for attorneys. As the public censure of petitioner for violating Rule
2-105(a)(3) violates the First Amendment, the judgment of the Illinois
Supreme Court is reversed, and the case is remanded for proceedings not
inconsistent with this opinion.

It is so ordered.

EXERCISES

1. Using Martindale-Hubbell, find a law office in your area that indicates some concentration on federal tax law.
2. Find an advertisement in your local yellow pages for a law office
   and analyze its effectiveness.
3. Obtain samples of letterhead stationery and business cards from
   three different law offices and discuss the impression each makes
   with respect to the image of the office.
4. Indicate the types of subjects that should be included in a law office newsletter to generate new clients.

5. Develop a client evaluation form.
6. What is your opinion of the appropriateness of lawyer advertising?
7. Create your own newsletter on the courses you have taken thus far.
8. Discuss how a law office can market its services without violating Rule 7.3 regarding solicitation.
9. Discuss the appropriateness of hiring an outside firm to market a law office.
10. Discuss the concept of "truth in advertising" with respect to law office advertisements.

SITUATIONAL ANALYSIS

Recently, in New York state a lawyer decided to advertise her law office. Wearing very low-cut and revealing clothing, she had pictures of herself taken lying across her desk and used these pictures to advertise her law firm. Her rationale was that she was working in a male-dominated area of law and needed some way of breaking into the ranks of attorneys who regularly practiced in that area in her community. The ads proved to be very successful, and the attorney was able to increase her clientele by a huge percentage. However, several of the local attorneys, as well as several citizens, filed complaints against her for her advertising tactics.

1. How would you argue for the attorney?
2. How would you argue for the complaining attorneys?
3. How would you argue for the complaining citizens?

7

Administrative Systems

Ethics and professional responsibility are critical elements in the management of a law office. A well-managed firm sets high standards of ethical and professional conduct for everyone in the firm. Management policies should cover the key areas in which ethical dilemmas arise: confidentiality, conflicts of interest, client relations and development, delegation and supervision, billing and the handling of client funds.

Therese A. Cannon
Ethics and Professional
Responsibility for
Legal Assistants

CHAPTER OVERVIEW

In order to be effective and productive, a law office must run like a well-oiled machine. The oil that keeps the machine functioning smoothly and efficiently is the administrative system established by the office.

The key element in the effective administration of an office is the ability to keep track of all of the personnel, files, and other materials that pass through the office on a daily basis. If information is not properly stored, its retrieval, although not impossible, becomes overly time-consuming, a time factor that cannot be billed.

The administration of a law office falls into three broad categories: personnel, filing and recordkeeping, and library management. In large law offices these areas are overseen by three separate individuals: the personnel director, the office manager, and the librarian. In smaller firms these functions become blended and may be administered by one person.

Personnel administration for a law office involves the hiring (and firing) of two distinct groups of individuals: the professional staff composed of the attorneys, law clerks, and paralegals, and the support staff consisting of secretaries, receptionists, and general clerks. The hiring and firing process is now semi-regulated by the advent of various federal statutes enacted over the past decades to provide equal employment opportunities to persons who had been discriminated against in job placement in the past. These laws have had a dramatic impact on the staffing policies of all businesses, but most especially on law offices because they are composed of persons obligated to uphold the law.

Not only have the general laws of the land had an impact on law offices but, to a much greater extent, the dramatic increase in technology has changed the way a law office prepares and stores documents. At one time all documents were primarily prepared by typists or secretaries; today the lawyers themselves directly create typed documents that are only "cleaned up" by the support staff. Retrieval of documents has also become a fairly acute problem for lawyers who, in many instances, are unfamiliar with or afraid of the technology at their fingertips.

Finally, because of the ever-increasing cost of renting or owning office space, management of an office library facility has become an important factor in the overall administration of the office. The computerization of many research materials has also led many law offices to reevaluate their library management systems.

This chapter will explain some of the most important elements of the proper administration of a law office. Although legal assistants are not necessarily directly involved in all of the administrative decisions of the office, they are the ultimate users of the systems established by the office and consequently must be familiar with the administrative process in order to work efficiently with the established system. The particular system adopted is less important than the ability of every member of the legal team to use and understand the system that is selected.

Personnel Systems

An adage states that "a chain is only as strong as its weakest link." This saying is directly applicable to a law office in that the office's legal team is only as strong as its weakest member. Consequently, it is imperative that the office hire and keep only the most competent persons available. Law office personnel system concerns fall into four main areas: hiring and firing issues, policies and procedures, compensation, and the creation of a staff manual. Each of these topics will be discussed in turn.

Hiring and Firing Issues

Historically, law firms, just like all other businesses, operated under an **employment-at-will** policy — that is, people could be hired and fired at the discretion, capricious or otherwise, of the employer. However, since the mid-1960s many federal statutes have been enacted that affect an office's hiring and firing decisions. These laws were created in order to eradicate inequality that existed in many employment situations, inequalities that go against the moral grain and the Constitution of American society. Today, employers must give full effect to these federal statutes in creating and implementing employment policies.

The most important of these employment laws are, chronologically, as follows:

The Civil Rights Act of 1964. The Civil Rights Act, also known as **Title VII,** was enacted in order to prohibit employers from discriminating against applicants or employees on the basis of race, color, religion, national origin, or gender. This act is a direct outgrowth of the civil rights movement that swept the country in the early sixties, and is designed to ensure that all Americans be given an equal opportunity to acquire employment and to be promoted within companies where they already work if their performance so warrants. Any employees or applicants who believe they were passed over for a particular job because of their belonging to one of the **protected categories** specified in Title VII may file suit against the employer based on illegal discrimination.

EXAMPLE:

Two people apply for a paralegal job at the law office. The office has only one opening. One of the applicants is a 35-year-old black woman, the other a 25-year-old white man. The office hires the man, and the woman claims that she has been unlawfully discriminated against based on her race and gender. Does she have a valid claim?

(1) Probably yes. Both she and the male applicant have equal educational backgrounds; they both graduated from their state university and have completed a certified paralegal program. Additionally, the woman has five years' experience as a legal secretary and three years' practical experience as a legal assistant. Under these circumstances, unless other factors can be shown, it would appear that the woman was discriminated against.

(2) Probably no. Assume the male applicant has a college degree and has a paralegal certificate from an accredited paralegal institution, but the woman left school at age 16 without ever receiving a high school diploma or GED. The woman married and never held a permanent job. In this situation it would appear that the office merely hired the best qualified candidate and did not unlawfully discriminate against the woman.

When dealing with questions concerning the Civil Rights Act, all factors must be taken into consideration before the existence of discrimination can be determined.

The Civil Rights Act was amended in 1991 to relax the burden of proof in cases involving discrimination under the Act and to allow for greater damages if discrimination can be proven.

The Age Discrimination in Employment Act of 1967.   Pursuant to this statute, an employer is prohibited from discriminating against an applicant or employee based on age if the applicant or employee is 40 years of age or older. In order to reduce operating costs, many businesses might fire middle-aged or elderly employees who are earning high salaries in favor of hiring less expensive younger employees who also, presumably, have fewer medical problems, thereby reducing medical insurance costs as well. This practice leaves many qualified individuals unemployed and uninsured — hence the creation of the Age Discrimination in Employment Act. Employees may now sue an employer if they can prove that they have been discriminated against because of age.

EXAMPLE:

A secretary has been with the law office for over 25 years and is now earning a fairly high salary. As a cost-reducing measure, the office decides to fire her and hire as her replacement a young graduate from a vocational school who will work for a much smaller starting salary. The secretary, who is 45 years old, may bring suit against the office based on age discrimination.

The Occupational Safety and Health Act of 1970.   The Occupational Safety and Health Act of 1970 (OSHA) was created to ensure employees a safe work environment. This statute improved on general negligence law by establishing specific workplace standards and by using inspections to monitor the creation and maintenance of a safe workplace.

EXAMPLE:

The law office decides to redecorate its facility. As a cost-saving measure, some old lead-based paint is used and nonlicensed electricians are hired to redo the wiring. Neither the paint nor the wiring meets safety standards, and the office may be fined and held responsible for resultant injuries to its employees due to the substandard work.

The Pregnancy Discrimination Act of 1978.   Under this statute a woman may not be fired from her job because she is pregnant. She is entitled to maternity leave and, at the termination of the period of leave, is guaranteed that she may return to her original position and that her absence will not be counted against her with respect to promotion and pay raises.

EXAMPLE:

An associate with the law office becomes pregnant and takes three months' maternity leave. At the end of this period she may return to the same position she had prior to her pregnancy. Her leave cannot count against her either in the determination of the clients she can work with or in her partnership potential.

The Americans with Disabilities Act of 1990. The Americans with Disabilities Act (ADA) was enacted to prevent employers from discriminating against persons with disabilities. The Act defines disabilities as any mental or physical impairment that substantially limits an employee from performing a major life activity, such as walking or seeing. Although primarily nonspecific in defining "disability," the Act specifically excludes minor or temporary problems such as a broken arm or a migraine headache.

If the employee's problem comes within the provision of the Act, the employer is required to make a **reasonable accommodation** for the person with the disability, such as providing physical access to facilities or modifying work schedules. The ADA became effective on July 26, 1992, for employers with 25 or more employees and on July 26, 1994, for employers with 15 or more employees. If employees with a disability can prove job discrimination, they may receive back pay, punitive damages, and reinstatement if they have been fired.

EXAMPLE:

A law clerk in a law office employing over 100 people is injured in a car accident and permanently loses the use of his legs. The office currently is not designed to accommodate wheelchairs, and the law clerk requests that the office's physical structure be modified to provide wheelchair access. This access is to include bathrooms, the main work area, and the employee lounge. If the office refuses, the law clerk may sue under the Americans with Disabilities Act.

The Family Medical Leave Act of 1993. Under this statute an employer must permit an employee a reasonable amount of time to take care of a family or medical emergency and may not discriminate against that employee. The employer may not fire the employee because of the medical time off nor may the employee be denied promotions or pay benefits that he or she has earned simply because of this leave. The statute permits eligible employees to be allowed 12 weeks of unpaid leave in any 12-month period for the birth or adoption of a child, to assist an immediate family member suffering from a severe illness, or for the employee's own severe illness. The Act applies to employers with 50 or more employees, public agencies, and private elementary and secondary schools.

EXAMPLE:

A file clerk in the office develops ovarian cancer and must take three months' leave for surgery and follow-up care. Under the Family and Medical Leave Act she is entitled to take this time without compensation and may not be discriminated against by the office because of her absence or condition.

In addition to the foregoing federal statutes affecting hiring and firing policies, federal standards also prohibit employers from allowing or permitting employees to be subject to sexual harassment. **Sexual harassment** is defined as unwelcome sexual advances that create an offensive work environment. The sexual harassment does not necessarily have to be a direct or indecent sexual proposition from a person in authority to an underling. Sexual harassment has a much broader application: It can include all comments, looks, touching, or displays of a sexual nature that intend, or have the effect of, intimidating or upsetting an employee.

An employer is required to take immediate action if any incident of sexual harassment comes to his or her attention. Probably the best method of approach, however, is to prevent sexual harassment before it occurs. Many offices have instituted training programs for all current and new employees that explain sexual harassment and indicate how sexual gestures and innuendo may make some employees uncomfortable. Additionally, many offices have an established policy against sexual harassment that is printed and distributed to all employees, indicating procedures for reporting, investigating, and correcting any such unwelcome conduct, including firing the offending employee. An intimidating or offensive workplace does not create the appropriate atmosphere to foster an effective legal team.

EXAMPLE:

A paralegal working for a law office has had a very sheltered background and is quite shy. Her supervising attorney has a much more freewheeling attitude toward sexual situations, and to pay her way through law school worked as an exotic dancer. The attorney thinks it amusing to leave copies of sexually explicit magazines around the office and to make jokes about sexual exploits in front of the paralegal. This conduct constitutes sexual harassment, even though it is between two women and does not involve sexual propositioning.

Policies and Procedures

It is a general rule that, to be effective and enforceable, a law must be disseminated to the public; a citizen cannot be expected to obey a law about which he or she has no knowledge. Similarly, with respect to a law office, a well-organized administration should have established policies and procedures that are disseminated to the entire staff.

These policies and procedures should include several areas of concern to employees. If the office wishes to establish a **dress code** in order to create a specific image, it should be established in a written policy statement, indicating appropriate and inappropriate attire as well as general dress guidelines. It is unfair to expect employees to second-guess the style the office considers appropriate.

EXAMPLE:

The office has a written dress policy indicating that dress should be "conservative." A receptionist comes to work one day in a bright pink suit that is the latest style. The office manager sends her home because the dress is "inappropriate." To the receptionist, the suit *is* conservative, a direct copy of a suit appearing in a well-respected fashion magazine. The policy established by the office left too much room for interpretation to be effective.

In order for the legal team to work effectively, everyone must be present and performing his or her function. Consequently, a specific policy should be established with respect to tardiness and absenteeism. A person who is habitually late, but who gets all of his work done, may see nothing wrong in arriving 45 minutes late. However, if that person is needed by another member of the legal team, and the team's project is delayed, the tardy employee has directly affected the performance of the office. Specific policies, including consequences, must be written out and distributed to all employees.

EXAMPLE:

A paralegal at the law office has a project due on Friday. When Friday morning arrives, the weather is so nice that the paralegal decides to take the day off. Because the paralegal did not show up at the office, the attorney did not have the material she needed for a meeting with a client at 11 A.M., and the client decided to hire another firm. The paralegal's "day off" has lost the office a valuable source of income.

The facilities of the law office exist to further the business of the entire firm. Although the office may permit the private use of facilities at odd times, any office policy with respect to the use of the facilities should be stated to the employees. Most offices do not object to the occasional and minimal use of its facilities for the private purposes of its personnel, but such use on a regular basis constitutes a misuse of the office.

EXAMPLE:

The office manager has three children in school. Whenever the children need school papers done, he lets them use the office computer, duplicating facilities, and supplies. At the end of the school year the manager's children have used up thousands of dollars of office time and equipment. This has a direct adverse effect on the entire office, but because the office has no stated policy on the matter the office manager does not see anything wrong with his actions.

If an employee has any specific problem with respect to the workplace, the office should establish procedures for registering complaints. These procedures should also cover disciplining and firing employees. Once a specific format has been established, it is easier for employees to follow the procedures and to know what is expected of them.

Finally, employees are entitled to receive feedback as to how well they are performing their jobs, and whether they are following all of the office's policies and procedures. This feedback should take the form of a regular **performance evaluation** that can be used to document an employee's work progress. For a complete discussion of performance evaluations, see Chapter 8.

EXAMPLE:

A paralegal in the office has a sudden emergency at home. According to established office policy, the paralegal knows that she must contact the paralegal coordinator immediately and inform the coordinator of all the projects she is currently working on so that the coordinator can have the work reassigned. The paralegal also knows that she must bring in documentation to prove the emergency existed. Because these procedures were established and dis-

seminated well in advance of the emergency situation, the paralegal did not find them offensive and knew exactly what to do, and
the office could continue to function efficiently in her absence.

Compensation

A major concern of every employee is the manner and amount of
compensation he or she will receive for work performed. The law office
should establish set policies with respect to the amount of remuneration
each category of employee will receive, including vacation and sick leave,
bonuses and incentive plans, and timing of payment (weekly, bi-weekly,
monthly, etc.). These policies must be explained to each employee at the
time the employee commences work, and should be documented in writing to avoid confusion or problems later on.

As a general proposition, each office is free to establish the amount
and method of compensation that it deems appropriate, but with two important caveats. The federal government has enacted two statutes that directly relate to employment compensation policies. The first, **The Fair
Labor Standards Act,** establishes the minimum wage scale and number of
hours an employee may work without adjustment to the minimum wage.
Second, in 1963, **The Equal Pay Act** was promulgated requiring employers
to give equal pay for equal work. The purpose behind this act was to eradicate discriminatory policies that existed with respect to salaries and
wages.

EXAMPLE:

The law office has two paralegals, a man and a woman. Both have
similar backgrounds and started working at the office at approximately the same time. The office pays the male paralegal $3,500 a
year more than the female. This appears to be discriminatory and
violative of the Equal Pay Act of 1963.

If the office establishes a pension plan as part of its total employment
compensation packet, it may be entitled to certain tax benefits, provided
that the plan is approved by the Internal Revenue Service and meets the requirements of **The Employee Retirement Income Security Act (ERISA).**
ERISA was enacted in order to secure employee pension plans so that the
funds may not by used by employers for any other purpose, thus guaran-
teeing the employee a pension when he or she eventually retires. The law
office must explain to its employees all of the provisions of its pension
plan, including the point in time when the employee has **vested,** or enforceable, rights in the plan.

EXAMPLE:

The law office establishes a pension plan for its employees. A few years after the plan is created, the office suffers a short-term cash-flow problem, and the senior partners want to use the money in the pension plan to cover the office's immediate shortfall. This is illegal under the provisions of ERISA; the funds belong to the employees who have contributed to the plan, not to the office.

The law office's entire compensation package should be documented, explained, and disseminated to all employees.

The Staff Manual

In order to disseminate all critical information to its employees, many law offices find it effective to write a **staff manual,** also called a **policies and procedures manual.** A manual helps the office define all of its administrative policies; once printed in black and white, many problems inherent in these policies may be easily discerned and corrected. Additionally, the manual becomes, in effect, the employment contract that exists between the office and all of its employees. Because it is a form of contract, the manual should be totally accurate and written in a clear yet comprehensive manner.

The manual should be divided into two main areas. The first establishes the **policies** of the office, stating specifically all rules by which the office expects all employees to abide. The second describes any specific **procedures** the office requires employees to follow in given situations, such as a sexual harassment complaint or the chain of command to be contacted in the case of an emergency situation. The manual can also be used to clarify any ethical concerns that might arise with respect to the administration of the office (see below). The manual should be distributed to all employees of the office and updated on a regular basis.

The staff manual should also specify **job descriptions** for the various functions performed by members of the legal team. Employees cannot be expected to perform work they do not realize is part of their specific job function, nor is it fair to have employees do different work or more work than their positions call for. By having definitive job descriptions in the staff manual, these sorts of problems can be avoided. Be aware, however, that many statutes prohibit describing jobs in a manner that would be discriminatory, such as requiring specific ages, genders, or so forth, unless the employer can prove a specific need for such designation. Such descriptions would most probably be inappropriate for most work performed at a law office.

The American Bar Association has created a sample manual that may be used by a law office, entitled Law Practice Staff Manual, 2d ed. For computerized offices, Greenleaf Software has created a form staff manual on a floppy disk, titled Cadence Policy and Procedure Manual, that can be placed in the office computer, personalized, and then disseminated to the employees by means of individual disks or programmed to the mainframe.

Creating a staff manual is probably the most effective method of establishing administrative policy and disseminating it to the employees.

EXAMPLE:

An associate in the law office has just been informed that one of the file clerks believes that she is being sexually harassed by one of the firm's security force. The associate takes out the office manual, looks in the table of contents for procedures with respect to dealing with problems of sexual harassment, and then follows the procedure established by the office. Having the manual can streamline the resolution of the alleged problem.

Always remember that the most important asset of a law office is its personnel; consequently, it is imperative that a law office establish specific policies and procedures to deal with hiring and firing issues and employment compensation, and to see that these rules are effectively communicated to every member of the legal team.

Filing and Recordkeeping

An army can travel on its stomach, but a law office travels on its documentation. The entire legal profession would come to a standstill if its members could not quickly and easily retrieve the multitude of papers and computer disks the legal field generates. Chapter 9 will concentrate on the preparation of these documents; this section is concerned with creating an effective method of filing and storing the documents.

Basic Filing Systems

Every law office must determine a method, or several methods that are cross-referenced, for filing all of the paper and computer work generated by a legal practice. Regardless of the method or methods utilized, all members of the legal team must agree to use the same system. There are basically five general filing system methods:

1. alphabetical
2. subject
3. geographic
4. chronological
5. numerical

Alphabetical

Maintaining alphabetical files is probably the simplest method for storage and retrieval of documents. The only information necessary to retrieve the document is the first name appearing on the file.

EXAMPLE:

The office is handling the merger of two corporations. The documents should be filed under the first letter of the first name of the corporation whose name appears first alphabetically.

Subject

Arranging material according to subject is a logical method of storage, provided that all parties agree as to the subject of any given file. For documents that cover a wide range of matters, such a system may create additional work to ensure that each file is stored according to each subject involved in the material.

EXAMPLE:

As part of a divorce proceeding, the law office is involved in the division of the spouses' business. These documents should be filed under both "Divorce" and "Business" in order to retrieve the information as needed.

Geographic

Although a geographic filing system may be appropriate for many types of businesses, for a law office this method might become confusing, unless the firm has many offices located in different locations. In such an instance it may be appropriate to file material according to the branch office that is handling the legal matter.

EXAMPLE:

The law firm has offices located in New York, Washington, D.C., and Houston, Texas. Research documents are stored according to the location of the office that is actually handling the matter.

Chronological

A chronological file is one that is kept according to the date on which the item was produced or received. For individual case matters, maintaining a chronological file can help the legal team keep track of the movement of the case; however, it is generally a good idea to cross-reference chronological files according to one of the other systems indicated in this section in order to facilitate retrieval of the information.

EXAMPLE:

The law office is involved in a civil litigation matter. As each document is prepared, filed with the court, or received, a copy of the document is placed in the client's file in chronological order, and the file itself is kept in alphabetical order according to the client's name. When the attorney wants to find out when an answer to her discovery request was made, the document can be found by checking the chronological file under the client's name.

Numerical

Numerical files may be kept for certain form documents that the office uses on a continuing basis, but numerical files would typically be inappropriate for general legal information. However, if a numerical filing system is used and the office is computerized, it is generally helpful to place a **bar code** on the document so that it can be filed quickly by a computer scan, similar to the method used in supermarkets.

EXAMPLE:

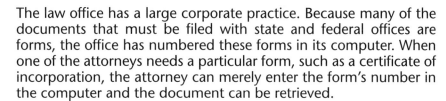

The law office has a large corporate practice. Because many of the documents that must be filed with state and federal offices are forms, the office has numbered these forms in its computer. When one of the attorneys needs a particular form, such as a certificate of incorporation, the attorney can merely enter the form's number in the computer and the document can be retrieved.

Most law offices rarely use only one filing method. For practical purposes it is easier to retrieve information if it is **cross-referenced** — that is, placed under several different systems, with each file indicating all the other systems under which it may be located. In this manner the information can be retrieved if the legal team is working on a particular subject, or if it is working on a matter for a specific client.

EXAMPLE:

As mentioned in a preceding example, if the office is working on a divorce matter that involves various business problems, the information could be filed under the client name as well as the subject matter. In this fashion the attorney can retrieve the appropriate information regardless of which filing system she is using at any given moment; if another client has a similar business problem, she can find the file by looking under the subject even if she cannot remember the name of the divorcing couple.

Preparing Documents

Once the office has decided on the filing system or systems it will use, the legal team must make sure that the documents are prepared for filing according to the system selected. Needless to say, the first task is to make sure that the document is physically ready for storage. This may mean checking the document for mending or stapling if necessary. Once the document is in good order for storage, it must be classified and cross-referenced. **Classifying** a document means deciding what importance the document plays in the life of the law office. **Vital** documents must always be stored and maintained. **Important** indicates that the information must be maintained for a significant period of time, but at some point in the future it may be destroyed. **Useful** information has a short-term life expectancy, whereas **nonessential** documents typically may be quickly destroyed. These classification methods are used in order to eliminate hoarding of unnecessary documents when space is at a premium.

Cross-referencing, as noted above, means placing a document in duplicate files in order to facilitate retrieval of the information. In order to cross-reference, one must be aware of the various filing methods the office utilizes and be able to determine the appropriate files for the information. Both classifying and cross-referencing require that the person preparing the document for filing be sufficiently analytical so as to determine the status of the document in question.

Storage

The final step in storing the document is the physical placement of the document in the storage option used by the office. Storage may be either nonelectronic or electronic, and there are several facilities available for each type.

Nonelectronic

Nonelectronic storage is the traditional method of maintaining records by employing a specific item of furniture designed for filing. There are six generally used nonelectronic storage systems.

1. Vertical Files.   Vertical files are traditional filing cabinets, usually with two or three drawers to each cabinet, and the drawers placed one above the other. Internally, the files are placed front to back.

2. Lateral Files.   Lateral files are a type of vertical file in which the drawers extend horizontally for several feet. The files are kept horizontally as well, either left to right or right to left.

3. Open Files.   Open files resemble bookcases in which material may be stored but with little or no security for the files. Most law offices do not use this type of filing storage system because of the confidential nature of legal work.

4. Rotary Files.   Rotary files are small desktop units that are capable only of limited storage. Some offices may use this type of storage for current work being performed by the members of the legal team. Once the work is completed, the information is placed into one of the other systems for permanent storage.

5. Mobile or Portable Files.   These units resemble the vertical or lateral files mentioned above, but are smaller and have wheels so that the files can be brought to the person who needs them rather than the person going to the files.

6. Card Files.   Card files, as the name would indicate, are small desktop units that hold index cards. This type of storage may be used as a quick reference until the complete file can be obtained or may be used as a substitute telephone directory.

Electronic

There are four basic methods of electronic storage currently used by law offices.

1. Microcomputer Disk.   A microcomputer, or floppy, disk contains a vast amount of information in a small, easily portable fashion. The disk is inserted into any computer capable of reading it, and the information then appears on the computer screen. The microcomputer disk may be duplicated and given to anyone who has need of the information it contains.

2. Mainframe Disk.   A mainframe disk is a computer disk that is used only in the main computer unit of the office. Anyone with a terminal can access the information by accessing the mainframe itself, but the information is not individually kept by members of the office, and access is usually secured by requiring the user to provide a special entry code.

3. Microfilm.   Microfilm is an older method of storing a great deal of printed information in a limited space — here, a roll of film. Because of the advent of computers, few offices still store information on microfilm, and most microfilm storage is being converted to computer disk.

4. Microfiche.   Microfiche is microfilm photographed on sheets or cards. Microfiche can store more information than microfilm in the same physical area, but, as with microfilm, microfiche is being rapidly replaced by computer disk.

Library Management

Most law offices cannot afford the luxury of maintaining full-fledged law libraries overseen by a law librarian and assisted by one or more library clerks. However, even the smallest law office maintains some sort of library for legal reference.

Because of the cost both of books and space, many offices only maintain the codes and reporters of the state in which the office is located, along with some federal materials. Many firms simply avail themselves of law libraries in the area that grant access to the public or members of the bar. Regardless of how limited the research materials in the office might be, all libraries must be properly maintained — that is, the material must be obtained, updated, and cataloged for easy reference.

As computers become more prevalent in all law offices, many firms are utilizing computerized legal research services such as **Lexis** and **Westlaw,** which will be discussed in Chapter 10. Be aware, however, that these computerized services are quite expensive and charge the firm on an hourly basis. Consequently, most firms limit the availability of these resources to very specific uses.

However, regardless of the extent, or lack thereof, of a particular law office's library, one of the greatest reference assets that a firm can maintain for its legal team is a **form file.** A form file is an index of all standard forms used by the office, as well as all briefs, memoranda, and other legal documents prepared by the members of the legal team. This form file provides a quick method of obtaining all of the legal work previously prepared by the office so that research can be streamlined and not duplicated. All members of a law office should maintain historical files of all their work, as well as copies of all legal work that crosses their desks. Having a format to follow is the key to performing work efficiently.

Administrative Systems and Ethics

Several ethical problems may arise with respect to a law office's administrative systems, especially in the area of hiring and firing and the confidentiality of stored documents.

As discussed above, many statutes exist that are designed to prevent employers from discriminating against protected categories of individuals. To circumvent these laws, many employers will try to put obstacles in the way of qualified employees in order to avoid hiring them or to facilitate firing them without legal repercussions. By making tasks overly unpleasant or the work environment unfriendly, employees may decide to leave on their own, thereby permitting the employer to get away with illegal discrimination. On the other hand, there are instances of incompetent or lazy employees who use these laws in order to sue or subtly extort funds from employers by claiming discrimination where none exists. Both employers and employees must be aware of the benefits of these laws and the appropriateness of their application.

There have been many instances in which law offices have been guilty of fostering or closing an eye to sexual harassment because the victim is a low-level or new employee and the harasser is a senior member of the firm. The office would rather cover up or ignore the particular situation than root out the problem. Sexual harassment creates a negative workplace environment, which in turn results in an unhappy and unproductive legal team. When dealing with these situations, the senior members of the office should look to the welfare of the entire team, not just that of an individual member.

Finally, as discussed in previous chapters, whenever any member of the office is dealing with records and documents pertaining to client matters, that information must be kept in the strictest confidence. Filing systems are designed not only to permit easy storage and retrieval of information but also to protect that information from prying eyes. No member of the legal team should be cavalier with respect to the confidentiality of stored documents.

CHAPTER SUMMARY

People are most comfortable when they are aware of all of the rules and procedures that establish the parameters of their work environment. The more specific and detailed the office's adminstrative systems are, the easier it is for the members of the legal team to function to the best of their abilities.

Hiring and firing of employees has become a matter influenced by various federal statutes designed to protect individuals from being unfairly discriminated against and to help all persons acquire and maintain decent employment. All members of the law office should be made aware of all laws applicable to employment questions, and training may be indicated in order to alert all members of the team as to how those laws are to be applied. All rules and procedures that concern a person's employment with the office should be written down and disseminated to all employees, and many offices find it most convenient to create a staff manual detailing all of its policies that can be distributed to everyone in the office. It is unfair to expect an employee to live up to a standard of which he or she is unaware.

Paperwork is the bane of every law office, and in the interest of efficiency it behooves the office to establish appropriate filing and record-keeping systems so that the members of the legal team have easy and ready access to information. Many different systems and means of storage exist. It is up to the managing personnel of the office to decide on a system that best suits the needs of its employees; once decided on, all employees must follow that established system.

Every law office must maintain some form of library facility for its members. The library may be as extensive as that of a good law school or as limited as a simple file cabinet containing the attorneys' past work product. Whatever the resources available, the library materials must be appropriately categorized, indexed, and updated to be of use to the legal team.

Key Terms

Age Discrimination in Employment Act of 1967:   Federal law prohibiting job discrimination for workers over the age of 40.

Americans with Disabilities Act of 1990 (ADA):   Federal law prohibiting job discrimination for persons with permanent mental or physical disabilities.

Bar code: Computerized method of scanning numerical information.

Card files: Storage method for index cards.

Civil Rights Act of 1964:   Federal law prohibiting discrimination based on age, race, sex, religion, or national origin.

Classification: Determining the importance of documents for the purpose of storage.

Cross-referencing: Method of filing information under more than one type of file to ease retrieval.

Dress code: Office rules with respect to appropriate work attire.

Employee Retirement Income Security Act (ERISA):   Federal law designed to protect employee pension funds.

Employment at will: Permitting employers to hire and fire at will for any reason.

Equal Pay Act of 1963:   Federal law requiring equal pay for equal work.

Fair Labor Standards Act: Federal law establishing minimum wage and work hours.

Family Medical Leave Act of 1993:   Federal law permitting employees to take leave for medical emergencies.

Lateral file: Horizontally designed storage system.

Lexis: Computerized legal research program.

Mainframe disk: Computer storage method for an entity's main computer.

Microcomputer disk: Computer storage method whereby every person in a law office may have his or her own computer file containing stored data.

Microfiche: Microfilm stored on sheets or cards.

Microfilm: Method of storing vast amounts of printed information on a single piece of film.

Mobile or portable file: Storage cabinet on wheels.

Occupational Safety and Health Act of 1970 (OSHA):   Federal law requiring employers to maintain a safe workplace for their employees.

Open file: Storage method similar to open bookshelves.

Performance evaluation: Method of giving an employee feedback on how well he or she is doing.

Policies: Statement of office rules.

Policies and procedures manual: Staff manual.

Pregnancy Discrimination Act of 1978:   Federal law prohibiting discriminating against a woman because she is pregnant.

Procedures: Methods of applying the office rules.

Protected categories: Specific groups of persons for whom antidiscrimination laws have been enacted.

Reasonable accommodation: ADA requirement that employers take reasonable steps to aid their disabled employees.

Rotary file: Desktop storage method.

Sexual harassment: Making unwelcome sexual advances, leers, touching, and so on in a work environment.

Staff manual: Book containing all of the office's rules and procedures.

Title VII: Another name for the Civil Rights Act.

Vertical file: Storage method in which file cabinets are placed one above the other.

Vested: Having legally enforceable rights.

Westlaw: Computerized legal research system.

Cases for Analysis

The following two cases are presented in order to highlight certain problems incident to hiring and firing procedures. Brown v. Ford, Bacon & Davis, Utah, Inc. concerns gender discrimination, and Elliott v. Montgomery Ward & Co. deals with age discrimination.

Brown v. Ford, Bacon & Davis, Utah, Inc.
850 F.2d 631 (10th Cir. 1988)

Linda Brown filed a complaint alleging her former employer discharged her from her position as an accountant because of her gender and her complaint of discriminatory treatment, in violation of Title VII of the Civil Rights Act of 1964. She further claimed the defendants breached her contract of employment by failing to comply with termination procedures specified in their personnel manual. The trial court found defendants had not discharged plaintiff for discriminatory or retaliatory reasons but had breached the contract.

Plaintiff appeals on the grounds that the court's findings on her civil rights claims were clearly erroneous and that damages for her contract claim were not properly calculated. We conclude plaintiff's objections to the court's factual findings merely go to the weight and credibility to be accorded the evidence, which amply supports the court's findings. We further conclude, in light of the peculiarities of this case, damages were improperly calculated. We therefore affirm in part but remand for further proceedings.

The unusual fabric of this case was first [raised] by the defendants when plaintiff's supervisors determined that Ms. Brown's continued employment was not desirable. The trial court found that this decision was [based] in two separate circumstances. The first of these circumstances was plaintiff's inability to function at a businesslike level, an inability reflected by her repeated tardiness, inattentiveness, and improper sociability. Plaintiff also made several mistakes in her work that proved detrimental to her employer. Although one of plaintiff's supervisors attempted to help her raise the level of her performance, these efforts met with no success.

The second, and equally important, factor leading to plaintiff's dismissal arose from defendants' acquisition of another company. This acquisition brought Amy Caputo, another accountant, into Ms. Brown's department. Ms. Caputo ultimately proved herself more competent than plaintiff. Plaintiff's supervisors determined there was insufficient work for both plaintiff and Ms. Caputo, and therefore decided to terminate Ms. Brown in a "reduction in force." Plaintiff was given the three weeks' severance pay her contract mandated for such a discharge.

This combination of circumstances led the trial court to conclude Ms. Brown was terminated both for cause and because of a lack of work. Plaintiff claims this finding is clearly erroneous, arguing that various inconsistencies in the evidence demonstrate these reasons are pretextual. We have examined the record and have concluded plaintiff's arguments do not satisfy her burden of demonstrating that a mistake was made by the trial court. Recognizing the arguability of plaintiff's view of the evidence, we nonetheless conclude the district court's findings are plausible when the record is viewed in its entirety. With this conclusion before us, we cannot find clear error. Equal Employment Opportunity Commn. v. Wyoming Retirement Sys., 771 F.2d 1425, 1429 (10th Cir. 1985). It is not the function of an appellate court to determine issues anew, nor will it disturb factual decisions supported by the evidence. State Distribs., Inc. v. Glenmore Distilleries Co., 738 F.2d 405, 411-12 (10th Cir. 1984).

While it is seemingly inconsistent that plaintiff was terminated both for cause and as a result of a reduction in force, the evidence supports this conclusion. We do not agree with plaintiff's contention that defendants have taken inconsistent positions to justify their acts. It is a simple matter of fact that when the company decided it had insufficient work for two full-time accountants, it chose to release the one whose performance was below that of the other.

Although there are many other threads within this fabric which could be explored, and indeed have been in the briefs, we do not believe there would be profit in doing so. Suffice it to say that for each time plaintiff has asserted a "yin" argument, defendants have responded with a "yang," leading us to the conclusion that plaintiff's arguments go to the credibility of the witnesses and the weight of the evidence. These issues were resolved by the trial court, and we rely upon its resolution.

We are troubled, however, by the award of damages. By finding that plaintiff was discharged both for cause and as part of a reduction in force, the district court has created an unintended dilemma. If plaintiff was discharged as part of a reduction in force, there was no breach of contract and plaintiff is entitled to no damages whatsoever. If plaintiff was discharged for cause, however, defendants breached her contract by failing to afford her the "progressive discipline" procedures her contract required as a precondition to discharge for cause. Plaintiff would then be entitled to her accrued salary for the period between her procedurally defective discharge and the time when her employer "substantially complied"[1] with the required procedures, subject to her duty to properly mitigate. Piacitelli v. Southern Utah State College, 636 P.2d 1063, 1067-69 (Utah 1981).

The district court's resolution of this dilemma required some measure of judicial legerdemain. The court found that plaintiff was entitled to the "progressive discipline" procedures because defendants showed there was "just cause" for her discharge. With no apparent factual foundation, the court concluded that as a matter of law it would have taken only six weeks for plaintiff's supervisors to give her the necessary "two warnings with related timetables." It found plaintiff could then have been terminated "without cause" even if her job performance had improved during this period. Based upon these findings, the court restricted plaintiff's damages to six weeks' salary plus interest.

The district court's efforts to forge a just and equitable result have produced an unsupportable judgment. If plaintiff's discharge was in fact based on her unsatisfactory job performance, she is entitled to back pay and reasonable front pay consistent with *Piacitelli*. If, however, the determinative factor in plaintiff's discharge was the lack of work she was quali-

---

1. The Utah Supreme Court has held that an employer substantially complies with "progressive discipline" procedures when "the purpose of the procedural requirements was fulfilled and the substantial interests of the parties were satisfied." Piacitelli v. Southern Utah State College, 636 P.2d 1063, 1066 (Utah 1981).

fied to perform, defendants' breach did not actually damage plaintiff. We therefore remand for a determination of whether plaintiff is entitled to damages consistent with our reading of *Piacitelli,* or whether her damages for breach of contract are curtailed by the absence of work she was qualified to perform.

Affirmed in part and remanded for further proceedings.

Elliott v. Montgomery Ward & Co.
967 F.2d 1258 (8th Cir. 1992)

John R. Gibson, Circuit Judge.

Marilee Elliott, after holding a number of department management jobs with Montgomery Ward, was told she must either transfer to a store twenty-four miles from home at a $9,000 per year salary reduction or accept a severance package. She accepted the severance package and brought this action alleging: (1) discrimination under the age discrimination provisions of the Minnesota Human Rights Act, Minn. Stat. §363.03 subd. 1(2)(b) and (c) (1990); (2) intentional infliction of emotional distress; (3) emotional distress under Minn. Stat. §363.03 subd. 1(2)(b) and (c); and (4) breach of contract. The district court granted summary judgment in Ward's favor on all claims. On appeal, Elliott argues that the district court erred in granting summary judgment on her age discrimination and breach of contract claims. We affirm the district court's dismissal of the breach of contract claims, but reverse the summary judgment on the age discrimination claim and remand this claim for further consideration.

Elliott began working for Ward as a cashier in 1964. Two years later, Ward promoted her to assistant manager. Beginning in 1968, she served as department manager of several different departments in Ward's Apache Plaza store. In 1982, when she was 43, Ward gave Elliott the option of a severance package or reassignment. She chose reassignment and became group merchandiser of ten departments for approximately two years, and then over a three-year period was transferred on several occasions. She received favorable job evaluations and numerous awards from Ward based on her job performance.

In February 1987, Ward began reorganizing its Minneapolis and St. Paul operations. Elliott's district manager and store manager told Elliott that her position had been eliminated and the responsibilities divided among two younger employees, Nancy Harris, age 33, and Julie Grant, age 26. During the meeting, the district manager told Elliott that "the company was growing so rapidly that she would not be able to keep up with how fast the company was growing." Ward gave Elliott the option of involuntarily transferring to a Ward store some twenty-four miles from her home at a $9,000 salary reduction, or accepting a severance package. Ward gave Elliott two days to make a decision, and she accepted the severance package. She was 47 years old at the time of her resignation and had worked at

Ward for 23 years. She brought this action in Minnesota state court under the age discrimination provision of the Minnesota Human Rights Act and also asserted claims for emotional distress and breach of an employment contract.

Ward removed the case to district court on diversity grounds, and filed a partial motion for summary judgment. The district court first considered Elliott's age discrimination claim. It analyzed Elliott's claim as a disparate treatment case and applied the analysis set forth in McDonnell Douglas Corp. v. Green, 411 U.S. 792, 93 S. Ct. 1817, 36 L. Ed. 2d 668 (1973), as adopted by Schlemmer v. Farmers Union Central Exchange, 397 N.W.2d 903, 907 (Minn. Ct. App. 1986). Elliott v. Montgomery Ward & Co., No. 4-89-646 slip op. at 4 (D. Minn. Nov. 27, 1990). Under that analysis, a discharged employee carries the initial burden of establishing a prima facie case of age discrimination by showing: (1) she is a member of a protected class; (2) she was qualified for the job from which she was discharged; (3) she was discharged; and (4) the employer assigned a nonmember of the protected class to do the same work. Slip op. at 5 (citing Hubbard v. United Press Intl., 330 N.W.2d 428, 442 (Minn. 1983)). Because this case involved a reduction in force, the district court applied this court's decision in Holley v. Sanyo Manufacturing, Inc., 771 F.2d 1161 (8th Cir. 1985). In reduction in force cases, *Holley* requires an employee to also make "some additional showing" that age was a factor in the employer's decision to establish a prima facie age discrimination case. Id. at 1165.

The district court concluded that Elliott carried her initial burden of satisfying the first four elements under *McDonnell Douglas*. Slip op. at 5-8. See also Elliott v. Montgomery Ward & Co., No. 4-89-646, slip op. at 13 (D. Minn. May 29, 1991). Nevertheless, the court concluded that Elliott failed to produce "other evidence" of discrimination as required by *Holley*. Slip op. at 8-9 (Nov. 27, 1990). The court ruled that the statement Ward "was growing so rapidly [plaintiff] would not be able to keep up with how fast [the company] was growing," did not suffice as other evidence, concluding that the statement did "not directly relate to [Elliott's] age." Id. at 8. As Elliott relied on this single statement to satisfy the increased burden in a reduction in force case, the district court concluded that she failed to carry her burden of proof and granted summary judgment in favor of Ward. Id. at 9. The court also granted summary judgment for Ward on Elliott's claim of intentional infliction of emotional distress, id. at 9-11, and emotional distress under Minn. Stat. §363.03 subd. 1(2)(b) and (c). Id. at 11.

Elliott filed a motion for reconsideration. The court denied reconsideration of the age discrimination claim, rejecting Elliott's arguments that discovery was incomplete on the date of the hearing, and that Elliott and the other two employees were not uniformly evaluated. Elliott v. Montgomery Ward & Co., No. 4-89-646, slip op. at 17-18 (D. Minn. May 29, 1991). The district court also concluded that Ward was entitled to summary judgment on Elliott's breach of contract claim because no breach occurred. Id. at 16. Elliott appeals the district court's dismissal of her age discrimination and breach of contract claims.

I

Elliott attacks the propriety of summary judgment on the age discrimination claim by first arguing that she complied with *Holley* and set forth additional evidence to show that age was a factor in Ward's employment decision.[1] In the alternative, Elliott argues that this court should modify the rule in *Holley* by eliminating the fifth requirement of showing that age was a factor in the employment decision. Elliott particularly relies on the Seventh Circuit's decision in Oxman v. WLS-TV, 846 F.2d 448 (7th Cir. 1988), and asks that we follow *Oxman*. Ward responds that this court properly decided *Holley* and that we should adhere to it.

In *Holley*, this court concluded that "some additional showing" of discrimination is required to make a prima facie case in reduction in work force cases. 771 F.2d at 1165. This court later applied the additional element in cases brought under the Minnesota Human Rights Act, Kypke v. Burlington Northern R.R. Co., 928 F.2d 285, 286 (8th Cir. 1991). We are bound by *Kypke* under principles of stare decisis. Only the court en banc could grant the relief Elliott requests.

There are at least two additional reasons why we should not embark on the path suggested by Elliott. The first is that the issue before us is one of Minnesota state law; the issue is material here only because *Kypke* applied our decision in *Holley* to claims under the Minnesota Human Rights Act. If *Holley* is to be reconsidered, and we are not persuaded that it should be, it should be in a case in which the federal Age Discrimination in Employment Act is an issue, not when the issue is only indirectly involved in determining a Minnesota claim. The other reason is that, as we will shortly explain, we are convinced that Elliott has complied with *Holley*.[2]

For purposes of appeal, Ward concedes that Elliott satisfies the first three elements of a prima facie age discrimination case.[3] Ward argues,

---

1. Elliott concedes that this is not a disparate impact case. Elliott claims that this is a disparate treatment case, and that Ward treated her less favorably with respect to the terms of her employment during its 1987 reduction in force.

2. If we wrote on a blank slate, we would question whether Minnesota courts have applied *Holley* in reduction in force cases. We read Rademacher v. FMC Corp., 431 N.W.2d 879 (Minn. Ct. App. 1988), to incorporate the reduction in force consideration in the second stage of the *McDonnell Douglas* analysis dealing with the articulation of a nondiscriminatory reason for discharge. Id. at 882-83. Although *Rademacher* cited *Holley*, it set out only four elements of a prima facie age discrimination case and made no mention of the fifth factor we announced in *Holley*. Id. One unpublished Minnesota Court of Appeals decision has specifically applied *Holley*, Hartzell v. Patterson Dental Co., No. C9-91-1322, slip op. at 8, 1992 WL 20742 (Minn. Ct. App. 1992). Minn. Stat. §480A.08 subd. 3 (1990) states, however, that "[u]npublished opinions of the court of appeals are not precedential." Certainly, Minnesota state courts are at liberty to define the requirements of a prima facie case as they see fit. Insofar as *Hartzell* may be contrary to *Rademacher*, this is an issue for Minnesota courts to resolve. While *Kypke* applied *Holley* to an age claim brought under the Minnesota Act, we are not altogether sure that the issue of whether or not it should do so was squarely raised.

3. Despite this concession, Ward devotes substantial attention in its brief to the issue of Elliott's qualifications. Elliott produced evidence that she received favorable evaluations, promotions, and numerous awards from Ward based on her job performance. In addition, she worked for Ward for 23 years. Thus, Elliott's qualification for the job is a disputed fact question.

however, that Elliott failed to prove that a non-member of a protected class was assigned to do the *same* work because the job responsibilities for the two newly created positions changed. This argument is disingenuous. The "same work" requirement obviously refers to the newly created position. See, e.g., Johnson v. Minnesota Historical Society, 931 F.2d 1239, 1242 (8th Cir. 1991) ("proof necessary will vary according to the circumstances of the case."); Leichihman v. Pickwick Intl., 814 F.2d 1263, 1270 (8th Cir.) (when company eliminated position entirely, plaintiff may show that company had "some continuing need for his skills and services"), cert. denied, 484 U.S. 855, 108 S. Ct. 161, 98 L. Ed. 2d 116 (1987).

Elliott argues that the district court erred in concluding that she failed to show that age was a factor in Ward's employment decision. Elliott points to the statement made by her manager that "the company was growing so rapidly that she would not be able to keep up with how fast the company was growing." The district court concluded that this statement "does not directly relate to plaintiff's age," and thus, concluded that Elliott failed to establish a prima facie case. Slip op. at 8-9 (Nov. 27, 1990). We conclude, however, that the statement is sufficient to establish a prima facie case. We believe that this statement is sufficiently close to the line that in the light most favorable to Elliott, and given all favorable inferences, a factfinder could reasonably conclude that this statement demonstrated that age was a factor in Ward's employment decision. We held that similar statements were sufficient to establish a disputed fact question as to whether age was a factor in an employer's decision in *Johnson*, 931 F.2d 1239. In that case, the employee had been called a "blind old bat," and mocked about his back problems. Id. at 1244. A superior also testified that "younger" archaeologists had "new ideas [and] fresh enthusiasm." Id. Based on this testimony, we concluded that a question of fact existed as to whether the employee's age was a determining factor in the employer's actions. Id. Likewise, here, we conclude that a question of fact exists as to whether Elliott's age was a factor in Ward's employment decision. Accordingly, the district court erred in concluding that Elliott failed to establish a prima facie case of age discrimination.

Under the *McDonnell Douglas* analysis, establishing a prima facie case of age discrimination does not end our inquiry. After an employee establishes a prima facie case, the burden of production shifts to the employer to "articulate some legitimate, nondiscriminatory reason" for its employment decision.[4] *McDonnell Douglas*, 411 U.S. at 802, 93 S. Ct. at 1824; Williams v. Valentec Kisco, Inc., 964 F.2d 723, 726 (8th Cir. 1992). If the employer comes forward with such a reason, the burden shifts back to the employee to demonstrate that the proffered reason was merely a pretext for intentional discrimination. The employee may succeed in this "either directly by persuading the court that a discriminatory reason more likely motivated the employer or indirectly by showing that the employer's prof-

4. As we recently explained in Williams v. Valentec Kisco, Inc., 964 F.2d 723 (8th Cir. 1992), such an analysis is not necessary in direct evidence cases. Op. at 728. Elliott, however, does not argue that this is a direct evidence case.

fered explanation is unworthy of credence."[5] Texas Dept. of Community Affairs v. Burdine, 450 U.S. 248, 256, 101 S. Ct. 1089, 1095, 67 L. Ed. 2d 207 (1981). The plaintiff at all times retains the burden of production. Id.

Elliott argues that pretext is shown by Ward's evaluation process. Elliott claims that the evaluation process is "inherently subjective," and therefore, "subject to abuse." Elliott also says that the same manager did not evaluate her, Harris and Grant in Ward's 1986 mid-year performance reviews, and that Harris was subject to a different evaluation and that these facts demonstrate that Ward failed to apply uniform methods of evaluation.

The district court concluded that Ward's evaluation process is "inherently subjective in that the person conducting the evaluation must decide on the rating the employee is to receive. . . ." Slip op. at 8 (Nov. 27, 1990). Nevertheless, the court found that the same manager evaluated Elliott, Grant, and Harris, and that the three were rated according to the same objective performance scale. Id. Based on this, the district court concluded that no genuine issue of fact existed that Elliott "was fairly compared to the two employees who were selected to replace her and that they were better qualified" than Elliott. Id.

We see nothing in Elliott's claim that raises a genuine issue of material fact as to Ward's evaluation process. Contrary to Elliott's implication, *Rademacher*, 431 N.W.2d 879, does not hold that a subjective evaluation process demonstrates pretext. *Rademacher* does not condemn subjective evaluation processes; rather, it requires that such evaluation processes be uniformly applied. Id. at 883. Here, there is no evidence that Ward's evaluation process was not uniformly applied. It is undisputed that Elliott, Harris, and Grant, at the time they were all group merchandisers, were subject to the same performance reviews and evaluated by the same manager. That an evaluation process contains some subjective components cannot in and of itself prove pretext or discriminatory intent. See Goetz v. Farm Credit Serv., 927 F.2d 398, 404 (8th Cir. 1991). Likewise, that Harris's 1986 mid-year evaluation differed in format and criteria from Elliott's is of no consequence. Harris was not a group merchandiser at that time.

Elliott also argues that the supervisor's statement that she could not "keep up" with the company demonstrated pretext. Evidence used to establish a prima facie case in some cases may also establish pretext. Haglof v. Northwest Rehabilitation, Inc., 910 F.2d 492, 494 (8th Cir. 1990). This circuit also recently held that a statement analogous to the one here bordered on direct evidence and was further support for establishing pretext.

---

5. Elliott based her breach of contract claim on the alleged age discrimination. In its analysis of this claim, the district court concluded that Ward's reduction in force constituted a legitimate, nondiscriminatory reason for discharge. Slip op. at 13 (D. Minn. May 29, 1991). Elliott does not dispute this finding. The district court further concluded that Elliott failed to show that a genuine issue of fact existed that Ward's reason was pretextual, and thus, entered summary judgment for Ward on Elliott's breach of contract claim. Id. at 15. That the analysis went this far demonstrates some potential inconsistency in the prima facie case requirements between the age discrimination and breach of contract claims and is further support for our holding that Elliott established a prima facie case of age discrimination.

Williams, 964 F.2d at 728 (Supervisor asking why "an old man [was] carrying the boxes"). Accordingly, we conclude that Elliott met her burden of proof, and the district court erred in entering summary judgment on Elliott's age discrimination claim.

II

Elliott next claims that the district court erred in entering summary judgment on her breach of contract claim. Elliott claims that the employee handbook and personnel policies constituted an employment contract.[6] The district court did not decide whether Ward and Elliott formed a contract based on the employee manual or personnel policies. Slip op. at 11 (May 29, 1991).

In Minnesota, a personnel policy handbook may become enforceable as an employment contract if it meets the requirements for formation of a unilateral contract. Pine River State Bank v. Mettille, 333 N.W.2d 622, 627 (Minn. 1983). An offer must be more definite than an employer's general statement of policy. Id. at 626; Fitzgerald v. Norwest Corp., 382 N.W.2d 290, 292-93 (Minn. Ct. App. 1986).

Elliott specifically claims that Ward breached two provisions of its employee manual. First, she points to a provision of the manual which provides that "[a]ll personnel actions . . . are administered without regard to race, color, sex, national origin, [or] age. . . ." Second, she relies on the personnel policy which says that all employees will be evaluated on a "uniform method." Based on these provisions, Elliott contends that Ward breached its employment contract by discriminating against her on the basis of age and by failing to apply uniform methods of evaluation.

Reviewing Elliott's state law claim de novo, Salve Regina College v. Russell, — U.S. — , 111 S. Ct. 1217, 1221, 113 L. Ed. 2d 190 (1991), we first conclude that the nondiscrimination provision of the manual is nothing more than a general policy statement, and thus, is insufficient to give rise to a unilateral employment contract. *Pine River*, 333 N.W.2d at 626. The Minnesota Court of Appeals considered a nondiscrimination policy in *Fitzgerald*, 382 N.W.2d at 292-93, and concluded that the language in the employee handbook was definite enough to raise a genuine issue of fact about whether the provisions constituted an offer of employment. Id. at 293. The provisions were similar to the one in issue here, but also provided that the nondiscrimination policy was "more than just a statement," explained a specific affirmative action program, and encouraged persons to seek employment with knowledge of the program and policy. Id. These latter provisions of the policy formed the basis for the court's decision in *Fitzgerald*, and are not contained in the Ward personnel manual.

---

6. Ward responds that Elliott was an at-will employee who could be terminated at any time and without cause, and thus, cannot maintain a breach of contract action. Elliott's status as an at-will employee does not necessarily preclude her from bringing a breach of contract action based on specific provisions of an employee manual. See Pine River v. Mettille, 333 N.W.2d 622, 629-30 (Minn. 1983).

Elliott also claims that Ward breached its employment contract by failing to provide and apply a uniform method of evaluation. Elliott again claims that evidence of lack of uniformity is proven by Ward's failure to evaluate Elliott, Grant, and Harris according to the same criteria or by the same supervisor.

We reject Elliott's argument. First, the language in the policy manual is general, and thus, cannot form the basis for a contract. Moreover, even if the language were sufficiently definite to form a contract, as we have previously discussed, no evidence suggests that Ward breached this provision. As the district court found, Elliott was subject to the same evaluation process as Harris and Grant. Accordingly, we affirm the district court's dismissal of Elliott's breach of contract claim.

We affirm the district court's dismissal of Elliott's breach of contract claim, reverse the district court's order as to the age discrimination claim, and remand this claim for trial.

EXERCISES

1. How would you document the fact that the law office fired an employee based on discrimination? How would you document the fact that the office justifiably fired the employee?
2. Discuss some of the ethical problems in maintaining office files.
3. Locate a law library facility in your area that grants access to the general public.
4. Draft a sample table of contents for a staff manual.
5. In addition to the laws mentioned in this chapter, which other statutes have a direct impact on office hiring and firing procedures?
6. How would you document the fact that an employee in a protected category was fired for incompetence rather than because of discrimination?
7. Discuss how far a law office should go to make "reasonable accommodation" under the ADA.
8. Locate a judicial decision indicating that dress codes may be discriminatory and discuss its impact on the creation of a law office's image.
9. Argue that maintaining timesheets may be a form of discrimination against slower employees.
10. Analyze the court's decision in Brown v. Ford, Bacon & Davis, Utah, Inc.

SITUATIONAL ANALYSIS

A law office employs over 20 paralegals. In a recent hiring frenzy the office hired three paralegals who graduated from three different schools in the area. Two of the paralegals have turned out to be excellent employees, but the third has difficulty in understanding and completing assignments. This paralegal requires instruction far in excess of all the other paralegals and does not appear to understand complex concepts. The office wishes to fire the paralegal, but the paralegal claims that, under the Americans with Disabilities Act, she is protected because the lack of intellectual ability is a "disability."

Similar situations have arisen under the ADA in other areas of employment, but there is no definitive judicial decision on the matter.

1. Argue the case for the law office.
2. Argue the case for the paralegal.

8

Management Concepts

The real challenge in managing paralegals is to encourage, inspire and reward excellence across the entire paralegal task spectrum — which ranges, in our practice group, from the highly analytical to the crushingly mundane.

> Joyce E. Larson
> Legal Assistant Coordinator
> Brown & Wood
> New York, New York

CHAPTER OVERVIEW

First and foremost, a law office is people. The people who comprise the law office are more than just a group of random individuals sharing the same geographic location. To work effectively, they must act collectively as a single unit. How well these people work together as a legal team constitutes the group dynamics of the office. **Group dynamics** are the interactions of two or more persons who work collectively to advance a common goal.

The law office must not only be concerned with the proper production and maintenance of its records; it must also recognize that it will only be productive if all the members of the legal team can function as a unit. To facilitate this collective common work ethic, the person in charge of office personnel must be aware of the gradations of office politics and the gentle art of negotiation and persuasion. Several management techniques, theories, and strategies are available to accomplish this objective.

This chapter will concentrate on the inner workings of the personal relationships between and among the members of the legal team. It will focus on some basic management principles and methods of organizing work tasks and evaluating performance, and on how to negotiate and

solve problems. Finally, the chapter will discuss some of the ethical considerations that are encountered with respect to law office management.

Basic Management Principles

Management Concepts

There are two primary functions of effective management: planning
and organization. Planning is the setting of specific goals and objectives
for the work force and the office as a whole, and determining the most efficient method of ensuring that these goals are achieved. In determining the
desired goals of the office, the manager must be able to differentiate between immediate, short-term, and long-term goals. An **immediate goal** is
one that must be accomplished within a few days at the outside. An example of an immediate goal would be finding additional temporary space to
accommodate an emergency project. A **short-term goal** is one that should
be achieved within a three-year period, such as expanding the client base
or hiring additional personnel. Finally, a **long-term goal** is one to be completed beyond three years, such as moving the office to different or larger
quarters to accommodate the increased client base and staff resulting from
the completion of the short-term goals. Effective management requires as-
sessing a need, determining an effective method of meeting it, and then
setting a time frame for accomplishing the goal. This is often referred to as
strategic planning.

EXAMPLE:

New technology has been introduced by several computer companies, and the office has decided to upgrade its information technology. A goal is set to modify or change the existing system within
one year. This is a short-term goal.

Organization refers to the ability of the manager to garner all of the
resources of the office in an effective manner to ensure that the goals of the
office can be reached. This includes finding the best qualified people to
staff the office, seeing to it that the team is appropriately managed, and
motivating all members of the legal team sufficiently that they remain productive and valuable employees. Each of these aspects of organizing the
office will be discussed in turn.

Recruitment and Hiring

Many law offices actively recruit new personnel by advertising open-
ings directly at law schools, paralegal institutions, and secretarial colleges.

Generally, new attorneys are recruited during their last year at law school, with most of the major law firms sending people directly to the schools to interview prospective associates. Typically, new associates begin work after Labor Day after graduating law school and taking the bar exam during the summer.

Paralegals and other support staff are usually recruited throughout the year; however, the greatest period of new employment is usually in September, corresponding to the arrival of the new associates. Most law offices do not visit paralegal and secretarial schools but rather contact the schools' placement offices and indicate a specific need.

The recruitment process involves three main methods of selecting new employees:

1. a written application and resume
2. an interview
3. a test

Application and Resume

The first impression that a prospective employee makes is by means of a written application and resume. In establishing the hiring goals for the office, the manager will have certain needs in mind with respect to the education and other qualifications of new employees. The application and resume are used to eliminate those persons whose backgrounds do not meet the needs of the office. Additionally, the physical presentation of the application and resume can indicate the seriousness and maturity of the applicant: A sloppy or badly written document may indicate a lack of interest or ability.

EXAMPLE:

The law office wishes to hire an entry-level paralegal who has completed an accredited paralegal program. The office notifies various schools in the area and begins to receive resumes. The person in charge of recruitment can immediately screen out those students who have not yet completed their courses of study because that information can be confirmed by the resume.

See Exhibit 14, which is an example of a standard employment application.

Exhibit 14: Sample Employment Application

Blumbergs Law Products B 605—Application for employment, 7-92   PUBLISHED BY JULIUS BLUMBERG, INC.

The Civil Rights Act of 1964 prohibits discrimination in employment practice because of race, color, religion, sex or national origin. P. L. 90-202 prohibits discrimination on the basis of age. The laws of some States prohibit various types of discrimination. The Americans With Disabilities Act prohibits asking job applicants about disabilities.

FOR OFFICE USE	
Possible Positions	Locations

EMPLOYMENT APPLICATION

Date ....

Please Print

FOR OFFICE USE	
Location	Rate ....
Position	Date ....

Last Name   First Name   Middle Name   Social Security No.

Present address ....
Number   Street   City   State   Zip

How long at this address ....   Phone (.........) ....

Prior address ....   How long at prior address ....

Number of dependents ....   Relatives, other than spouse, employed by the company.........

Do you hold a valid drivers license? ....Do you own a car? ....Will you travel? ....Will you relocate? ....

Give three references (no relations), name, address and telephone number:

1. ....
2. ....
3. ....

Position desired? ....Salary or hourly rate expected? ....

Can you work full-time ....Part-time ....if part-time, specify days and hours.........

Are you legally eligible to work in the United States? ☐ Yes ☐ No

Have you worked with computers? ☐ Yes ☐ No Explain ....

Can you type? ☐ No ☐ Yes: How many words per minute? ....

What machines can you operate? ....

Have you worked here before? ☐ Yes .... ☐ No Dates   Have you applied here before? ☐ Yes .... ☐ No Dates

Have you served in the Armed Forces? ☐ Yes ☐ No Branch ....

Dates of duty: from ....to ....rank at discharge ....

Type of discharge ....special training ....

Do not answer the following questions unless the box in front of the question is checked. Answers to the questions checked are needed for bona fide job qualification, national security, business necessity or other reasons legally permissible.

☐ Height......... Weight ....   ☐ Are you between 18 and 70 years of age? ....   If not, state your age.........

☐ Are you a citizen of the U.S..........If not, do you intend to become a U.S. citizen ....and can you produce evidence from the Immigration and Naturalization Service to permit your employment in the United States? ....

☐ What languages do you speak and write.........

☐ Have you ever worked for this company under a different name? ....Is any additional information relative to change of name, use of assumed name or nickname necessary to enable a check on you work record? If yes, explain ....

☐ Have you ever been bonded? ....If yes, for what job(s) ....

☐ Have you ever been convicted of a crime?.........If yes, give details.........

Exhibit 14: *(continued)*

FORMER EMPLOYMENT (Including Civil Service)

FROM	TO	FIRM NAME—ADDRESS (START WITH LAST CONNECTION)	REASON FOR LEAVING	Salary or Hourly Rate
/ / / /		Name		
Supervisor		Address		
Tel. No.		Nature of business		
Position - duties				
/ / / /		Name		
Supervisor		Address		
Tel. No.		Nature of business		
Position - duties				
/ / / /		Name		
Supervisor		Address		
Tel. No.		Nature of business		
Position - duties				
/ / / /		Name		
Supervisor		Address		
Tel. No.		Nature of business		
Position - duties				

If you do not wish us to contact an employer listed above indicate which one and state why ....

SCHOOLS ATTENDED, ADDRESS	NO. OF YEARS	COURSE STUDIED	GRADUATE?	DEGREE
			☐ Yes ☐ No	
Elementary			☐ Yes ☐ No	
			☐ Yes ☐ No	
High			☐ Yes ☐ No	
College			☐ Yes ☐ No	
			☐ Yes ☐ No	

Additional comments you wish to make about your qualifications ....

We assure you that this application will be evaluated solely on its merits and we thank you for your interest in our company.

PLEASE READ CAREFULLY BEFORE SIGNING

I understand that if I am offered a job, employment is at will, unless the employer and I sign a separate employment contract. This means that I can be discharged at any time if the employer wishes to do so, for any cause or for no cause.

The answers given and the statements made by me in this application are true and complete. I understand and agree that misrepresentation or omission of facts called for is cause for dismissal. You may make any investigation of my personal history and my credit or financial record that you think necessary.

Date .... 19 ....
                                                                                  Applicant's signature

No representation is made by the publisher that the printed questions or requests for information in this application conform to or comply with State and Federal Laws although every effort has been made to do so.

Interview

Once the applicant's background has been intitially screened by means of a resume or application, the office will arrange a personal interview with the applicant. The purpose of the interview is to assess the physical appearance of the applicant in terms of grooming and demeanor and to study the person's verbal skills and body language, as discussed in earlier chapters. During this interview process the manager can evaluate how well the applicant will fit in with the office and the image it wishes to project.

EXAMPLE:

The office manager arranges an interview with one of the applicants for the entry-level paralegal position because of her outstanding credentials. At the interview the applicant is poised, well-groomed, well-spoken, and outgoing. The manager has learned much more about the applicant than could be discerned on the basis of a resume alone.

Test

Many people may appear to be qualified for a particular position on paper, but if the office requires special skills, such as minimum typing speed or familiarity with editing legal documents, a test may be in order to determine that the particular applicant does possess the necessary skills to do the job successfully. These desired skills must be determined before the recruitment process begins, and must appear as part of the job requirements in any notice of potential employment. After, or in conjunction with, the personal interview, the applicant may be asked to demonstrate his or her abilities by taking a job-related test.

EXAMPLE:

The office requires that the paralegal it hires be knowledgeable about correct Bluebook citation forms. In order to determine the applicant's skills, the office administers an exam in which the paralegal is required to correct several standard citations. In this manner the office can determine the prospective employee's ability.

One important caution with respect to the recruitment process: As discussed in the last chapter, there are many protections against discrimination in the hiring process, particularly bias based on age, sex, race, religion, or national origin. No question or restriction in selection can be used to unlawfully discriminate against persons who fall into these protected categories.

Employment Contracts

Once a person has been hired by the office, he or she is obligated contractually to the firm. The contract may be either oral or written. Written contracts may take the form of an employee handbook that applies universally to all employees or individually negotiated agreements that affect only particular persons. Regardless of the format, all employment agreements should cover several areas to provide guidance for the employee. The specific details of employment contracts are beyond the scope of this book, but the following are some clauses that must be considered:

Job Description.   In order to avoid uncertainty on the part of the employee, the manager should specify all of the duties that are incident to the employee's position. The more detailed the job description, the better. This can minimize stress on the part of the employee and provide a basis for establishing both work and career goals.

Compensation.   Probably the most frequently used motivating factor in management is the monetary payments made to employees. The employee should know exactly what his or her yearly salary is to be and the method of payment (weekly, monthy, etc.), as well as any potential bonus plan the office has. Compensation also includes reimbursement of expenses the employee undertakes on behalf of the employer, as well as expense accounts to which the employee may be entitled.

Leave.   The employee must understand how much sick, vacation, and family leave he or she is entitled to, including any restraints on the use of such leave, such as vacation time that may only be taken during certain months. The employee should be made aware of any office policy with respect to deducting leave for tardiness or absenteeism.

Employee Benefits.   Special benefits given to an employee in addition to regular monetary compensation should be described in the contract. Examples of such benefits are health and dental insurance, life insurance, pension and profit-sharing plans, and so forth.

Termination.   If the employment is expected to be for a specified period, the employee should know the last date of employment. More important, a well-drafted employment contact will specify all grounds that may give rise to the termination of the employment, both for and without cause. By establishing the grounds for termination at the outset, the office may be able to avoid potential litigation later on. See the section below on firing.

Restrictive and Proprietary Covenants.   Restrictive and proprietary covenants are special clauses in employment contracts that concern the confidentiality of office data and prohibitions against going into direct competition with the office after employment is terminated. These clauses are legal and enforceable, provided that they do not completely and irrevocably prohibit the employee from earning his or her livelihood. Courts also will not enforce such clauses if the period of their restriction is too long or if they cover a geographic area beyond that from which the office draws its client base.

A good manager will see that all employees are aware of these contractual provisions and, preferably, will have them in writing for the employee to keep for reference. Once an employee is hired as a permanent member of the legal team, the manager can then return his or her focus to the continued efficiency of the entire legal team.

Time Management

Time management refers to the ability of the members of the legal team to organize their work time so that all necessary tasks are performed efficiently, accurately, and — hopefully — within the confines of the work week. For many businesses, and especially service industries such as law offices, time is a resource, the primary resource that the office has. There are only so many hours in a day, and a law office typically charges for work on an hourly basis. The more efficient the members of the legal team, the more work that can be performed within a set period of time.

The first approach taken in effective time management is to eliminate or reduce factors that are **time wasters** — activities that do not further the business goals of the office. Some of the most familiar time-wasting factors in an office are socializing, procrastination, disorganization, and ineffective communication.

Socializing refers to the time that the office personnel spend simply enjoying each other's company and discussing events that have nothing to do with office work. Although some socializing is important to the creation of a relaxed and productive work environment, a problem may arise if too much time is spent on non-work-related chatter. The optimum scenario is to keep the atmosphere relaxed but limit social intercourse to work breaks, lunches, and occasional small talk.

EXAMPLES:

1. Elaine and Rochelle, two attorneys with the office, have just returned from their summer vacations. On the first day back they spend about an hour discussing the details of their trips. This socializing wasted valuable work time. The conversation would be less wasteful had it occurred over lunch.

2. Mary and Suzanne, two paralegals with the office, have just returned from their summer vacations. On the first day back they spend ten minutes catching up on how the vacations went, and then arrange to meet for a coffee break later in the morning. This social intercourse creates a friendly atmosphere and does not waste office time.

Procrastination is putting off work until the last possible moment rather than sitting down to accomplish tasks as soon as possible. Many people would prefer to postpone onerous or boring work, but in an office all work must be monitored so that is is completed by the date it is due. An unforeseen problem may arise with respect to fulfilling a task, and deferred work may create problems later.

EXAMPLE:

Vivien, a young lawyer with the firm, is given her first complaint to draft and file. Vivien is very nervous about the task and postpones doing the work until the day the complaint must be filed. Once she starts the drafting, she realizes that she needs additional information but is unable to locate the client, and the complaint is not filed. This was the last day the suit could be filed before the statute of limitations expired, and now the firm may be liable for malpractice for not filing the complaint in a timely manner.

If the law office has not established set policies and procedures, accomplishing tasks may become difficult because the members of the office are uncertain as to how to complete their work. This failure to have established procedures creates disorganization, which in turn wastes time because the members of the legal team have to determine which steps to follow.

EXAMPLE:

The law office wants to maintain an image as one happy family working as a single unit. To this end, the support personnel are not assigned to any particular attorney or paralegal. When work needs to be typed or filed, the attorneys and paralegals have to waste time finding support staff who are free to assist them. This wastes valuable work time.

Finally, if the goals of the office are not effectively communicated to the legal team members, they do not know what is expected of them or which work is to take priority, and therefore cannot function effectively. Time is wasted in trying to determine which tasks are important and who is responsible for seeing that they are accomplished.

EXAMPLE:

Helen is hired as a paralegal for the law office, working for three different attorneys. One morning she arrives at work to find piles of papers on her desk from all three lawyers, but no one has indicated the order of importance for the work or when the work must be completed. The attorneys are all out of the office, and Helen starts working on one of the projects only to learn later that it was the least important and the last one due.

In order to avoid these time-wasting factors, several time management strategies should be employed by the office. The most common of these strategies are as follows:

Set Priorities.   As indicated in the example above, each task has a different degree of importance and due date. In order to avoid confusion and wasting time, specific orders of importance should be assigned to each task so that the employee knows where his or her effort should be spent.

Use Effective Communication Techniques.   Never assume that the employee intuitively understands the wishes of the person who is assigning the work. Make sure that all tasks are specifically described, and be open to questions to avoid misunderstandings.

Organize Paperwork and Work Areas.   Make sure that there is "a place for everything and everything in its place." Too much time can be wasted simply looking for the materials necessary to perform the given task. By having specific areas for all materials and work, the entire operation of the office can run smoothly. Think of the efficiency of a factory conveyor belt.

Plan Ahead.   Anticipate problems and organize work *before* it is communicated to the employee. Tasks and procedures that have been thought through ahead of time can be communicated faster and more efficiently.

Reduce Socializing and Utilize Slack Time.   Try to limit interoffice socializing to set periods during the day, such as coffee breaks or lunch time, or arrange for group social activities after office hours. If there is a slow or slack period during the work day, try to use that time efficiently by organizing files, doing routine paperwork, or otherwise keeping the office in smooth operation.

As the saying goes, "time is money" and wasting time means wasting money for the office.

Personnel Management

Personnel management refers to the ability of the office to maintain a happy and relaxed workplace so that the employees may work effectively and productively. Probably the greatest hindrance to effective personnel management is stress. An employee who feels burdened by stress in the workplace is not going to be a productive worker. Consequently, the primary goal of personnel management is to relieve job-related stress.

Stress in the workplace may be caused by several factors. First, if employees are uncertain as to what function they are expected to perform, they will constantly feel pressured because they will be unsure that the task being performed is the appropriate task. In order to avoid this cause of anxiety, the supervisor should establish specific goals for each employee. By having a specified goal, he or she can know what is expected and work toward accomplishing that objective.

 EXAMPLE:

As stated in the previous example, Helen, the office paralegal, was given a pile of work to perform but no guidance as to which tasks should be performed in which order, or any indication as to how the work must be done. This uncertainty creates stress, making Helen less efficient than she could be.

Second, employees will always be anxious if they feel that there is no job security with the office. Obviously, no one can be guaranteed lifetime employment, but employees like to feel that there is some longevity associated with their employment. Therefore, the office should indicate not only the goals it expects an employee to accomplish, but also provide for evaluation of the employee's work. The evaluation should disclose clearly whether the employee is performing well or not. To accomplish this, many offices use standard employee evaluation forms, which will be discussed below.

 EXAMPLE:

Jeannette has been working as a secretary with the law office for three months. During that entire time no one has ever commented on her work. She does not know what the office thinks of her performance and fears that she may be fired at any time. This anxiety could be reduced simply if the supervisor would assess the quality of Jeannette's work.

Third, if there is an unpleasant work atmosphere or problems with relationships with fellow workers, an employee will feel job-related stress. As discussed in Chapter 7, many stress-related problems can be associated with interpersonal issues at work, from sexual harassment to attempting to accommodate physical infirmities. All of these problems must be worked out with the parties involved and not unilaterally decided by the office management. The employee must feel that he or she has some control over the work situation.

EXAMPLE:

A secretary in the office believes that she is being sexually harassed by one of the associates. The head of the firm must establish procedures for dealing with this situation, and work with both parties involved to come to some appropriate resolution.

Finally, if an employee is given too much work, work that requires constant concentration and overtime, the employee eventually will become "burnt out" — exhausted from work overload. Office managers must be aware of the number and complexity of the tasks that are being assigned to the workers, and make sure that each employee is afforded enough time to recuperate, mentally and physically, from an overabundance of work.

EXAMPLE:

Larry is a paralegal with the office. He is assigned to assist three partners in the firm, and for the past four months has been working until nine o'clock every night, every Saturday, and several hours every other Sunday. Larry is exhausted and for now needs fewer tasks to perform in order to recuperate.

Of course, there is no set answer that can be used to solve every stress-related office situation. However, the goal of effective personnel management is to get all the employees to participate in the decision-making process that leads to problem resolution. Another stress factor at work is the feeling that one has no control over a situation. By having the employees participate in the resolution process — called **participatory management** — each employee feels that he or she is a vital and important member of the legal team.

EXAMPLE:

The office is establishing some new policies on time management and billing. The person in charge of creating the policies should meet with every member of the legal team to hear his or her input. In this fashion the employees feel that they are a vital part of the organization and have some say in office policies that directly affect their work.

Motivation Techniques

Motivation is the ability of a manager to inspire employees to perform to the best of their ability. There are several techniques available to motivate employees to achieve optimum performance.

Establish Specific Goals. Employees work best when they know exactly what is expected of them. Additionally, employees will be more productive if they find their work stimulating and challenging. Of course, not every task in a law office is exciting, but a good manager will see to it that goals are set that enable an employee to "stretch" — go beyond what he or she has done before. In this manner the employee grows intellectually and looks forward to meeting new challenges on the job.

 EXAMPLE:

A paralegal in the office is interested in improving her research and writing skills, though they are only a small percentage of her usual work. In order to stimulate her, her supervising attorney gives her small but increasingly difficult research assignments to challenge her abilities. The assignments are well thought out and incremental in their difficulty so that the paralegal is merely challenged, not overwhelmed.

Reward Accomplishments. Everyone desires some form of recognition for work well done. A good manager will frequently acknowledge an employee's contribution to the office. This recognition may take the form of verbal acknowledgment, time off, a bonus, or any other means of letting the employee know that he or she is doing a good job and is appreciated.

 EXAMPLE:

A secretary in the office is asked to stay late to help out with an emergency project. At the end of the evening her supervisor congratulates her on the work she has done, and tells her that she can come to work late the next day because of the extra time she has put in. The secretary feels that she and her work are appreciated.

Provide Variety. To the extent possible, a good manager will try to give employees diversified work. Varied tasks ensures that, no matter how boring one project may be, there is always the prospect of other assignments that are more interesting. Varying the nature of the work also creates more energy in the worker.

EXAMPLE:

Rather than having the receptionist just answer telephones, the office manager assigns her some light typing and filing, and occasionally has her deliver papers to the courthouse. In this way the receptionist's job does not become mundane or routine, and the variety keeps her motivated and interested.

Create a Team.   As will be discussed below, creating a team helps motivate people because they develop a group identity by working together toward a common goal. The more cohesive the group is, the more of a motivating factor teamwork becomes. Most offices work on the basis of groups or teams, and this collective morale helps boost the motivation of each participant in the group.

Work Organization

Creating an Effective Team

The first step in creating an effective team is to determine the purpose for which the team is needed. Specific goals should be established before a team is created. When goals are set, the manager can assemble the most suitable people available to accomplish the goal.

In assembling the team, the abilities that each person brings to the group must be assessed. If several people are expected to provide the same skills, a conflict will be created. Consequently, areas of expertise should be established when forming the office group.

People work in different time schedules, and a problem may arise if members of the team work at different speeds. Unless the work can be performed separately, people should be selected whose work efficiency is compatible. When a team member's performance is dependent on other peoples' production, conflicts may arise if all members do not function at the same rate.

Some people are leaders; some prefer to follow direction. A team will not be effective if all the members fall into just one of these categories. When a team is formed, someone should be selected as the group leader, and the other members must feel comfortable in following his or her direction.

Finally, a good manager will select people who get along well with each other. If the manager knows that certain people are antagonistic to each other, they should not be placed on the same team.

Just like a good recipe, a good team is created by a perfect blending of just the right ingredients put together with careful planning.

EXAMPLE:

The managing partner in the office must assemble a team to pre-pare for a trial. She selects an experienced litigator who is known for his skill in the courtroom, two young associates who have demonstrated ability and a desire to learn courtroom procedures, and a paralegal who has been with the firm for a short period of time but has been involved in several trials for the firm. This team combines experience, ability, and a desire to learn with an able leader.

Team Operation

A law office operates as a **team** — a group of individuals who work together toward a specific goal. Even a sole practitioner usually has some sort of support staff who collectively constitute that office's team. Each member of a team has certain obligations to all other members of the group. These obligations must be understood by each team member; fail-ure to meet these responsibilities affects the performance of the entire group. These basic obligations are:

1. *Respect.* Each team member must respect the ability and integrity of other members.
2. *Dependability.* Every member of the team must be accountable for his or her actions and be expected to perform the tasks assigned when due.
3. *Loyalty.* The team operates as a group, a single unit, and every member must work toward the group goal rather than fulfilling individual wishes or obligations.
4. *Understanding.* Each team member must be understanding of the problems and concerns of the other members, and must accept human frailty in others.

Just like a family, the legal team must be able to put aside any differ-ences and work toward the common good. In order to work effectively as a group, needs and goals must be communicated to each member of the team. The communication may be **formal,** either by written or oral means, or **informal,** in which the information is passed on in casual give-and-take. The team can only achieve the group goal if the goal is understood by each member of the group.

Rarely do groups work in a totally democratic fashion. In most groups some hierarchy is formed, either formally or informally. A **hierar-chy** is a specified chain of command with specific divisions of tasks and functions. Having a hierarchy helps create specific goals for each member of the team and establishes a communication link for task assignment and evaluation. An example of the hierarchy of a typical legal team appears in Chapter 1.

Group Dynamics and the Office Team

Group dynamics are the interactions of two or more people who are working collectively toward a common goal. From grade school through retirement homes, human beings generally feel most comfortable in a group
situation. Groups serve several important functions in a work environment:

1. The group or office provides an identity for the members. The office staff members identify themselves as members of the legal
   team.
2. The group offers affiliation or relationships with other individuals
   with similar characteristics.
3. The group affiliation gives the individual members a sense of
   power. Ten people working together collectively can achieve
   greater strength than one person working alone.
4. The group establishes goals, and meeting these goals gives the
   members a feeling of accomplishment.

Basic management techniques endorse the effectiveness of group inter-
action. However, although there are definite benefits to group organization,
there are certain detriments as well. The benefits of group dynamics are:

1. Groups make more accurate decisions than individuals because
   several people can bring several areas of expertise and experience
   to help solve a given problem.
2. Communication is easier because the members are not working as
   separate individuals but collectively as a single unit.
3. The members of the group feel that they are part of the decision-
   making process and that they have helped accomplish the specific
   group goal.
4. Because each member of the group can feel that he or she participated in completing the task, there is more acceptance of whatever solution is arrived at than is generally felt if decisions are
   made unilaterally.

The disadvantages of working in a group are:

1. The group may develop **groupthink** — acting as a unit and losing the individual identity of each of the members, thereby negat-
   ing the potential input of each participant.
2. Groups are time-consuming, simply in terms of scheduling and
   holding regular group meetings.
3. There is the potential that members will compromise on solutions
   they do not believe in simply to save time.
4. The group may be dominated by one individual who leads the
   group by force of character, not necessarily because of knowledge
   or ability.

However, after all is said and done, every office works in groups, either formally or informally, and good management accepts this reality and works with it to make the group productive. Groups are generally characterized by a cohesiveness among their members plus a certain degree of conformity, resulting in a group "norm," that is, standard behavior exemplified by the particular group. Effective management utilizes the group to establish group goals, and rewards every member of the group when the goal is accomplished. Everyone in the group must feel that he or she is playing an effective and important part in the fulfillment of the office goal.

Performance Evaluations

Performance evaluations are an effective and common method of communicating to employees how well they are performing their assigned tasks. Evaluations may either be in writing or oral. These evaluations play an important role in defining an employee's function, establishing goals, and eliminating anxiety with respect to job security.

Performance evaluations help strengthen the bond between the employee and the employer, giving each the opportunity to discuss and identify potential problems, arrive at solutions, and define obligations. To be effective, the evaluations should be performed on a regular basis, either annually or twice a year, and standards should be established at the outset as to what is expected of the employee. It is also important that the evaluation be objective and avoid any personal hostility unrelated to work performance. In this context, the evaluation itself should be nonconfrontational. It is important to reinforce the employee's identity as a member of the legal team, and the evaluation should be presented as a method of improving the performance of the entire office.

Many offices create specific performance evaluation forms that are used as the basis for an actual face-to-face evaluation. These forms can either be general, focusing on attitude and ability, or very job-specific, focusing on actual work performed, and become a permanent part of the employee's record. The employee should be given the opportunity to review the form prior to meeting with the supervisor, and after the meeting a memorandum reflecting their discussion should be written, reviewed, and signed by both the employee and the employer, then placed in the employee's personnel file along with the evaluation.

EXAMPLE:

In her first performance evaluation, the office paralegal was censured for coming to work late. The paralegal always arrived between 9 and 9:30 A.M., never left before 6 P.M., and was unaware that there was a required starting time. At the meeting with her supervisor this matter was discussed. They agreed that, because of the failure of communication and the merit of the paralegal's overall job performance, the tardiness should not be weighed in the past evaluation period. The evaluation form was amended, and the paralegal felt that she was able to participate in reaching a fair solution to a potential conflict.

At the evaluation meeting, the employee and the employer should discuss areas that could be improved and mutually set goals to improve the employee's performance. This technique is known as **management by objectives,** where both parties are involved in establishing joint goals. It is always important that the employee feel that his or her input is important to the decision-making process.

Prior to the formal evaluation, many employers attempt to forestall potential conflicts by providing frequent informal feedback to the employee so that the employee gets a sense of how well he or she is doing. **Feedback,** a response to a particular task performed, is important to encourage the employee. Giving praise for a job well done acts as an incentive for the employee to continue such performance. Shortcomings in job performance should also be acknowledged, but in a positive manner with suggestions for improvement. This alerts the employee to potential problems and indicates a means of rectifying the situation before a problem actually does arise. This management technique is known as **coaching** because the employer guides the employee toward a desired goal.

 EXAMPLE:

A paralegal in the office has just written her first research memo for her supervising attorney and is anxious about her performance. The attorney, after reading the memo, compliments the paralegal on her effective and thorough research, and makes some suggestions with respect to rewording certain phrases to convey a clearer meaning. The paralegal has been "coached." She knows what she has done well and has been given guidelines to improve areas that need work. She was treated as an intelligent professional and will respond accordingly.

The most important factor to remember when dealing with performance evaluations is that everyone needs to establish specific goals, should be encouraged when goals are reached, and be given guidance when he or she has missed or lost sight of the objectives. The goals should be established by both parties and be reasonable. In this manner the employee knows what is expected and can work toward that goal.

A sample performance evaluation form is provided for reference.

Exhibit 15: Performance Evaluation Form

5-Excellent;   4-Very Good;   3-Good;   2-Fair;   1-Poor

WORK HABITS

Tardiness:	5	4	3	2	1
Absent:	5	4	3	2	1
Dress:	5	4	3	2	1
Demeanor:	5	4	3	2	1
Attitude:	5	4	3	2	1
Cooperation:	5	4	3	2	1

Comments:

JOB SKILLS

Knowledge of Area:	5	4	3	2	1
Preparedness:	5	4	3	2	1
Time Management:	5	4	3	2	1
Clarity/Organization:	5	4	3	2	1
Interest in Area:	5	4	3	2	1
Ability to Convey Information:	5	4	3	2	1
Overall Rating:	5	4	3	2	1

Comments:

AREAS FOR IMPROVEMENT

GOALS FOR NEXT PERIOD

Problem Solving

In any group situation problems will arise, both with respect to the work to be performed and interpersonal relationships. This is especially true in a law office where the business of the office itself, the practice of law, is concerned exclusively with solving problems. In terms of management practices, the members of the team must be able to differentiate between conflict and controversy. **Conflict** results when there is a person or group of persons who are blocking action. In order to forward the desired action, some resolution must be achieved. A **controversy** exists when there is a difference of opinion as to which action is appropriate. With a controversy some compromise must be attained.

One of the primary rules in solving problems in the workplace is never to be confrontational; one must never assign blame for the problem to another person. Instead, one should employ words that suggest a group problem requiring a group solution. Plural pronouns, as in phrases such as "our problem" and "we need to solve the problem," indicate a collaborative effort. Using singular pronouns indicates blame: "It's your problem, you fix it." Effective problem solving requires a group effort and consensus. When all members of the team participate in formulating the solution, they are more willing to see that the solution is carried out.

 EXAMPLE:

A client presents a legal problem to the office, and two of the attorneys on the team assigned to the client differ in their views of the appropriate course to take. Rather than permit a confrontational situation, the leader of the group should present the alternative strategies to the group for a discussion and group decision.

There are five basic steps involved in solving any given problem:

1. Define the problem. Know exactly where the conflict or controversy is, and focus only on that situation.
2. Gather information and data to help reach a decision that will resolve the problem.
3. Work out several different approaches to solve the problem based on the information gathered.
4. Test the effectiveness of an alternative by implementing some part of its plan.
5. Evaluate the alternative selected to determine that it does in fact resolve the problem.

EXAMPLE:

Two secretaries in the law firm share an office. One secretary always arrives at 9 A.M., the other at 9:30. The first secretary is angry; she believes that the other secretary is doing less work, even though the second secretary stays later than the first. The second secretary is also upset, believing that the first secretary always leaves early. The problem is one of insecurity. The solution is to get both secretaries together, indicate that the second secretary stays late, and perhaps introduce the concept of "flex time" in the office. In this fashion both secretaries know that they are working the same amount of time but at different intervals.

Negotiations

Unfortunately, not all problems are easily or readily resolved. Sometimes the problem is solved by **authority decision** — the unilateral decision of the person in power. In many instances, however, achieving resolution of the problem may require **negotiation.** In a successful negotiation both sides in a controversy present their arguments, and then mutually compromise and agree on a solution. In this manner the people who have the problem can arrive at their own solution, which is generally considered more productive than an authority decision.

In any negotiation strategy, the most important factor is that the negotiators leave some latitude for compromise. Negotiation does not mean one side conceding to all of the opposing side's demands; rather, it is an endeavor in which two sides reach some mutually acceptable solution. If one side leaves no room for alternatives, no compromise can take place, and the entire process becomes fruitless. Additionally, it is imperative that each party to the controversy treat the other as an intelligent being who is capable of reaching a fair conclusion.

There are basically three negotiation techniques that are employed in most situations:

Lose-Lose.   In the lose-lose technique, both sides feel as though they have lost. It is a true compromise, but a compromise in which each side gives up something. This is generally not the most effective negotiation strategy.

EXAMPLE:

Two law firms are representing adversaries in a lawsuit. One office is in Sacramento, the other in Washington, D.C. At some point the lawyers feel that a face-to-face meeting would be helpful, but each side wants the conference at its own office. In the end, the attorneys decide to continue the representation without the face-to-face meeting. The problem has been solved, but both sides have lost.

Win-Lose.   With this technique, one side is victorious and the other side is the loser. In this situation the losing party may feel resentful, which could create additional problems later on.

EXAMPLE:

Continuing the situation posited above: The D.C. lawyer eventually convinces the California lawyer to come to Washington because most of the important evidence is located in the East. The problem is solved, but the California law firm feels as though it has lost its edge and equal bargaining position.

Win-Win.   By far the most effective negotiation technique is to find some solution that provides a winning scenario for each side. In this fashion no one is the loser, and both parties feel victorious. Additionally, because the solution has been arrived at together, there is more of a chance that both sides will be desirous of seeing that it is effectuated.

EXAMPLE:

The parties now agree that they will try meeting by telephone conference call. They also decide that, if an actual physical meeting becomes necessary, they will alternate meeting sites between the two offices or, if more convenient, will hold the meeting in St. Louis, halfway between both parties. Now both sides feel as though they have won the negotiation; each side benefits.

How effective a person is at coming to some negotiated solution is dependent on that person's negotiation style. In this context "style" is the manner one negotiator uses toward the other: friendly and caring; cool and detached; experienced and wise; naive. This choice is totally dependent on the personality of the party and the particularities of the situation; no one style is appropriate to every scenario. The basic premise to bear in mind, however, is that a negotiation process will not be effective if both sides do not feel that they have contributed to its resolution. Furthermore, each side should believe that the solution is beneficial to itself. Negotiation is an art, not a science.

Firing an Employee

Chapter 7 discussed many of the federal laws that protect employees from unlawful discrimination and provide workers with certain guaranteed rights. This section will focus on some of the management concerns involved when an employee must be fired.

First, the employment contract should specify the grounds that the manager can use to terminate the employment. If an employee is unaware of potential areas of conflict, it is unfair to use such grounds as reasons for firing the employee. Having the grounds for termination delineated in the contract puts employees on notice as to what is expected of them.

Second, the employee must be made aware of the problems as they arise and be given the opportunity to correct any behavior that might cause termination. If the employee does not realize that he or she is doing anything wrong, there is no way that the situation can be corrected.

Third, and most important, the manager must document every instance that the manager believes may result in firing the employee. Because of the proliferation of new employment laws protecting workers, many fired employees are now suing former employers for illegal discrimination with respect to the firing. In order to prevent or minimize the impact of potential litigation, a well-documented file is the manager's best defense against an unwarranted lawsuit.

Finally, when the decision has been reached that an employee must be fired, it should be carried out as soon as possible. It is unfair to the office and the employee to prolong the situation. Also, if at all possible, the situation should be tempered by helping the employee make the transition and perhaps locate a new job. However, the manager must never apologize, but be firm and friendly.

Firing an employee is probably the most difficult task that a manager must face, but sometimes it is necessary for the good of the entire office and the legal team.

Management and Ethics

The management of the law office must make all members of the legal team aware of the ethical responsibility they share as members of the legal profession. The ethical standards established for lawyers, paralegals, and members of a law office must be communicated to the staff, and copies of the ethical standards should be distributed and made available to each member of the firm.

The sources for the ethical rules governing lawyers and legal assistants are the American Bar Association's Code of Professional Responsibility and Model Code of Professional Conduct. Specific reference to these guidelines have been made throughout this text where appropriate. In addition to the ABA codes, attorneys are also governed by various state codes of ethics enacted by the legislatures in each jurisdiction.

There are two primary sources of ethical standards for paralegals. The first is promulgated by the National Federation of Paralegals Association (NFPA) as an Affirmation of Responsibility, and the second is formulated as a code of professional behavior by the National Association of Legal Assistants (NALA).

These various codes and rules of professional conduct establish ethical goals for the members of the legal team. The management of the law office should make sure that every member of the office is not only aware of these ethical rules but understands that the office expects them to be upheld. Once the members of the office have had these ethical rules established as office and group goals, they are easier to attain.

CHAPTER SUMMARY

Because a law office is a service industry, its success or failure depends on the ability of the office to manage its personnel in a manner that is effective and conducive to excellent performance. Probably the most important factor in good management is providing every employee with an established set of goals that are capable of being achieved, and making sure that the employees receive feedback on their performance. Without specific goals and guidelines people feel adrift, which is counterproductive to an efficient workplace.

To achieve the goals established by the office, each member of the legal team must be able to manage time efficiently. Lost time represents lost income, which in turn results in the failure of the law office. To manage time productively, each member of the legal team must be able to set priorities for the work to be accomplished and must maintain a strict organization of his or her workload.

The law office is a team, a group working together toward a common goal. The dynamics of the group can either streamline or hinder the advancement of the goal, and effective management will ensure that the members of the legal team feel as though they are contributing to the group effort. The best approach is to negotiate productive activity within the group, not impose restrictions on the group from above. Participatory management is the best management.

Key Terms

Authority decision: Decision made unilaterally by a person in a supervisory position.

Coaching: Management technique in which the supervisor gives frequent informal guidance to the employee.

Conflict: Situation in which one person blocks progress.

Controversy: Situation in which two people have a difference of opinion on how to proceed with a goal.

Disorganization: Work situation in which employees have no structure or policy with respect to what is expected.

Feedback: Response by employer to a particular task of an employee.

Formal communication: Written or oral information shared at set periods by members of a legal team.

Group dynamics: Interactions of two or more persons working to advance a common goal.

Groupthink: Individuals acting as a unit, but in doing so sacrificing the identity and input of each member of the group.

Hierarchy: Chain of command and responsibility.

Immediate goal: Objective that can be accomplished in a few days.

Informal communication: Dialogue occurring casually.

Long-term goal: Objective to be accomplished in more than three years.

Lose-lose negotiation: Negotiation technique in which both sides lose.

Management by objectives: Management technique of setting goals.

Motivation: Method of inspiring employees to work.

Negotiation: Method of compromising and resolving problems.

Participatory management: Management technique in which the employees provide input in setting work goals.

Performance evaluation: Method of giving feedback to employees on how well they are doing.

Personnel management: Techniques for managing a staff.

Procrastination: Putting off work until the last minute.

Restrictive covenant: Contractual clause prohibiting an employee from competing with the company.

Short-term goal: Objective that can be accomplished within three years.

Socializing: Potential time-wasting activity; engaging co-workers in non-work-related activities.

Strategic planning: Establishing and planning goals for an office.

Time management: Method of organizing time efficiently.

Win-lose negotiation: Negotiation technique in which one side benefits and the other side does not.

Win-win negotiation: Negotiation technique in which both sides benefit.

Case for Analysis

The following case is presented to underscore some ethical problems that may arise with respect to the management of, or failure to manage, a law office.

State ex rel. Nebraska State Bar v. Kirshen
441 N.W.2d 161 (Neb. 1989)

PER CURIAM.

This is an original proceeding wherein the Nebraska State Bar Association (NSBA), relator, filed formal charges in this court against respondent,

Alan H. Kirshen. The formal charges were based on three separate complaints made to the Counsel for Discipline for the NSBA. . . .

Respondent attended law school at the University of Chicago from 1968 through 1971 and was admitted by examination to the Iowa bar. He spent 6 years "processing fraudulent things for the Federal Government." He was admitted to the bar in Nebraska on motion in 1979. . . .

Respondent first objects to the referee's finding that he violated DR 1-102(A)(6) by failing to provide management, supervision, and control of his office staff and procedures, contending that DR 1-102(A)(6) is unconstitutionally vague in failing to specify conduct or the nature of specific action which will result in sanctions. Respondent also claims that various procedural and substantive due process violations occurred at virtually every stage of these proceedings.

A lawyer is entitled to due process of law in a disciplinary proceeding.

> Disbarment, designed to protect the public, is a punishment or penalty imposed on the lawyer. . . . He is accordingly entitled to procedural due process, which includes fair notice of the charge. . . . [O]ne of the conditions this Court considers in determining whether disbarment by a State should be followed by disbarment [in federal court] is whether "the state procedure from want of notice or opportunity to be heard was wanting in due process."

In re Ruffalo, 390 U.S. 544, 550, 88 S. Ct. 1222, 1226, 20 L. Ed. 2d 117 (1968).

> The term "due process of law" has been often defined as such an exertion of the powers of government as are sanctioned by the settled maxims of the law and under such safeguards for the protection of individual rights as those safeguards prescribed for the class of cases to which the one in question belongs . . . but is satisfied by a proceeding applicable to the subject-matter and conformable to such general rules as affect all persons alike.
> . . . Due process of law may be said to be satisfied whenever an opportunity is offered to invoke the equal protection of the law by judicial proceedings appropriate for the purpose and adequate to secure the end and object sought to be attained.

State ex rel. Nebraska State Bar Assn. v. Jensen, 171 Neb. 1, 28-29, 105 N.W.2d 459, 476 (1960). This court has held: "Due process requires that adjudication be preceded by notice and an opportunity to be heard which is fair in view of the circumstances and conditions existent at the time." (Syllabus of the court.) Kirshen v. Kirshen, 227 Neb. 479, 418 N.W.2d 558 (1988).

We also have held that "[t]he established test for vagueness in a statute is whether it either forbids or requires the doing of an act in terms so vague that people of common intelligence must necessarily guess at its meaning and differ as to its application." Cunningham v. Lutjeharms, 231 Neb. 756, 763, 437 N.W.2d 806, 812 (1989). See, also, Weiner v. State ex rel. Real Estate Comm., 217 Neb. 372, 348 N.W.2d 879 (1984). However,

> [s]ince a disciplinary rule is promulgated for the purpose of guiding lawyers in their professional conduct, and is not directed to the public at large, the central consideration in resolving a vagueness challenge should be whether the nature of the proscribed conduct encompassed by the rule is readily understandable to a licensed lawyer.

People v. Morley, 725 P.2d 510, 516 (Colo. 1986). Similarly, the Iowa Supreme Court held that the standard for determining whether a provision of the Code of Professional Responsibility was unconstitutionally vague was "whether a 'reasonable attorney' would understand certain conduct to be prohibited. . . ." Committee on Professional Ethics v. Durham, 279 N.W.2d 280, 284 (Iowa 1979). See, also, Matter of Sekerez, 458 N.E.2d 229 (Ind. 1984).

DR 1-102(A)(6), when assessed in light of other terms of the Code of Professional Responsibility, has been determined not to be vague. See, e.g., Committee on Professional Ethics v. Durham, supra. In counts I and II, respondent was formally charged with violating a disciplinary rule by failing to respond to letters of complaint. Respondent was required to respond pursuant to Neb. Ct. R. of Discipline 9(E) (rev. 1986). A reasonable attorney would understand that this type of conduct is prohibited and adversely reflects on his fitness to practice law. The record supports a finding that respondent violated DR 1-102(A)(6) in this respect.

We note that respondent was not charged with failure to provide management, supervision, and control of his office staff and procedures. Respondent's own testimony suggested, however, that his failure to respond to . . . complaints is the fault of his secretary, whom he knew to be incompetent.

In In re Ruffalo, supra, the petitioner, an Ohio attorney, was charged in disciplinary proceedings with 12 counts of misconduct. During the hearing, a 13th count was added, based on testimony adduced at the hearing. The attorney was disbarred based, in part, on the misconduct charged in count 13. The Court determined that the attorney had not received fair notice as to the reach of the grievance procedure and the precise nature of the charges, depriving the attorney of procedural due process.

> In the present case petitioner had no notice that his employment of Orlando would be considered a disbarment offense until *after* both he and Orlando had testified at length on all the material facts pertaining to this phase of the case. . . .
> These are adversary proceedings of a quasi-criminal nature. . . . The charge must be known before the proceedings commence. They become a trap when, after they are underway, the charges are amended on the basis of testimony of the accused. He can then be given no opportunity to expunge the earlier statements and start afresh.
> How the charge would have been met had it been originally included in those leveled against petitioner by the Ohio Board of Commissioners on Grievances and Discipline no one knows.

390 U.S. at 550-51, 88 S. Ct. at 1225-26.

Even though we conclude that the referee's finding that respondent violated DR 1-102(A)(6) by failing to provide management, supervision, and control of his office staff and procedures was in error, respondent's reliance on his secretary's alleged incompetence as a defense is entirely misplaced. While respondent's failure to properly supervise his employee was not charged against the respondent, such conduct does not constitute a defense to the misconduct charged. A lawyer may not avoid responsibility for misconduct by hiding behind an employee's behavior and may not avoid a charge of unprofessional conduct by contending his employees are incompetent.

The preliminary statement to the Code of Professional Responsibility as adopted by this court states, "A lawyer should ultimately be responsible for the conduct of his employees and associates in the course of the professional representation of the client." "A lawyer also has responsibility to be aware at least of the major areas of responsibility and the actual work habits of employees and to exercise effective supervision." C. Wolfram, Modern Legal Ethics §16.3.1 at 893 (West 1986).

In State ex rel. NSBA v. Statmore, 218 Neb. 138, 142-43, 352 N.W.2d 875, 878 (1984), we said: "A lawyer's poor accounting procedures and sloppy office management are not excuses or mitigating circumstances in reference to commingled funds." (Citations omitted.) Similarly, "[a]n attorney may not escape responsibility to his clients by blithely saying that any shortcomings are solely the fault of his employee. He has a duty to supervise the conduct of his office." Attorney Griev. Commn. v. Goldberg, 292 Md. 650, 655-56, 441 A.2d 338, 341 (1982). We hold that a lawyer is ultimately responsible for the conduct of his employees and associates in the course of the professional representation of the client.

Respondent's testimony shows only that his failure to supervise his employee directly contributed to his failure to timely respond to the . . . complaints. He may not use his secretary's alleged incompetence to shield him from the consequences of his unprofessional conduct. . . .

Judgment of disbarment.

EXERCISES

1. Create your own version of a performance evaluation form.
2. Devise a different win-win situation for the problem of the D.C. and California law offices described at pages 215-216.
3. Form a group and create, as a unit, a proposal for reorganizing your paralegal program.
4. Devise a negotiation strategy to convince your teacher to change the requirements for this course.
5. Discuss the most important ethical consideration involved in the management of a law office.
6. Discuss the drawbacks that may be incident to participatory management.
7. Are groups always an effective management device? Discuss.
8. Prepare your own resume and have the class discuss its effectiveness.

9. Go to the library and find a sample employment contract and analyze its provisions.
10. Discuss effective methods for discharging an employee.

SITUATIONAL ANALYSIS

Your law office has limited space and two people must share each office.

Two workers who share an office are in constant conflict. One of the workers is always warm and insists on keeping all doors and windows open and constantly turns off the heat. The other worker insists on playing music, which she claims she needs to reduce stress and perform her job efficiently. Additionally, the second worker frequently talks on the telephone and invites in other office workers for both work and non-work-related matters.

These two people are getting on each other's nerves and are creating tension in the office, but no other space is available to move one of them. You are a member of the firm's grievance committee and must help resolve this problem. Which are the most appropriate techniques to employ, and how do you think the situation could best be handled?

9 Document Preparation

Dependence on computer spell-checks or thesauruses are extra guides, but there can be no excuse that "I did not learn it in school." There are enough self-help English Language textbooks available which allow improvement of skills. Life is a continual learning.

> Barbara Chozahinoff
> Paralegal Student (Retired Teacher)
> Queens College
> Flushing, New York

CHAPTER OVERVIEW

As stated previously, a legal practice is dominated by paperwork. At some point, all work generated by the law office will be reduced to a written format. It is the responsibility of every member of the legal team that the writings created by the office be clear, effective, and reflective of the intent of the author. The law is concerned with linguistic precision, and nowhere is this more evident than in the documents prepared by a law office.

Generally, there are three categories of documents prepared by members of the firm. The first is the regular business letter. The business letter is used to confirm oral communication, to convey basic information, and to accompany and explain other materials. If the letter is externally sloppy or internally incoherent, the effect is to create a negative image for the office. In most instances the first contact that people have with the office is by means of a simple business letter; therefore, it is imperative that the letter present the firm in the best possible light.

The second category of document prepared by the law office is memoranda. These memos may take the form of interoffice communications or analyze the result of intensive legal research performed for a client. The memo, like the business letter, must be clear and precise and frequently may require a persuasive manner — that is, it must be written in a fashion that convinces the reader of the writer's point of view. Whatever its style, the memo is the backbone of all legal work. The legal memo sums up the office's legal theory, based on applicable cases and statutes, that will be the focus for representing the client's interests. Without this form of legal document, the members of the legal team would be working without an organized plan.

The third classification of document produced by the law office is the legal form. These forms are preprinted or have been entered in the office computer or word processor. Typical examples of legal forms are court orders, basic motions, affidavits, and releases. Even though office forms are written in an established format, each document must be checked for its appropriateness to the client's particular matter.

Once the initial draft of a document has been prepared, it must be edited for correctness of content and format. Because of the required precision of language in the law, an unusual word or misplaced comma can dramatically change the meaning and effect of any given document. As a consequence, editing and proofreading documents become two of the most important tasks involved in document preparation.

Not only is it necessary that the members of the legal team understand the physical creation of a legal document; they must also be cognizant of the ethical problems associated with the creation of a document. Concerns such as plagiarism and the unauthorized practice of law are intimately involved in the creation of written legal materials, and every member of the office is held to a high standard to ensure that no ethical violations occur. This chapter will focus on the proper method of preparing and editing the various types of legal documents mentioned above, and will also highlight some of the ethical problems that may arise with respect to document preparation.

Business Letters

Format

A business letter is generally written on office letterhead stationery. Typically, the date of the communication appears on the upper right-hand corner of the page under the letterhead. If no letterhead is used, the office's name and address appear on the upper right-hand side of the page, and the date appears immediately below, with a line space between the address and the date.

On the upper left-hand side of the page, two line spaces below the date, the recipient's name and address appear. The address must be complete, including the zip code. Two line spaces below the recipient's address is the **salutation** or **greeting,** commencing with the word "Dear." In a business letter, unless the sender and recipient have established a personal relationship, the recipient's title and surname should be used, not a first name. A business salutation ends with a semicolon or colon, not a comma as is traditional in nonbusiness correspondence.

 EXAMPLE:

Smith & Jones, P.C.
1000 Barrister Drive
Suite 2400
Lubeck, Texas 00000

December 30, 1997

Janice Green
Arnold & Green
8 Plymouth Road, Suite 7
Fall River, Massachusetts 00000

Dear Ms. Green:

The body of the letter should contain all of the information the sender wishes to convey to the recipient, but in as short and concise a manner as possible. There are certain general principles that should be kept in mind when drafting a business letter:

Plan the Contents of the Letter Carefully.   As stated above, a business letter should be concise and inform the reader immediately of the reason for writing the letter. Avoid run-on or rambling sentences, and be careful to insert all pertinent information.

Write in a Clear, Effective, and Positive Manner.   When faced with committing something to paper, many people use words that they do not use in their ordinary conversations. The result is a letter that is pompous and generally ineffective because the words rarely convey the author's true meaning. When writing a business letter, emphasize simple, straightforward words. It is most effective to employ positive, action-oriented verbs rather than passive verbs. Action-oriented verbs are in the present or future tense and are used without qualification. When selecting the appropriate word, always err on the side of simplicity.

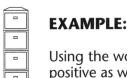

EXAMPLE:

Using the words "I might have attended but" is not as effective or positive as writing "I did not attend because."

Be Sure That Each Letter Is Complete.   Business letters are primarily used to convey information; if the information is incomplete or inaccurate, a result different from the one intended may occur. It is always important that any business communication convey *all* the information the sender needs to state.

EXAMPLE:

"This is to confirm our telephone conversation concerning our meeting next Thursday. I am looking forward to seeing you then."

This message is incomplete: Where is the meeting to take place? At what time? What is the topic of the meeting? Should any materials be brought? Even though the correspondent is confirming an oral communication with the recipient, the parties may have misunderstood each other, which is one of the reasons for confirming oral communications in writing. The written confirmation must be explicit and detailed.

Be Sure That Each Paragraph Is Complete.   A paragraph is composed of a group of sentences that together convey one complete thought. Make sure that each paragraph concerns only one major idea; if several ideas are contained in one paragraph, the result will be confusing. If this does occur, simply divide the paragraph into two or more paragraphs. Also, keep the paragraphs as short and concise as possible.

Edit and Proofread the Letter.   Probably even more important than planning the letter is editing and proofreading the letter. By editing and proofreading, any errors contained in the document can be discovered and corrected, including grammar, punctuation, and confusing or ineffective word selection. The purpose of editing and proofreading documents is to make sure that they are well organized, that they are accurate, that the style is appropriate to the subject matter, and that the appearance of the writing is attractive.

For a detailed discussion of the methods of editing and proofreading documents, see below at page 240.

Once the body of the letter is completed, the letter must be closed. The closing statements for business letters are "Sincerely," "Sincerely yours," and "Very truly yours." This closing appears two lines below the last paragraph of the body of the letter, and is lined up to correspond to the point at the top of the letter where the date is set. Each office uses its own standard form of closing, and all communications from the office should bear the same closing.

After the closing, blank lines are left for the sender's signature, and the sender's name is typed directly under the signature. If any courtesy copies are to be sent, this is indicated two line spaces after the sender's typed name on the left-hand side of the page; the abbreviation "cc:" is typed, followed by the names and addresses of all persons to whom copies of the letter are to be sent. Office policy should be that all correspondence is filed for future reference, if necessary, and copies of all correspondence are sent to the client.

 **EXAMPLE:**

> Smith & Jones, P.C.
> 1000 Barrister Drive
> Suite 2400
> Lubeck, Texas 00000
>
> December 30, 1997

Janice Green
Arnold & Green
8 Plymouth Road, Suite 7
Fall River, Massachusetts 00000

Dear Ms. Green:

This is to confirm our telephone conversation of this morning. We have agreed to meet next Tuesday, January 6, 1998, at 10 A.M. at our firm's Boston office located at 3 Charles Street, Room 1001, to discuss the employment contract of Elizabeth Borden.
I am looking forward to meeting with you next week.

> Sincerely yours,
>
> Ellen Jones

cc: Elizabeth Borden
      2 Hatchett Lane
      Fall River, Massachusetts 00000

Good News/Bad News

Not every business letter is a simple recitation of an oral communication or used as a cover for enclosing documents. Very often the business letter is used to convey specific news to the recipient. This news can either be good or bad news for the receiver.

Good news letters are fairly easy to draft. Because the content itself is positive, the tone is generally positive as well, and usually these letters are written in a concise and straightforward manner. Examples of good news would be informing a job candidate that she has been hired or informing a client that his lawsuit has been settled.

EXAMPLES:

Dear Prof. Crevelle:

This is to inform you that the State University has accepted our offer to settle your case against it for $1,000,000. The University has agreed to send a certified check within two weeks. When the check arrives, we will telephone you immediately.

We are pleased to have been of assistance to you in this matter. If you have any questions, or we can help you in any other matter, please do not hesitate to call us.

Congratulations on the successful outcome of your lawsuit.

Very truly yours,

_____

Dear Ms. Williams:

We are pleased to offer you a position at Smith & Jones, P.C. as a paralegal in our corporate law division. Your starting salary will be $30,000 per year, and your starting date is January 2 of this new year.

Please call Barbara Price in our office at extension 2525 to confirm your acceptance and to discuss the details of our employee benefit package. Ms. Price will also inform you of the rules and policies of the office.

We are looking forward to working with you.

Sincerely,

Bad news letters, on the other hand, present a more difficult drafting situation. Even though the content of the letter is negative, it still must be conveyed to the other party. As with all business communication, the letter itself must be short and concise, but with bad news it is always recommended to include some words that will buffer the negative impact of the communication. Never apologize for the bad news, but always try to find some positive aspect in the situation or at least de-emphasize the negative content as much as possible.

EXAMPLE:

Dear Mrs. Small:

After a careful review of your resume we are unable to offer you a position as a paralegal at Smith & Jones, P.C. However, we are sure that with your fine background you will be able to find suitable employment in the near future.
We wish you the best of luck for all future success.

Sincerely,

Regardless of whether the content of the letter contains good or bad news, all letters should be carefully planned before they are written. Three basic rules should be kept in mind when planning the letter:

1. Know exactly what information must be communicated.
2. Make sure the information is presented at the beginning of the letter. Do not hint about the letter's intent in the opening paragraph — this only makes the letter ramble.
3. When the information is communicated, end the letter. Do not continue to write just because the letter appears to be short.

Follow the advice from Alice in Wonderland: "Start at the beginning, go on until you come to the end, then stop."

Courtesy Copies and Filing

A **courtesy copy** is a duplicate of a letter sent to someone other than the addressee who has an interest in the matter contained in the letter. For example, a law office may send a copy of all communication between attorneys involved in a lawsuit to the client represented. (See the sample letter above at page 229.) Whenever it appears that a person other than the sender and the recipient should be aware of the letter's content, a courtesy copy should be sent.

All documents prepared by the law office should be filed according to the system adopted by the office, as discussed in Chapter 7. Only by making a file copy can the office have any evidence of letters sent, since the original is in the hands of the recipient. All letters received should also be filed. At some point in the future it may be necessary to refer back to various letters, and unless copies have been retained, such reference is impossible.

Keep in mind that once oral communication has been reduced to writing, the writing is the evidence of the discussion or agreement between the parties. If no copy of the writing exists, the parties are at a disadvantage should a problem subsequently arise.

Memoranda

Generally, a law office will generate three types of memoranda: interoffice memoranda, opinion memos, and persuasive memos. Each type of memo will be discussed in turn.

Interoffice Memos

An **interoffice memo** is one that is prepared for dissemination only to the members of the law office. Generally, it is not prepared specifically to describe a client problem but usually concerns office policies and procedures. Interoffice memos also may be used to document oral communications between members of the legal team. These memos must be distributed to all of the appropriate people, and then filed according to the office filing system.

Many offices have in-house formats that are used for the interoffice memo. If this is the case, all members of the legal team are expected to use that format. If there is no prepared form, the members of the legal team can create the memo in any manner that is appropriate to the purpose, content, and recipient of the memorandum.

 EXAMPLE:

INTEROFFICE MEMO

TO: All members of the firm

FROM: The Office Manager

RE: Tardiness and Absenteeism

As with all documents generated by the office, the writing should be clear and concise, the content well-planned and thought-out, and the final version edited and proofread. Remember that *every* document prepared by the legal team reflects on the image of the entire office.

Opinion Memos

An **opinion memo** is the result of legal research. It indicates the opinion of the author as to the status of the law in a given area or the possible outcome of a legal situation based on cases and statutes. Typically, opinion memos are used to keep members of the legal team informed of new changes in the law and problems that might arise with respect to a given area of law.

Opinion memos are not meant to convince the reader of a particular point of view. They are intended primarily to represent the author's perception and interpretation of the law. As with all research memos, an opinion memo is usually divided into four main sections: (1) facts; (2) issues; (3) statement of law; and (4) conclusion.

The **statement of facts** is a concise recitation of the factual background that gave rise to the need for the memo. For example, if a new bill has been introduced in Congress, the effects that its enactment might have on the firm's clients would be the reason why the memo was required.

 EXAMPLE:

FACTS

On March 2, 19 —, Rep. Bullock introduced a bill to the House Ways and Means Committee that purports to establish a flat income tax on all domestic corporations and limited liability companies. This flat tax is to be equal to 50 percent of the entity's gross income.

The **issue** is the particular question of law that is raised by the facts presented; it is the legal problem that gives rise to the memo.

 EXAMPLE:

ISSUE

Whether the imposition of a flat income tax rate of 50 percent on the gross income of a limited liability company is violative of current U.S. tax policy stipulating a graduated tax and therefore unconstitutional as violating the Equal Protection Clause.

The **statement of law** requires research into all current law, including all statutes on point with their legislative histories and all judicial and administrative decisions that have interpreted the particular area of law. This text is not designed to be a treatise on legal research and writing, and so all of the details of researching a legal question are not discussed here. However, for the purpose of document preparation, this section may be viewed as equivalent to the body of a business letter — that is, it must be well planned and thought-out and written in a manner that can be easily understood by the reader. Additionally, all of the legal authorities used by the author must be clearly identified and cited according to the format utilized by the office.

Finally, the **conclusion** represents the ultimate analysis of the situation arrived at by the author. The conclusion must be extremely brief — it is not the place to add additional arguments or legal authorities. Generally, one sentence for each issue discussed is appropriate for a conclusion.

EXAMPLE:

CONCLUSION

Based on the requirements of the Equal Protection Clause of the U.S. Constitution, the imposition of a flat income tax on limited liability companies would be unconstitutional and violative of all current tax laws and policies.

In terms of format, the opinion memo should be divided both in terms of content and visual appearance into the four headings indicated above: Facts; Issue; Statement of Law; Conclusion. In this manner readers can easily focus on the areas of most concern to them.

Persuasive Memos

In contrast to an opinion memo in which the state of the law is presented in a straightforward manner, a **persuasive memo** is used to convince the reader of the correctness of the author's legal conclusion. The author hopes to persuade the reader of the validity of a particular point of view, presumably one that favors the author's client. As with the opinion memo, the persuasive memo is the result of careful and thorough legal research.

The persuasive memo's structure is similar to that of the opinion memo. It too is divided, conceptually and visually, into four main sections: Facts; Issues or **Questions Presented; Argument;** and Conclusion. However, in a persuasive memo the body of the document is used to indicate how the law favors a particular position. To accomplish this, the author must select his or her words very carefully. It is considered an ethical violation to fail to mention facts that go against one's client, and it is also considered unethical to fail to mention cases or statutes that go against the writer's position. However, these negative elements can be de-emphasized by effective word selection, or distinguished on the basis of differences in fact situations by a careful analysis of the case or statute itself. This drafting requires the same careful planning and forethought given to all documents prepared by the office, and special consideration must be given to the language and tone used to persuade the reader. The writer must avoid all conclusionary statements unless supported by the law, and must be sure to provide full citations for all materials used in the memorandum.

As stated above, this is not a text on legal research and writing; however, basic writing skills apply to all documents prepared by members of the legal team.

Legal Forms

Legal forms are documents that can be used by different persons who find themselves in similar situations. Many courts, such as county probate courts handling estate matters, use standardized forms, and every jurisdiction provides texts called **form books** that include standardized language and formats for common legal documents.

In addition to the forms that are generated by public institutions such as the courts, judicial authorities, and government agencies, most law offices maintain their own files of standardized forms that they have created themselves. The firm uses these forms in multiple situations, with some slight variations. These forms may be entire documents or selected standardized paragraphs used for particular types of documents. Internal forms are generally filed in the office and are available for use by any member of the legal team.

Having a format to follow greatly streamlines the preparation of the document; however, caution must be exercised when using a standardized format. Not all of the language may be appropriate for a particular client or matter, and some analysis of the form must be made for its suitability to the particular problem. Additionally, when drafting documents for which standardized forms exist, it is usually a good idea to compare two or three of the forms and then select wording from each that appears to be most effective for the given situation. It is usually a bad idea to assume that because a form exists, it must be appropriate for all applications.

Before drafting any document for the office, always check to see whether there are standardized forms that the office typically uses. If not, begin to develop such a file.

The following exhibits provide examples of standardized forms. Exhibit 16 may be drafted and filed within the law office. Exhibits 17 and 18 are available from a publisher of legal documents.

Exhibit 16: Sample Standardized Form

Certificate of Limited Partnership

1. The name of the limited partnership is _____
(the "Limited Partnership").

2. The office of the Limited Partnership is to be located in _____

_____ County.

3. The Secretary of State is designated as the agent of the Limited Partnership
on whom process against it may be served. The post office address to which
the Secretary of State shall mail a copy of any process served on him against

the Limited Partnership is _____.

4. The name and street address of each general partner is:

_____   _____

_____   _____

5. The latest date on which the Limited Partnership is to dissolve is

_____ . The Limited Partnership may be terminated
sooner in accordance with the Limited Partnership Agreement.

6. The effective date of the Limited Partnership shall be _____ .

IN WITNESS WHEREOF, the undersigned has executed this Certificate of
Limited Partnership this _____ day of

_____ , and affirms the statements contained herein as
true under penalties of perjury.

_____
General Partner

Exhibit 17: Accident Report Form

T 490—Accident Report, Retainer, Request for Hospital Record, Transcript of Police Blotter.   JULIUS BLUMBERG, INC., LAW BLANK PUBLISHERS

Name of Injured..Age............Single-Married..............Phone............

Name of Father..Mother............................Wife-Husband..................

Address ....Floor..................................Apt. No............

Occupation ....Salary............................

Employer ....Address ....

Dr.............................Address............................Phone No............

Dr's visits to house............................Visits to Dr's office............................Amount of Bill, $............

Hospital ....Address............................

Ambulance Dr. ....House Dr. ....

Police officer's Name............................Badge............Precinct and Address............

DEFENDANT ....Address ....

Employed by ....Address ....

DEFENDANT ....

INJURIES ....

DATA ....

Date of Accident............................Time............M. Day............

Location ....

Weather Condition............................Street Condition............

On What Stairway............................Floor............Step............

Kind of Step............................What defect............

Floor Covering, Kind of Floor Covering............................

Condition of Lights............................What kind (gas or electric)............

If ceiling fell—give size of the piece............................Room............

Was notice given............................To whom............

By whom given............................Date given............Received reply............

Number of apartments in house............................Owner of House............

CAR No............Run No............What R. R. Co............What Line............

Conductor's Name ....Motorman's Name ....

MOTOR VEHICLE ....LICENSE NO............YEAR............

Automobile (Private)............Truck (Commercial)............Taxicab............Bus............Motorcycle............

Color............Number of occupants............Trailer............Coupe............Sedan............Touring............Passenger Capacity............

HORSE-DRAWN VEHICLE............No. on wagon............How many horses?............

Chauffeur or driver:............License No............

Name ....Address ....

I, the undersigned, residing at............................

do hereby retain............................as my attorney   to prosecute and adjust for me a claim for damages

arising from—personal injuries sustained by............................; loss of services of

............................; property damage—on the............day of............19............

through the negligence of............................

or other persons and do hereby give my said attorney the exclusive right to take all legal steps to enforce my said claim and I hereby
further agree not to settle this action in any manner without the written consent of my attorney.

In consideration of the services rendered and to be rendered by my said attorney   I hereby agree to pay   h   and   he
authorized to retain out of any moneys that may come into h   hand, fifty per cent of all sums received or recovered by
me by suit, settlement or otherwise by reason of the above claim.

Dated,............................19............   ....(L. S.)

WITNESS............................   ....(L. S.)
                                                                                      Signatures

Kindly furnish my attorney ,   or   representative
with a copy of the Police Blotter / Hospital Record in reference to the accident in which

was injured by   on the   day of

Dated,   19

STATE OF
COUNTY OF   } ss.:

On this   day of   19   , before me personally came and appeared
to me known and known to me to be the individual described
in and who executed the foregoing instrument, and who duly acknowledged to me that   he executed the same.

Forms may be purchased from Julius Blumberg, Inc., NYC 10013, or any of its dealers. Reproduction prohibited.

Exhibit 17: *(continued)*

RULE 41

MANNER OF ACCIDENT..

Date Filed:.............................

Reg. Rec. No.:.........................

Ret. Rec. Rec.:........................

WITNESSES—Name............................... Address.................... Phone..............

REMARKS ....

TRANSCRIPT OF POLICE BLOTTER

Accident Number	Surname		First Name and Initials	Sex
Aided Number	Address			Age
Date	Time	Place of Occurrence		

Accident	No.	Sick	Injured	Dead	Found Drowned	Lost Child	Foundling

Nature of Illness or injury		Fatal / Serious / Slight / Unknown

School (Name or Number) Attended by Injured, if Child

To	Hospital	Home	Morgue	Claimed	S. P. C. C.

STRUCK BY	COLLISIONS	Runaway or Stopping Runaway	Stealing Ride	Crossing Street Not at Crossing
Railway Train		Boarding, Riding In, or Alighting from Street Car	Motor Vehicle	Other Vehicle
Private Auto		Violation Traffic Regulation	Pedestrian Crossing Against Lights	
Taxicab		Defect in Vehicle	Defect In Pavement	Vehicle Making Left Turn	Right Turn
Auto Bus		Police Action	None	Arrest	Summons	Submitted To Court
Commercial Auto		City Involved	Officer a Witness	U. F. 18 Forwarded ?	
Motorcycle		Driven by 1	Name	Address	Lic. No.	Owner Chauffeur Employee
Street Car						
Horse Drawn Vehicle Private, Commercial		Driven by 2				Owner Chauffeur Employee

Traffic Controlled by Officer ?   Name   Shield No.   Command

Traffic Controlled by Lights ?   Lights in Operation ?   At time of accident in what direction was traffic moving on lights ?   North and South / East and West

Position of Vehicle or Vehicles in Street After Accident

DETAILS

Names and Addresses of Witnesses (if none, so state)

Cause	Responsibility

Telegraph Bureau Notified	Time a. m. p. m.	Received by	Sent by

Reported by Patrolman   Certified as Correct

Name

Shield No.   Pct.   Lieutenant   Pct.

Exhibit 18: Closing Statement Form

CLOSING STATEMENT

TO: OFFICE OF COURT ADMINISTRATION
    Retainer and Closing Statements
    Post Office Box 2016
    Church Street Station
    New York, NY 10008

1. Code number appearing on Attorney's receipt for filing of retainer statement (if statement filed with Clerk of Appellate Division prior to July 1, 1960, give date of such filing).

....
Code Number

2. Name and present address of client ....

3. Plaintiff(s)   4. Defendant(s)

5. If action commenced, state date .... 19.. Court
.... County. Was note of issue or notice of trial filed? .... If "Yes," was action disposed of in open court? .... If not disposed of in open court, state date stipulation of discontinuance was filed with CALENDAR CLERK of the court in which the action was pending................................. 19..........

6. Check items applicable: Settled [   ]; Claim abandoned by client [   ]; Judgment [   ]. Date of payment by carrier or defendant .... 19........... Date of payment to client .... 19...........

7. Gross amount of recovery (if judgment entered, include any interest, costs and disbursements allowed) $...............

8. Name and address, of insurance carrier or person paying Judgment or claim and carrier's file number, if any ....

9. Net amounts: to client $ ....; compensation to undersigned $............................; names, addresses and amounts paid to attorneys participating in the contingent compensation ....

10. Compensation fixed by retainer agreement [   ]; under schedule [   ]; or by court [   ].

11. If compensation fixed by court: Name of Judge..., Court .... Index No. .... Date of order .... 19...........

12. Itemized statement of payments made for hospital, medical care or treatment, liens, assignments, claims and expenses on behalf of the client which have been charged against the client's share of the recovery, together with the name, address, amount and reason for each payment ....

13. Itemized statement of the amounts of expenses and disbursements paid or agreed to be paid to others for expert testimony, investigative or other services properly chargeable to the recovery of damages together with the name, address and reason for each payment ....

14. Date on which a copy of this closing statement has been forwarded to the client .... 19..........

Dated:...................................... NY, ... 19...........

Yours, etc.   Yours, etc.

....
Signature of Attorney   Signature of Attorney

....
Attorney   Print   Attorney
                                   or
....   Type   ....
Office and P.O. Address   Office and P.O. Address

.... Dist. .... Dept.................. County   .... Dist. .... Dept.................. County

**NOTE – Court Rules require that the attorney for the plaintiff file a stipulation
or statement of discontinuance with the court upon discontinuance of an action.**

(If space provided is insufficient, use Blumberg's Rider number B 539.)   Fold as indicated to fit window envelope.

Editing and Proofreading

Once a draft of the document has been prepared, it is necessary that the draft be edited and proofread. **Editing** involves making corrections to the content of the written work. As part of the editing process the document must be both redlined and blacklined. Although the two words are generally used interchangeably, there is in fact a slight difference between the two. **Redlining** is the internal editing of a document, including such corrections as grammar, spelling, punctuation, and reorganization of the writing. All changes are made in red pencil. **Blacklining** is the comparison of two or more versions of the same document to locate any changes or differences between the versions. Blacklining is extremely important, especially when documents are changed while parties continue negotiations, or when legal documents are translated and revised into different languages. Both of these processes are extremely time-consuming but ultimately extremely important. A computer program for blacklining, COMPARE-RIGHT, is available; however, to use COMPARE-RIGHT both documents must be input into the computer. Although this system is very time efficient, most blacklining is done manually, either by paralegals or attorneys in the office. Although every word processor has some editing ability, the software usually modifies only basic spelling and punctuation mistakes.

Proofreading is different from editing. Although it also involves checking the document for accuracy with respect to spelling, grammar, and puncuation, **proofreading** concerns itself with the overall content and appearance of the writing, verifying that the document in its final version is an exact copy of the edited draft. If the document contains references to legal materials, all citations must be carefully checked and **bluebooked** — that is, the citations must conform to the requirements of the current edition of A Uniform System of Citation. Proofreading is very detail-oriented work and must be performed with great precision. Improperly proofread documents will reflect negatively on the image of the law office.

Legal documents require the editing and proofreading skills of a legal technician. Some of the most important symbols used in proofreading and editing appear on page 241.

Document Preparation and Ethics

Several ethical concerns are involved in the preparation of documents by the members of the legal team. If any of these ethical standards are breached, the entire law office is held responsible, either legally or morally.

The primary ethical problem in preparing documents is plagiarism. Plagiarism is the unauthorized and uncredited use of another person's writing. By plagiarizing, a person is in practice stealing another person's ideas and converting them into his or her own. All material gathered from a source other than the writer of the document must be acknowledged and

Symbol	Meaning	Symbol	Meaning
‖←	Align	⎯⎯ (transpose)	Transpose
+ or &	Ampersand	score	Underline
≡	CAPS	wf	Wrong font
⌣	Apostrophe	⊙	Insert period
✻	Asterisk	[	Move left
∨ or ∧	Insert	]	Move right
(bold)	**Bold**	⌐	Move up
{ }	Bracket	⌐	Move down
] [	Center	Stet	Do not change
⌒	Close	ℙ	Paragraph
ℓ	Delete	no ℙ	No paragraph
#	Space	ital	Italicize
sp out	Spell out	regular	Regular type
⌃a	Subscript	=	SMALL CAPS
⌄	Superscript		

credited. Copyright infringement, another aspect of plagiarism, will be discussed in Chapter 10.

Because forms are so prevalent in the practice of law, it is very tempting for persons who are not licensed to practice law to fill out these forms on behalf of others. This can occur in law offices when legal assistants and secretaries are so familiar with standardized forms that they believe that they can fill them out without supervision by an attorney. As discussed in previous chapters, this constitutes the unauthorized practice of law and may result in censure, fines, or imprisonment for the perpetrator. Note the *Furman* case in Chapter 2 and the case dealing with the Kentucky Bar Association, which appears below.

Anything that goes out under the office's letterhead is presumed to be a representation by the office. Anyone who uses the letterhead for unauthorized purposes, so as to add the weight and prestige of the firm to the communication, is also violating ethical responsibilities. If a secretary in the office is having trouble with her landlord, she cannot use the office letterhead to write an angry letter to her building's owner unless an attorney in the firm has agreed to represent her. Otherwise, it gives the appearance that the secretary is being represented by the law firm.

Finally, it is of the utmost importance that all documents prepared by the office be accurate with respect to the factual material they contain and the legal authorities they cite. No member of the legal team may make any change in documents that has not been completely authorized. Making such changes is a direct violation of the rules of ethics and may result in lawsuits for damages. See Latson v. Eaton, below.

CHAPTER SUMMARY

All documents prepared by the law office require careful planning and attention to detail, both in choice of words and physical format. The office is held to whatever is stated in its written communications, and it behooves the members of the office to see that every writing produced by the legal team is precise, effective, and appropriate. This is true regardless of the type of document prepared.

Generally, law offices produce three broad categories of documents: business letters, memoranda, and legal forms. Each of these requires the same attention to detail regardless of the recipient of the document or the amount of money involved in the matter covered by the writing. Every document prepared by the law office reflects on the image of the firm and, as discussed in the earlier chapters, projecting the appropriate image is one of the fundamental responsibilities of every member of the legal team.

Once a document has been drafted, it must be edited and proofread to determine whether it is accurate and suitable for its intended purpose. Unfortunately, many people view editing and proofreading as time-consuming and unimportant factors in document preparation; in fact, they probably form the most important aspect of effective writing. Editing a document is the only way writers can be sure that the document truly reflects the information they are trying to convey.

Finally, all work produced by the law office must meet the highest ethical standards of the legal profession. These documents are written evidence of the office's character and ability, and if the members violate any ethical consideration, from plagiarism to the unauthorized practice of law, it reflects badly on the firm as a whole and may result in unfavorable legal consequences.

Key Terms

Argument: The body of a persuasive legal memo, indicating how the law favors the writer's position.

Blacklining: Comparing two versions of the same document.

COMPARE-RIGHT: A computer program designed to compare documents.

Conclusion: The last section of a legal memo, indicating the result reached in the author's analysis.

Courtesy copy: Copy of a letter sent to someone with an interest in the matters discussed in the letter.

Editing: Reviewing a document for correctness.

Form book: Text with standardized versions of documents.

Greeting: The salutation of a letter.

Interoffice memo: Memo used for in-house purposes only.

Issue: Question of law raised by the facts presented in an opinion memo.

Legal form: Standardized document used in the practice of law.

Opinion memo: Legal memo indicating the author's view of the status of the law in a given situation.

Persuasive memo: Legal memo used to convince the reader of the author's legal conclusion.

Plagiarism: The unauthorized use by an author of someone else's thoughts or work.

Proofreading: Checking a document to make sure it follows the edited draft.

Questions presented: A section of a persuasive memo, indicating the issues involved in a legal problem.

Redlining: Editing a document for accuracy with respect to grammar, content, and so forth.

Salutation: The opening of a letter.

Statement of facts: Concise recitation of the factual background of a legal problem in an opinion memo.

Statement of law: Presentation of relevant cases and statutes in a legal memo.

Cases for Analysis

The following cases are included to highlight some of the ethical problems encountered in document preparation. Federal Intermediate Credit Bank of Louisville, Kentucky v. Kentucky Bar Association and Latson v. Eaton concern the unauthorized practice of law engendered by unlicensed persons completing legal forms for third persons. In re Schroeter involves the issue of altering the meaning of terms in a document.

Federal Intermediate Credit Bank of Louisville, Kentucky v. Kentucky Bar Association
540 S.W.2d 14 (Ky. 1976)

PER CURIAM.

Pursuant to RAP 3.530(e) Federal Intermediate Credit Bank of

Louisville (hereinafter called the Bank) has moved for review of Advisory Opinion U-11 issued by the board of governors of the Kentucky Bar Association in October of 1975 and summarized on page 24 of the October 1975 issue of Kentucky Bench and Bar.

According to its text, the advisory opinion was given in response to a question submitted by the general counsel and secretary of the Bank, as follows:

"*QUESTION:*   Does the completion of a printed real estate mortgage form by a lay employee of a governmental lending agency, using information furnished by an attorney, the form containing a printed facsimile of the signature of an attorney who is not an employee or officer of the specific agency as the preparer of the mortgage, constitute the unauthorized practice of law by the lay employee or by the agency?

"*ANSWER:*   Yes.

"The Kentucky Bar Association has been requested, by way of a voluntary application of the General Counsel and Secretary of the Federal Intermediate Credit Bank, to furnish an opinion as to whether the mortgage preparation procedure used by production credit associations (PCA) in Kentucky involves the unauthorized practice of law. . . .

"An examination of the blank mortgage form reveals the following information is filled in: date, name and address of borrower(s), legal description and source of title of property to be encumbered, if any, and completion of notary requirements. The form contains what appears to be standard mortgage language and reflects, at the foot thereof, a printed preparer's statement and a printed facsimile of the general counsel's signature. The general counsel concedes that he seldom personally sees or examines the completed document, although he prepared the printed form.

"It is well settled that preparation of mortgages is the practice of law. Howton v. Morrow, 269 Ky. 1, 106 S.W.2d 81 (1937) at page 82, Kentucky State Bar Association v. Tussey, Ky., 476 S.W.2d 177 (1972) at page 178.

"It is clear, further, that a corporation may not, through professional or non-professional salaried employees, draft mortgages. Frazee v. Citizens Fidelity Bank & Trust Co., et al., Ky., 393 S.W.2d 778 (1965) at page 784.

"Under the rule enunciated in the *Frazee* case, the proposed procedure of the PCA outlined above involves the unauthorized practice of law in the Commonwealth of Kentucky."

In its brief filed with this court the Bank has rephrased and broadened the question as follows: . . .

"II. Whether the Completion of Blanks on Standardized Mortgage Form By a Lay Employee, Pursuant to the Instructions of the Attorney Who Prepared the Form and Upon Which a Facsimile of His Signature as Preparer Appears, With Information Which IS Common Knowledge and With Information Provided by Another Attorney Constitutes The Preparation of a Legal Instrument and, Therefore, The Unauthorized Practice of Law?

(A) Whether Filling Uncompleted Spaces, Under the Facts and Circumstances of This Case, Requires the Exercise of Legal Knowledge or Legal Skills by the Lay Employee?
(B) Whether A Lay Employee Who Transcribed Information Into Blanks on Prescribed Legal Forms Pursuant to an Attorney's Instructions Is Practicing Law?"

. . . Addressing ourselves to the question as it was presented to and answered by the Bar Association, we are of the opinion that when a lending agency presents to the borrower for execution a real estate mortgage that has been completed on a form prepared by one lawyer, with information such as the property description and payment schedule copied by a lay person from a loan application and a title certificate furnished by another attorney, neither of the respective attorneys having examined the instrument in its final form prior to execution by the borrower, the lending agency is practicing law without a license.

As a corollary proposition, it is fundamental that no person, lawyer or not, can truthfully certify that he has drafted an instrument unless and until it is completed and ready for signature, because until then it is not an instrument, but merely a form that can be sold by the bundle at any bookstore. It is no answer in this particular instance to say that each of the parts has been prepared by a licensed attorney. The fact is that when the instrument is presented to the unschooled layman as a fit and proper subject for his signature neither attorney has seen or passed on it as a whole.

Of course we shall not be trapped into declaring that when a typist copies a property description into a deed or mortgage form she is practicing law. Cf. Carter v. Brien, Ky., 309 S.W.2d 748, 749 (1956). It is the person for whom she is doing the work, and who will pass upon and cause the completed product to be presented for signature, who undertakes the responsibility for its legal sufficiency. Cf. Pioneer Title Trust Ins. & Trust Co. v. State Bar of Nevada, 74 Nev. 186, 326 P.2d 408, 411 (1958).

In order to conform to the requirement that its mortgage be prepared by a licensed attorney it would be necessary for the local PCA (a) to return the final instrument to the Bank for approval and endorsement by its counsel or (b) to have the final instrument inspected and endorsed by local counsel as the responsible drafter. One or the other must be done after the instrument is ready for signature and before it is signed.

In summary, Advisory Opinion of the Kentucky Bar Association is affirmed.

Latson v. Eaton
341 P.2d 247 (Okla. 1959)

This is an appeal from a judgment for damages caused by defendant, a layman, improperly preparing certain legal documents for plaintiffs for hire. . . .

Title 5, Section 12, O.S.A. provides:

> The Supreme Court of the State of Oklahoma shall have exclusive power and authority to pass upon qualifications and fitness of all applicants for admission to practice law in the State of Oklahoma, and the qualifications of such applicants shall be those which are now or may be hereafter prescribed by the statutes of Oklahoma and the rules of the Supreme Court.

Paragraph two (2) of Article 3, Chapter 1 of the Rules creating, controlling and regulating the Oklahoma Bar Association, which were adopted by the Bar Association and the State Supreme Court, January 1, 1951, 5 Okl. St. Ann. c.1, Append. 1, provides:

> No person shall practice law in the State of Oklahoma who is not an active member of the Association, except as hereinafter provided. [Exceptions are then made as to non-resident attorneys at law.]

This rule was passed in the public interest and for the advancement of the administration of justice. It is regulatory in nature, limiting or licensing the practice of law. The practice of law is regulated for the benefit of the members of that class or segment of the public which might be injured if unskilled and untrained persons were permitted to practice the work or duties of the profession. A regulatory rule or statute is enacted for the benefit of those who might be injured in the absence of such regulation. Thus we are drawn to the inevitable conclusion that the plaintiff herein comes within the class of persons intended to be protected against the unlicensed and unlawful practice of law.

As to what constitutes the practice of law, we observe the case of Conway-Bogue Realty Inv. Co. v. Denver Bar Association, 135 Colo. 398, 312 P.2d 998, 999, when the court there held:

> Preparation of receipts and options, deeds, promissory notes, deeds of trust, mortgages, releases of encumbrances, leases, notice terminating tenancies, and demands to pay rent or vacate, by completing standard and approved printed forms, coupled with the giving of advice or explanation as to legal effects thereof, constitutes the "practice of law."

The acts of the defendant definitely would constitute the practice of law under the above authorities. Since our code is similar to that of California, the construction given by the California court might well be applied in this case.

The liability of an unlicensed person to perform duties which have been construed as legal services, has been determined in the case of Biakanja v. Irving, Cal. App., 310 P.2d 63, 64, wherein the court held:

> Where defendant, who was a notary public and not a licensed attorney, acted as attorney and not as a scrivener when he drew will, the draw-

ing of will was in violation of statute limiting practice of law to active members of State Bar, and this violation permitted sole beneficiary of will to recover from defendant the difference between amount beneficiary would have received had will been valid and amount actually distributed to her according to laws of intestate succession.

In view of the authorities above we are of the opinion that the trial court was not in error in overruling motion of defendant.

Since the second and third propositions argued by defendant are based upon the same theory as his first proposition, we are of the opinion that they are properly disposed of in the discussion hereinabove.

Defendant's fourth proposition is that the court erred in giving instructions numbered four and six. These instructions complained of are in harmony with the case of Biakanja v. Irving, supra, and we hold the trial court did not commit error in giving same.

Judgment affirmed.

In re Schroeter
489 P.2d 914 (Wash. 1971)

Per Curiam.

Leonard W. Schroeter was admitted to the practice of law in this state on September 30, 1954. Since that time, he has practiced primarily in the Seattle area, although he has also practiced in Alaska and California. Other than this proceeding, there are no disciplinary complaints on his record of practice in Washington.

On June 16, 1969, a formal complaint was filed against Mr. Schroeter at the direction of the Board of Governors. After several days of hearings, at which Mr. Schroeter was present and represented by counsel, the hearing panel made findings and conclusions, and recommended censure as to two items and a 6-month suspension as to the third. The Board of Governors accepted the recommendations of censure, but increased to 1 year the proposed suspension.

. . . The primary charge is that in July of 1964 respondent altered the transcript of a telephone conversation with a potential medical witness in a malpractice case, so as to give it a meaning opposite to that which was actually said by the witness. The altered transcript was given to opposing counsel in conjunction with settlement negotiations. The complaint also states that, when this matter was subsequently brought to respondent's attention, he took no steps to rectify the misrepresentation.

The gravity of this charge is not to be minimized. In their day-to-day dealings and communications, attorneys must constantly rely upon the candor and trustworthiness of their professional colleagues. Rule 1.1(j) of our Disciplinary Rules for Attorneys states that a ground for discipline is the violation of the Canons of Ethics of the legal profession. Canon 2 states:

> The conduct of the lawyer before the court and with other lawyers should be characterized by candor and fairness.

It is not candid or fair for the lawyer knowingly to misquote the contents of a paper, the testimony of a witness. . . .

It is unprofessional and dishonorable to deal other than candidly with the facts in taking the statements of witnesses, in drawing affidavits and other documents, and in the presentation of causes.

CPE 22, Candor and Fairness, RCW vol. O.

Canon 41 states:

When a lawyer discovers that some fraud or deception has been practiced, which has unjustly imposed upon the court or a party, he should endeavor to rectify it; at first by advising his client, and if his client refuses to forego the advantage thus unjustly gained, he should promptly inform the injured person or his counsel, so that they may take appropriate steps.

CPE 41, Discovery of Imposition and Deception, RCW vol. O. See also CPE 29 and 32.

Respondent cites the case of In re Dore, 165 Wash. 295, 4 P.2d 1107 (1931), wherein no discipline was imposed, as analogous. We disagree. That case involved an unconcealed alteration in a reporter's transcript for a *proposed* statement of facts. There was testimony that this was a common practice of the bar in that jurisdiction and that attorneys in the jurisdiction understood such documents as mere proposals and did not rely upon them as representations of fact. To the contrary, the case at bar involves deliberate misrepresentations of fact in documents perforce relied upon by other members of the bar, with attendant harm to the public. The two cases are not apposite.

Mr. Schroeter admits the substance of the charges, but calls our attention to mitigating factors: his intent to conform the transcript to earlier statements by the same witness; the surrounding disarray in the aftermath of the 1964 Alaska earthquake (the negotiations for settlement were in Alaska with Alaskan counsel); subsequently alleviated psychological stress which impaired his judgment; the eventual absence of serious consequence arising from this misconduct; that this incident was isolated and uncharacteristic; that this incident occurred 7 years ago, and that respondent's conduct has been good and trustworthy before and since that time; and respondent's cooperation and candor during these proceedings.

We agree that these factors should be considered in mitigation. We think that they have. But for the mitigating circumstances, the appropriate discipline for so serious a breach of the canons would be more severe. We think that the Board of Governors took these considerations into account, and we adopt the recommendation of a 1-year suspension on this item.

A second item of complaint charges that respondent used stationery which was misleading in two respects. First, letterheads indicating multistate connections named respondent and his partners, but failed to indicate that respondent and his partners were not authorized to practice in the other states. Second, billheads were used which named as partners persons who had since left the firm and discontinued any association with it. These assertions charge a violation of Canon 33 (CPE 33 Partnerships-

Names). See also American Bar Association Ethics Opinions 115 and 316. The exhibits in this case substantiate these charges. The record also indicates that this is the first time such aberration has been charged against respondent. The practices were brief and have since been discontinued. There is no evidence anyone was victimized by these practices. Respondent emphasizes that the letterheads were prepared by out-of-state attorneys in whom he had placed his reliance, and that he had ordered office personnel to dispose of the billheads and was unaware of their continued use.

Such matters, while they should be considered in mitigation, do not erase the fact of violation. Delegation in good faith of professional responsibilities and their implementation cannot relieve an attorney from his professional obligations. Compliance with the Canons of Professional Ethics is a personal duty of each attorney. Practicalities may suggest that mechanical matters be assigned to office staff or that professional colleagues be looked to for suggestions. But in no instance can an attorney delegate the final responsibility of his personal compliance with professional standards.

We are satisfied that the hearing panel and Board of Governors took these mitigating circumstances into account when recommending the discipline to be imposed. A letter of censure is the lightest form of discipline available under our rules. Respondent may complain that informal, nondisciplinary steps would have sufficed. But our rules do not include such informal steps as a matter of right. Rather, they are a matter of common courtesy. We agree that a letter of censure was the appropriate penalty. . . .

We confirm the statement and supplemental statement of costs claimed by the Washington State Bar Association pursuant to DRA 7.1.

EXERCISES

1. Go to the library and find two form books for your jurisdiction.
2. Write a letter for a law office telling a potential client that the firm will not handle her case. The potential client is a pro-life advocate accused of willfully destroying property at an abortion clinic.
3. Write a letter for a law firm representing an estate. You must inform a potential beneficiary that he will receive no bequest because the executor is required to sell off the property he was to inherit in order to pay estate taxes.
4. Write a letter for a law office confirming the settlement of a personal injury case for $213,000.
5. Find the first draft of an old paper of yours and edit it using the editing marks that appear at page 241.
6. Draft an interoffice memo for your school indicating a change in course scheduling.
7. Go to your county court house and acquire sample forms used by the court.

8. Write a letter to the Unemployment Office explaining why an employee was fired for cause and therefore is not entitled to full benefits.
9. Discuss the various uses that may be made of a fully researched legal memorandum.
10. Discuss why properly written documents are important for the effective practice of law.

SITUATIONAL ANALYSIS

The law office you work for has offices located all over the world. Two documents come in from one of the firm's European offices; they are two versions of a major trade agreement entered into by one of the firm's clients and the government of a European country. The documents represent one promulgated by the client, the other by the foreign government. You are asked to translate the documents, compare them for differences, edit the documents, and then analyze the differences. Discuss in detail how you would approach this problem in the most efficient and accurate manner.

10 Law Office Technology

First hire the MIS manager before you buy the tools.
Why have a room full of computers that no one knows
how to use. . . . I'm tired of having professionals sitting
in front of a screen yelling "Help!"

Jessica Bede
Vice President
Capintec, Inc.
Ramsay, New Jersey

CHAPTER OVERVIEW

The past ten years have seen dramatic changes in the operation of a law office because of the technological advances in office equipment. The creation of word processors and user-friendly computers has totally revolutionized the speed and efficiency of a law office's output.

In the not too distant past many functions now routinely performed by computers were performed manually by individuals. Typing, filing, reproducing, mailing, and so forth were all part of the regular work day of most office employees. Although these functions still exist, because of computerization they are performed quickly, efficiently, and in a cost-effective manner, releasing office workers to perform more creative tasks. This is not to say that the introduction of computers to the workplace was easily accomplished. For many years computers were large and cumbersome machines that required special climatic conditions and a great deal of floor space. As computers became smaller and less expensive, and software was created for more ordinary office uses, more and more office acquired them. However, many people are still reluctant to use computers because of a fear of the unknown.

Today, every member of the legal team should be familiar with computers and general office technology. Because of increased costs of salaries and employee benefits, most offices now require the attorneys to perform many functions that were once the province of the support staff, such as typing initial drafts and reproducing documents. Every member of the office must be computer literate in order to be productive and efficient.

Currently, law office computers provide a variety of services for the legal team. Word processing, accounting timesheets and statements, legal research databases, and litigation support services are now available to every person in the office within seconds right at his or her own desk, as well as fax, e-mail, and conferencing capabilities. Manual dexterity in the ability to use a mouse and the computer keyboard has become almost as important as mental ability in providing accurate and efficient legal services.

Information on modern technology in computer services for the law office can be found in articles in the ABA Journal, state bar magazines, and legal computing periodicals. Offices are constantly updating their technology, and all law office staff must be able to keep up with these technological changes.

This chapter will focus on the basic computer technology currently used in most law offices. A general overview of information systems will be followed by a discussion of computer hardware, software, and ethical considerations.

Information Systems

Information systems is the term generally given to all methods of storing, maintaining, and retrieving information. More specifically, it has come to mean the use of computers to store, process, and retrieve data. There are three main types of computers in use at most law offices — the microcomputer, the minicomputer, and the mainframe.

Microcomputer

The **microcomputer** is commonly referred to as a **personal computer** or **PC**. It is the smallest type of computer. The microcomputer either operates on its own or may be connected to other computers to share information and peripheral devices such as printers and modems. Computers that are connected together become a **network.** A network of microcomputers is known as a **local area network (LAN).** The computers in the LAN are called nodes or workstations. In a peer-to-peer LAN, a workstation can access information stored on any of the other workstations in the LAN. In a client-server LAN, each workstation has access to the information stored on the computer controlling the LAN, called the file server.

Minicomputer

A **minicomputer** is a mid-size computer either used as a stand-alone unit, a file server for a microcomputer LAN, or as the main computer in a network that consists of the minicomputer and **display terminals.** A display terminal has only a **keyboard** and a **monitor.** Display terminals are completely dependent on the computer controlling the network and cannot function or store information independently. Minicomputers perform functions faster than microcomputers, but a minicomputer network with display terminals is more vulnerable than a microcomputer LAN. In the event of a failure of the main computer, a minicomputer network ceases to function. In the case of a microcomputer LAN, however, a failure of the main computer still leaves each workstation with a fully functioning stand-alone computer.

Mainframe

A **mainframe** is the largest type of computer, typically able to store large amounts of data. It is organized in a network configuration with display terminals or microcomputers at each workstation. Usually only a few people will have access to all of the information in the mainframe; most members of the office will only be capable of accessing information necessary for their own work needs. Access is controlled by the use of **passwords,** specific words or symbols that permit the user to enter the computer or specific information areas.

 EXAMPLE:

A law office maintains a mainframe computer to store all computerized information for the office. Every attorney in the office has a display terminal or microcomputer at his or her desk that is connected to the mainframe so that the attorneys can access the information. Additionally, the office has microcomputer notebook computers that can be checked out by the attorneys to take home or on business trips. The attorney can use the software available on the notebook computer, or plug the computer into telephone lines and contact the mainframe using the computer's modem. The attorney has a password that permits access to information only for clients to which he or she has been assigned. The password prevents unauthorized access to information. This type of system makes the computerized information available in the office or anywhere else by telephone. You will find similar setups with microcomputer and minicomputer stand-alones and networks.

Computer Hardware

Computer **hardware** is the term used to describe the physical components of the computer system. Hardware can be divided into three main categories: hardware used to process and store information, hardware used to input information into the computer, and hardware used to receive information from the computer.

The System Unit

The **system unit** is the physical unit that houses the majority of the computer's hardware. It contains the computer's main memory, its processor(s), its secondary memory storage devices such as hard disks and drives for diskettes, magnetic tapes, and CDs, and its communication devices such as a modem.

Main Memory

Main memory in the computer consists of **ROM** and **RAM.** ROM and RAM are located on chips in the system unit. ROM — "read-only memory" — is the memory that stores instructions for the computer that have been placed on the chips by the manufacturer. It is read by the computer and cannot be written to. RAM — "random access memory" — is the workspace that is available to hold programs while you are using them and documents that you are creating. RAM is temporary memory and is erased when the computer is turned off. To save documents and data, they must be stored on some type of secondary memory device such as a magnetic disk. The amount of RAM contained within the computer determines how many programs and documents that you can have open simultaneously.

Secondary Memory

Secondary memory is where information is stored. Most of the computer's information will be stored on an internal **magnetic disk.** This magnetic disk is often called the "hard disk" and will store the programs that you use on the computer and any documents that you create using the computer. Portable magnetic disks are used to store documents and software files outside of the computer. These portable magnetic disks can be removable hard disks or **diskettes.** Diskettes, sometimes referred to as floppy disks, come in two primary sizes, 3½-inch and 5¼-inch. They are inserted into a diskette drive in the system unit being used.

To back up the contents of the computer's hard disk, law offices often use **magnetic tape.** Magnetic tapes look like thick cassette tapes and can store the entire contents of the computer's hard disk. By keeping a copy of the hard disk on magnetic tape, the office can quickly retrieve lost information in the event of a failure of the computer's hard disk.

Another important storage device in the law office is the optical disk. Optical disks are used to store the images of evidentiary documents for quick access and trial exhibition. This type of optical disk is called a WORM (Write Once Read Many) disk. Once the image of the document has been placed on the disk, it becomes a read-only disk. Other optical disks used for the storage of files are rewritable compact disks (CDs). These rewritable CD drives are growing in popularity. The most common CD drive, however, is the **CD-ROM** (Compact Disk Read-Only Memory) drive. You cannot store information to a CD in a CD-ROM drive because the drive is read only. CD-ROM is taking the place of the bound volumes of books in the law office's library. An entire set of case reporters can be stored on three or four CD-ROM disks. An advantage to these CD-ROM libraries is that you can use keyword searching to locate cases that contain the words you are looking for.

Input Devices

Input devices are pieces of computer hardware that are used to input information into the computer. The original input device was the **punched card.** Holes were punched into the cards to represent the instructions to the computer. The cards were then stacked and run through a card reader to input the information. The most common input devices used today are the **keyboard** and the **mouse.** The keyboard consists of alphanumeric keys, cursor movement keys, special command keys, and function keys. The function keys are used with software programs to activate the programs' features. A mouse consists of a roller ball that moves the position of an arrow or other indicator on the screen. As the user moves the mouse, buttons on the top of the mouse can be pressed to activate features. Other devices that are similar to the mouse are the **trackball, touchpad,** and the **integrated pointing device.** These devices are mainly found on portable computers. A trackball looks like an upside-down mouse. The user moves the ball with his or her fingers and selects items with the trackball's buttons. A touchpad is a pad that is sensitive to a person's touch. Moving a finger across the touchpad will move the pointer on the screen. Tapping the touchpad or pressing a button will select items. An integrated pointing device looks like the head of a pencil eraser. It is moved like a joystick to move the pointer on the screen. Buttons are then used to select the items pointed to.

Other input devices that you will find in the law office are **scanners, bar code readers, touch screens,** and devices capable of recognizing speech and handwriting. Scanners are used to scan documents into a word-processing program for editing or to capture the image of a document onto an optical disk. Bar code readers are used to scan bar codes that are used with a bar coding system. Some law offices bar code their books and files. Bar coding is also found with imaging systems. When an office scans the images of documents onto optical disks for display at trial, bar codes can be set up for each of the documents. A bar code sticker for a document can be placed in the attorney's argument outline or witness questions. When the document is introduced at evidence, the attorney sweeps the bar code reader across the sticker and the document is displayed in the courtroom. Touch screens are special monitors that recognize the touch of a finger or an electronic pen. These touch screens can be used during trial to circle and highlight evidence displayed on computer screens. Speech recognition and handwriting recognition are just beginning to make their way into the law office. Speech recognition devices identify words and print them on the computer screen. Handwriting recognition devices can identify a person's printing and translate it into typed text.

EXAMPLE:

A lawyer for the office is holding a conference at the client's corporate headquarters. The lawyer is revising a contract for the client. She takes the original contract and faxes it to her law office. The office uses a scanner to input the contract, and the secretary types in the changes dictated by the lawyer using the computer's keyboard. The office is using two different input devices to streamline its work.

Output Devices

Output devices are pieces of hardware that are used to communicate the results of the computer's processing to the user. The most common output devices are monitors, printers, and speakers. Monitors resemble a television screen and are sometimes referred to as "cathode ray tubes" (CRTs) and "video display terminals" (VDTs). There are two main types of monitors, monochrome and color. Monochrome monitors are two-color displays similar to black-and-white television screens. Color monitors offer three or more colors and allow for enhanced graphics.

If the user wishes to have the accessed information written on paper — what is known as a "hard copy" — a printer may be used to print the document. There are two categories of printers currently in everyday use. The first category is **impact printers** in which the characters appearing on the screen are "typed" onto a piece of paper in a manner similar to a typewriter, with some part of the printer impacting the paper. Impact printers include dot matrix and daisy wheel printers. The second category is **nonimpact printers.** With nonimpact printers, the printer's hardware does not actually impact the paper. This category includes laser and inkjet printers. Generally, nonimpact printers are faster than impact printers.

With the advent of multimedia presentations, speakers have become an integral part of the computer system. While they are not likely to be found on the standard law office computer, they will be found on the computers in the office that are used to create presentations for trial.

Communication Devices

Communication devices are used to contact the office's computer from a remote location, access electronic mail (e-mail), and access on-line services and databases. The most common communication device is the **modem.** The modem translates the digital signals of the computer into analog signals that can travel through the telephone lines. The modem in the receiving computer translates the incoming analog signals back into digital signals.

On-line capability has been the buzzword of computer use in the nineties. On-line services have greatly increased the amount of information that is readily available to computer users by giving them access to large databases and the "information superhighway." Many services that are appropriate to law offices are available on-line. These services can provide constantly updated legal materials to the user, as well as access to a wide variety of nonlegal information. The major legal research services are discussed later in this chapter.

On-line capability also means that the user can be connected to an ever-increasing network of offices and persons. One outgrowth of this capability is the use by the courts of on-line access for the filing and distribution of court documents and viewing of docketing calendars. There are a few drawbacks to using on-line services. First, on-line services can be costly. General access is acquired by a monthly charge as well as charges for actual time usage in many cases. However, these services are cost-efficient when used to locate authority quickly or to locate material in a source that is not readily available in your office. Second, linking to some networks may create a problem with unwarranted access to files, resulting in breaches of confidentiality and other ethical concerns. Third, on-line capability may be daunting to people unused to computer technology, resulting in those people limiting their use of the computer because of their fear of the unknown.

EXAMPLE:

An attorney with the office is negotiating a contract for a client. The attorney representing the other contracting party lives across the country. Rather than meeting personally or talking on the telephone, the attorneys use on-line services to communicate, discussing changes in the contract by e-mail, inputting changes and faxing the updated document to each other's terminals, and performing legal research on the matter by using on-line legal research sources. The ability to communicate through the computer has streamlined their work.

Computer Software

Computer software is the instruction codes that run the computer's hardware. Computer software can be divided into four categories: computer languages, operating systems, utility programs, and applications. Computer languages are the language codes used to write the other three categories of programs. Computer languages include BASIC, Fortran, COBOL, C++, and many others. Operating systems manage the storage, utilization, and movement of files on the computer system. An operating system is necessary in adding computer programs to your computer. Operating systems include Unix, DOS, Windows 95, OS/2 Warp, and System 7 for the Macintosh. Utility programs are pieces of software that enhance your computer system. Utility programs include screen savers, virus scanners, and undelete and unformat programs. Applications are software programs that produce a product. Applications include word processors, electronic spreadsheets, databases, and graphics programs. This section will focus on the applications that you will be using in the law office.

Word Processors

Word processing is a computer function that uses the computer's capabilities to create written documents. It is a form of super typewriting, editing, proofreading, and printing. The basic word-processing computer system requires a keyboard, monitor, printer, hard drive, and a word-processing application program.

Word processing operates in the following fashion:

1. The user, utilizing the computer keyboard, types the material into the computer. Most word-processing programs include a spell-checking feature that will spot misspelled words, alert the user to the error, and offer alternatives. However, if the typographical error creates an actual word, the error will not be picked up by the processor.

EXAMPLE:

The office secretary is typing a complaint. The secretary misspells both the word "hair" and the word "complaint." The computer finds the misspelling of "complaint" and offers alternatives. The word "hair," however, was misspelled "hare," which is also an English word and is therefore not indicated as wrong.

2. The user can use a menu or function keys to utilize special word processing functions. These functions could include changing the margins of the page, adding page numbers, and adding footnotes.
3. Once initially typed into the computer, the document may now be edited, using several functions included in the program. Words, sentences, or paragraphs can be moved, materials from other documents that are already inputted into the computer may be merged with the document being typed, and the user may space the document as desired.

EXAMPLE:

A secretary wishes to use a standard paragraph that she has used before on other documents. These documents are already stored on the computer's hard disk, and the secretary can retrieve them and move the desired paragraphs into the complaint without having to retype them.

4. Once the document is finished to the user's satisfaction, the document may be stored for future reference. Storage may either be to the computer's hard disk or to a portable diskette.

EXAMPLE:

Once the complaint from the previous example is finished, the secretary has the complaint stored on the main computer of the office network. Now anyone in the firm who has access to that client's file may view or edit the document.

5. Once completed and stored, the computer can output the document either on the monitor or as a printed hard copy.

EXAMPLE:

When the attorney has approved the complaint, the secretary prints up a final hard copy to file with the appropriate court.

Because of the widespread use of word processing, most members of the legal team in the modern law office are expected to create their own drafts of documents on the computer. Secretaries usually create the final version of the document, "cleaning it up" by making any necessary changes and putting the document in the proper format. Consequently, it behooves all persons who wish to work in a law office to be familiar with its word-processing program. Although the many available word-processing programs are basically similar to each other, there are sufficient differences that make it necessary to learn each system separately. Each office selects the program deemed most appropriate for its use.

WordPerfect and Microsoft Word are the two word-processing programs that are used by most law offices. Not only do the law offices use these programs to create letters and pleadings, but they also link them to other programs to import spreadsheets, databases, and legal forms. There are also **desktop publishing** features that allow for professional-looking newsletters, manuals, and brochures.

EXAMPLE:

The law office wants to publish a newsletter as a marketing tool to attract new clients. Rather than having the newsletter printed by a professional printing service, the office is able to use the desktop publishing features of its word-processing program to create a professional-looking newsletter with several different typefaces, graphs, and colors. This use of the computer is more efficient and cost-effective than paying an outside printing service.

Database Management Software

Database management software is used to manage large amounts of data such as all of the evidentiary documents in a large litigation case, the firm's client list, and the contents of the firm's library. A **database** is an organized collection of related information. There are two main types of databases: summary databases and full-text databases. A **summary database** is one that utilizes a digest or abstract of the information stored. An example of a summary database would be a legal digest system or the local telephone directory. A **full-text database,** as the name would imply, stores the complete text of a particular document. **Imaging databases** can fall into either category of databases. Imaging databases are used to store an image of a document or photograph on an optical disk. When the image is scanned onto the optical disk, a summary database can be used to record the document number, title, date, and other specifics about the document. If a full-text database program is available, the full text of scanned documents can be stored on a separate disk.

In addition to the differences in the ways that summary and full-text databases store their data, there are differences in the way that information is retrieved from these databases. To find information in a summary database, the user searches within the fields of that database. For example, an evidentiary database might have the following fields:

Document Number
Document Type
To
From
Date
Summary
File Number

To enter a document into the database, these fields would be filled out from information found on the document. A sample is shown below.

Document Number	**125**
Document Type	**Letter**
To	**Smith, John**
From	**ABC Corporation**
Date	**3/12/97**
Summary	**A letter terminating the employment of Mr. Smith stating that he had not been performing to the level of his position and citing many days that he arrived more than an hour late for work.**
File Number	**9123.1.5**

To locate documents within the summary database, the user must identify the field to be searched in and the information to be searched for. To perform these searches the user utilizes relational operators and connectors. The relational operators most often used in summary databases are

=	equal to
>	greater than
<	less than
>=	greater than or equal to
<=	less than or equal to
<>	not equal to

Connectors are used to connect two or more search requests. The most common connectors are

AND
OR
NOT

A sample search that would locate all of the documents contained in the summary database from ABC Corporation would look as follows:

From = ABC Corporation

The user identifies the field name, uses an operator, and identifies what he is looking for. A sample search using a connector that would find all of the documents with dates in March of 1997 would look as follows:

Date>=3/1/97 AND Date<=3/31/97

To search within a full-text database, the user utilizes keywords, proximity operators, connectors, and root expanders. For example, to locate all documents that mention Mr. Smith's level of performance, the user would want to look for the word "level" within a certain proximity of some form of the word "performance." The search could look as follows:

level w/6 perform!

This search would locate all documents in the database in which the word "level" is within six words of any word with the root "perform." The connectors that you use with full-text databases are the same as those used with summary databases: AND, OR, and NOT. To locate all of the documents within the database that mention level of performance and also refer to some form of the word "termination," the following search could be used:

level w/6 perform! and terminat!

To make sure that all of the desired materials are retrieved, it is important to remember that not every person is going to use the same words to describe a situation. Therefore, it is often necessary to think of synonyms or alternatives for the keywords and include them within the search. For example, someone may have used the words "fire" or "discharge" instead of "terminate." Alternatives are connected with the OR connector. One example would look as follows:

level w/6 perform! and terminat! or fir! or discharg!

This would be a very good search to locate any documents within the database that refer to Mr. Smith's level of performance and the ending of his employment.

Legal Research Databases

After accounting and word processing, probably the most significant use of modern computer technology by law offices is in the area of legal research. Ever since the beginning of the 1970s, legal research materials have been available through computers with modem capabilities. Over the years the number and variety of these materials have increased tremendously. Today, almost all government agencies and law firms have some computerized legal research tools available for their legal teams. These include the on-line databases of Lexis/Nexis and Westlaw, other on-line databases that are not particularly legal in nature but that can be of value to the legal researcher, legal databases available on CD-ROM, and the growing information sites that are found on the Internet.

Lexis/Nexis

Lexis/Nexis was the first of the computerized legal research databases developed. The Lexis portion of the database contains legal-specific materials. The Nexis portion of the database provides access to newspapers, magazines, wire services, and broadcast transcripts. The Lexis/Nexis database is divided into Libraries. Each Library contains many files of materials in which the user can perform full-text searches. After a user selects a Library, such as the GENFED Library (containing general federal materials), she is prompted to select a file such as Supreme Court decisions, statutes from the United States Code, or the decisions of a specific district court. Once the file has been selected, a search is drafted using keywords, proximity operators, connectors, and root expanders.

EXAMPLE:

An associate in the office is using Lexis to research a problem concerning a shareholder's derivative suit. After selecting the appropriate Library and File, she types in the word "shareholder" and processes the search. This retrieves too many cases for her to read so she narrows the search by adding the proximity operator **w/10** and the word "derivative." However, a major decision in this area used the word "stockholder" in place of "shareholder." Therefore this synonym is added for the most accurate search as shown below:

shareholder or stockholder w/10 derivative

Westlaw

Westlaw is very similar to Lexis/Nexis. It also contains legal-specific materials as well as periodicals, news, and business information. To search within Westlaw, you select a database and then use your full-text searching tools. Both Lexis/Nexis and Westlaw have added natural language searching to their databases. This allows the search to be typed as a regular sentence instead of requiring the keywords, proximity operators, and connectors. A sample natural language search based on the shareholder suit referred to in the previous example could be entered as follows:

shareholder or stockholder derivative actions

Databases Containing Nonlegal Information

Databases that can be valuable to the legal researcher do not always contain legal information. Databases containing periodicals, medical, and business information include the Dow Jones News/Retrieval Service, DIALOG, and Vu/Text.

CD-ROM

Many law books are available on CD-ROM. For a law office that mainly uses its state's supreme and appellate case reporters, purchasing these on CD-ROM for full-text search abilities can be much more cost-effective than subscribing to Lexis/Nexis or Westlaw. These law books on CD-ROM provide the text of the books plus the ability to use full-text searching and to travel to a cited case by clicking on its highlighted citation.

The Internet

The Internet is a collection of computer sites throughout the world. They are all connected together and can be accessed by subscribing to an on-line service such as America Online or to a direct Internet provider. Most legal information can be obtained by using Telnet or the World Wide Web. Telnet is a feature that lets you travel to another computer and use it as though you were sitting in front of it. Many libraries have Telnet addresses that you can access to utilize their library card catalogs. To access the World Wide Web you need a Web browser program such as Netscape. The World Wide Web contains Internet sites that utilize HTTP or "Hypertext Transfer Protocol" to enable you to click on highlighted and underlined text to travel to different sites. New legal information sites appear daily on the World Wide Web. To find these sites you need to use a "search engine." Two of the most popular search engines are Yahoo and Lycos. Yahoo is located at *http://www.yahoo.com.* Lycos can be found at *http://www.lycos.com.* Once you reach these search engines, you type a key-word such as "law" into the search box and click on the search button. This will provide you with a list of sites that mention "law." You may want to use other words to narrow the search. When you see a site you wish to travel to, you simply click on its highlighted name. From that site you can travel to others by clicking on highlighted references, or you can go back by clicking on a "Back" button that is found at the top of most Web browsers. Be careful about using legal information that you find on the Internet. You do not always know who has posted the information, whether it is accurate, or when it was last updated. Therefore, always check the information in the official books to make sure that your information is accurate.

Electronic Spreadsheets

Electronic spreadsheets are used by law offices to perform some accounting functions, for estate and tax planning, and for matters such as guardianships, conservatorships, and marital dissolutions that require an accounting of assets. An electronic spreadsheet looks just like an accountant's pad — basically, a large page full of columns and rows just like a graph. Each column, a vertical division of the screen, is labeled with a letter. Each row, a horizontal division, is numbered. The intersection of a column and a row forms a **cell.** A cell is where information is entered. Each cell is identified by its **cell address,** the column letter followed by the row number (e.g., B12 or D3). A sample spreadsheet is shown below.

	A	B	C	D
1	**Biller**	**Rate/Hr.**	**January Hours**	**January Income**
2	Berman, T.	$250	180	$45,000
3	Crawford, D.	$225	175	$39,375
4	Devon, L.	$225	210	$47,250
5	**Totals**		565	$131,625

This sample is a portion of a firm's spreadsheet that multiplies the biller's rate times the number of hours worked to calculate the amount of income the biller generated for January. The advantage of an electronic spreadsheet is that the numbers do not have to be calculated using a calculator.

Instead of placing the totals in cells D2, D3, and D4, the user enters a formula that multiplies the entry in column B by the entry in column C. The actual entries in these cells would look like the following example:

	A	B	C	D
1	**Biller**	**Rate/Hr.**	**January Hours**	**January Income**
2	Berman, T.	$250	180	+B2*C2
3	Crawford, D.	$225	175	+B3*C3
4	Devon, L.	$225	210	+B4*C4
5	**Totals**		565	$131,625

The formulas shown in column D would not show on the screen; rather, the actual computed totals would appear. In cell D5 a function would be used to add the **range** (group) of cells, which would be identified as D2..D4. This function could look as follows if entered in the Lotus 1-2-3 or Quattro Pro electronic spreadsheet programs: *@sum(D2..D4)*

Another advantage of the electronic spreadsheet is that it can be used to perform "what if" scenarios. Once the formulas and functions have been entered into the spreadsheet, the numbers within the spreadsheet can be altered to see how the changes would affect the spreadsheet totals. For example, changing D. Crawford's billing rate to $250 per hour would immediately display the difference in his January income to the firm if his billing rate were raised.

Litigation Support

Law offices that are heavily involved in litigation are depending more and more on specific computer applications to maintain and streamline all of the documentation and information necessary to manage multiple complex lawsuits. The various uses that can be made of computer technology with respect to litigation are explained below.

Creation of Documents

There are several software programs that provide standard formats for complaints, answers, motions, orders, and so forth. By using these programs, the time involved in producing the standard forms used in litigation can be minimized.

Manage the Calendar

Calendaring software can help the user manage a calendar and lawsuit dockets. These programs operate like a technological tickler system, organizing and alerting the user to time limits and due dates for various court and discovery items.

Case Management

Case management software can be used to maintain all information with respect to a particular lawsuit, including the calendar, parties, documents, witnesses, and so forth. This keeps the lawsuit information quickly available on the computer screen.

Perform Calculations

Software is available that can perform damage calculations to help the attorney determine the potential monetary outcome of a lawsuit. Personal injury damage calculation software will take the injuries suffered, the life expectancy of the plaintiff, the work-life expectancy of the plaintiff, and the potential loss of wages to the plaintiff, and compute an amount of damages that should be claimed in the lawsuit.

Conduct Legal Research

As discussed previously in this chapter, computerized legal research can be performed on-line and through the use of CD-ROMs. This computer technology assists and streamlines traditional legal research that is necessary for all litigation.

Managing Evidence

All types of lawsuits involve huge amounts of evidence. Using a computer can help sort, index, cross-reference, and provide quick access to evidentiary information. Using an imaging database stored on optical disks can free up the office space that was used to store the litigation documents and make it very easy to locate a document.

Court Automation

Many courts are using computers to allow law offices access to calendars and case indexes. In some jurisdictions, pleadings can be filed by computer. These courts usually require that an original signature page be filed in person or by mail.

 EXAMPLE:

The law office is involved in a major lawsuit involving maritime law. The office uses its computer to perform legal research, prepare and file its pleadings, maintain its calendar, and manage its evidence. Rather than maintain several drawers in a file cabinet to store the evidence in the case, the evidence has been scanned onto an optical disk. The hard copies of the documents have been sent to storage. Now when someone needs a copy of a document, its image can be located on the optical disk and a copy can be printed on the firm's laser printer.

Technology and Ethics

Three main ethical problems exist with respect to the use of computer technology. The first concerns copyright infringement. A **copyright** is a government grant of exclusive use of an artistic or literary work to the creator of the work. Computer programs are subject to copyright protection. This means that when a firm purchases a specific computer software program, that program is protected by copyright law in the same fashion that a book is protected. The law office may not use that software in any unauthorized manner, such as copying the program without paying the owner of the copyright. The unauthorized use of copyrighted material acts as a conversion of the copyright holder's property.

The second ethical concern involves the security of the data stored in the computer. As discussed previously, all information gathered from a client is expected to be kept confidential. If that information is stored in the office computer, the office must take specific steps to safeguard the client's privacy. One method that can be used to secure the data is to keep the information in specific areas on the computer that require a password to enter. Another way to protect client confidences is to prohibit the duplication of disks containing client information.

Finally, many computer files may be destroyed or lost due to **bugs** or **viruses** that can be passed from one computer to another through an online connection or a portable diskette. These bugs and viruses can destroy and erase computer files, and the infliction of such viruses into a program is both an ethical and legal violation. To protect itself from bugs and viruses, a firm should protect its computer system with virus scanning software that will check for viruses and inoculate the computer's disks so that they cannot receive viruses.

CHAPTER SUMMARY

The modern law office is becoming increasingly dependent on computer technology. For many years offices have been using word-processing and accounting software to speed up their document creation and billing systems. Today, computers are used to perform legal research, provide litigation support, and facilitate a myriad of other functions once performed by a multitude of persons and machines. Anyone who is entering the legal field must be familiar and comfortable with the various computer programs used in most law offices.

However, along with these advances, modern technology has also created various ethical problems. Security of access to the computer database, infringement of copyright laws, and the potential for inserting bugs and viruses to destroy computer files have become concerns that must be addressed as the law office increases its automation.

Key Terms

Bar code reader: A bar code reader is used to scan bar codes that are used with a bar coding system.

Bug: A problem with a software program that can result in information being improperly stored or corrupted.

CD-ROM: Compact Disk Read-Only Memory. An optical disk that can only be read. Similar to music CDs, these disks require a special disk drive to be read by the computer. Many legal reference books are available on CD-ROM.

Cell: The intersection of a column and a row within an electronic spreadsheet in which data is placed.

Cell address: The address of a cell indicated by the column letter followed by the row number, such as "A1."

Copyright: The right to the exclusive use of an artistic or literary work given to the creator.

Database: An organized collection of related information. Databases can be summary databases or full-text databases.

Desktop publishing: Using computer capabilities to create documents with the quality of professional printing.

Diskette: A magnetic disk that can be inserted and removed from disk drives at the front of the computer's system unit.

Display terminal: A keyboard and monitor frequently found connected to minicomputer and mainframe computer systems.

Electronic spreadsheet: A computerized accountant's pad frequently used for accounting purposes and the analysis of alternatives.

Full-text database: A database that contains the full text or image of documents or other information stored within the database.

Hardware: The physical components of the computer system.

Imaging: The storing of a picture of a document or photograph on an optical disk.

Impact printer: A printer that impacts the page with some part of the printer's hardware.

Information systems: Term generally given to all methods of storing, maintaining, and retrieving information.

Input devices: Hardware devices that allow the user to input information into the computer for processing.

Integrated pointing device: An integrated pointing device looks like the head of a pencil eraser. It is moved like a joystick to move the pointer on the screen. Buttons are then used to select the items pointed to.

Keyboard: The primary input device of a computer, it contains alphanumeric keys and keys that perform other computer functions.

Lexis: The computer-assisted legal research database provided by Mead Data Central.

Local Area Network (LAN): Two or more microcomputers cabled together to share information and peripheral devices.

Magnetic disk: Also called the "hard disk"; stores the programs used on the computer and any documents created on the computer.

Magnetic tape: A tape that stores data magnetically on its surface. Can be stored on reels or within cartridges.

Mainframe: The largest type of computer in terms of size, storage capacity, and speed.

Microcomputer: The smallest type of computer in terms of size, storage capacity, and processing speed. Sometimes referred to as a personal computer or PC.

Minicomputer: The intermediate type of computer in terms of size, storage capacity, and processing speed.

Modem: A device that allows a computer to contact another computer through the telephone lines.

Monitor: A hardware device that displays data on a television-like screen.

Mouse: An input device that rolls on a ball located on its bottom surface.

Network: Computers cabled together to share information and peripheral devices.

Nonimpact printer: A printer that prints characters without impacting the paper with the printer's hardware.

Optical character recognition: The computer's ability to recognize text from a scanned document.

Output device: A hardware device that stores or displays the results of a computer's processing.

Password: Letters, numbers, and characters that identify a user to the computer in order to obtain access to a computer, a disk drive, or a file.

Personal computer (PC): A microcomputer.

Printer: An output device that prints data onto paper or other medium.

Punched card: Cards upon which holes are punched to represent data or instructions.

Random Access Memory (RAM): Temporary memory that is utilized while the computer is operating to store data that is being processed or awaiting storage on a secondary storage device.

Read-Only Memory (ROM): The computer's permanent memory that can be read but not written to or altered during normal computer operations.

Scanner: A scanner is used to scan documents into a word-processing program for editing, or to capture the image of a document onto an optical disk.

Secondary memory: Place where information is stored in the computer.

Summary database: A database that stores the summary or an abstract of data from a document or item.

System unit: The computer's main unit that houses the processing unit, circuit boards, main memory, and disk drives.

Touch screen: Touch screens are special monitors that recognize the touch of a finger or an electronic pen.

Touchpad: A pad that is sensitive to a person's touch. Moving a finger across the touchpad will move the pointer on the screen. Tapping the touchpad or pressing a button will select items.

Trackball: A device that looks like an upside-down mouse. The user moves the ball with his or her fingers and selects items with the trackball's buttons.

Virus: Software code created intentionally to damage a computer system.

Westlaw: The computer-assisted legal research database operated by West Publishing Company.

Word processing: The use of a computer to create a document.

Cases for Analysis

The following cases are included to highlight certain points discussed in the chapter. West Publishing Co. v. Mead Data Central Inc. involves a case of copyright infringement by the two major sources of legal research databases, and Smollen v. Dahlmann Apartments, Ltd. concerns the use of computer records in billing and litigation.

West Publishing Co. v. Mead Data Central, Inc.
616 F. Supp. 1517 (D. Minn. 1985)

ROSENBAUM, District Judge.

In this action, plaintiff West Publishing Company (West) alleges copyright infringement by defendant Mead Data Central, Inc. (MDC) on the basis of MDC's proposed introduction of "star pagination" keyed to West's reports in its LEXIS legal research system. West is before the Court seeking a preliminary injunction enjoining this introduction pursuant to Rule 65 of the Federal Rules of Civil Procedure (F.R. Civ. P.). MDC has answered, and moves for dismissal of all counts, alleging plaintiffs failure to state a claim upon which relief may be granted, pursuant to Rule 12(b)(6), F.R. Civ. P. The Court heard oral argument on September 17, 1985. Based upon the files, briefs, affidavits, arguments of counsel, and all other matter submitted, the Court grants plaintiff's motion for preliminary injunction and denies defendant's motion for dismissal.

Background

For all purposes relevant to these motions, West is engaged in the business of collecting, selecting, compiling and reporting the judicial opinions of state and federal courts. West arranges these opinions into a series of books collectively known as the "National Reporter System" publications. Each case report West publishes (West report) is assigned to one of the individual series within the overall National Reporter System. This is done on the basis of court and/or subject matter of the opinion. West reports are further categorized, arranged and assigned to a volume within the series. The volumes and pages are then sequentially numbered to allow detailed reference to West's reports. The exact location of each West report in the overall arrangement of case reports, can be found ("cited") by stating the volume number, series designation, and page number of the report. West represents that upon completion of each volume it registers a copyright claim with the Register of Copyrights and receives a separate Certificate of Registration. (See, Affidavit of Arnold O. Ginnow; Affidavit of Darrin Pepper.) Copies of the Certificates of Registration were provided during argument of the present motion. For purposes of this decision, the validity of the documents are not in question.

The Court takes notice of West's success in its field. Judicial decisions are routinely identified by the names of the parties and the West citation, i.e. volume numbers, series designation, and first page of the opinion.

MDC owns and operates LEXIS, a computer-assisted legal research tool containing decisions of state and federal courts (LEXIS reports) in its database. The judicial opinions stored in the LEXIS database note the citations to the first page of the judicial opinions as reported in West's National Reporter System. This is done by displaying at the top of the LEXIS computer screen a West series designation, volume number, and page number on which the opinion begins.

In June of 1985, MDC announced its plan to include "star pagination" within the text of LEXIS reports by October of 1985. MDC's announcement and subsequent advertisements of this new feature indicate that star pagination will consist of "the addition of the official page cites to the full text of online case law material." (See defendant's Exhibit E.) Star pagination was acknowledged at oral argument to be the insertion of numbers from West's National Reporter System publications within the body of LEXIS reports. This will permit the LEXIS user to determine the West page number coinciding with the text of a LEXIS report taken from the LEXIS screen or computer printout, without the physical necessity of referring to the volume of the National Reporter System publication in which the report appears.

West claims that MDC's intended star pagination constitutes an appropriation of West's comprehensive arrangement of case reports in violation of the Copyright Revision Act of 1976, 17 U.S.C. §101 et seq. On this basis, West seeks this preliminary injunction to enjoin MDC's alleged infringement.

Discussion

... Neither party questions that some parts of West's National Reporter System publications are appropriate subjects for copyright protection. The focus is on which portions of those publications are under the protection of the copyright laws. West claims that its arrangement of cases in its volumes and the page numbers it sets forth can be copyrighted. MDC denies West's claim. The Court finds two cases of particular interest and importance in providing an analytic framework in which to consider the claims of the parties. They are Callaghan v. Myers, 128 U.S. 617, 9 S. Ct. 177, 32 L. Ed. 547 (1888) and Banks Law Pub. Co. v. Lawyers Co-operative Pub. Co., 169 F. 386 (2nd Cir. 1909). It is to these two cases that the Court must first turn.

In *Callaghan,* the plaintiff, Meyers, became the owner of several volumes of the reports of the Supreme Court of the State of Illinois. These volumes were prepared by and acquired from the official reporter of the Supreme Court of the State of Illinois. The volumes contained not only the opinions of the Court, but also considerable matter original to the reporter including the title page, table of cases, headnotes, statements of facts, arguments of counsel, indices, etc. The Court held that all the matter in the law reports, excluding the opinions of the Court, were the appropriate subject matter of copyright protection. *Callaghan,* 128 U.S. at 647, 9 S. Ct. at 184.

The Court in *Callaghan* specifically delineated the copyrightable portions of the law reports, saying:

> Such work of the reporter, which may be the lawful subject of copyright, comprehends . . . the *order of arrangement of the cases, the division of the reports into volumes, the numbering and paging of the volumes,* the table of cases cited in the opinions, (where such table is made,) and the subdivision of the index into appropriate, condensed titles, involving the distribution of the subjects of the various headnotes, and cross-references, where such exist. (Emphasis added).

Callaghan, 128 U.S. at 649, 9 S. Ct. at 185.

It is clear the Supreme Court found that under appropriate circumstances pagination and arrangement ascend to a level appropriate for copyright protection. If the arrangement of cases and the paging of the book depend simply on the will of the printer, or the order in which the cases have been decided, or upon other accidental circumstances, they of course are not subject to copyright protection because they then involve no labor, talent, or judgment. *Callaghan,* 128 U.S. at 661, 662, 9 S. Ct. at 189, 190.

West's comprehensive arrangement of cases satisfies the Supreme Court's *Callaghan* test of labor, talent, and judgment. West collects cases from every state and federal court in this country. West does not then simply take any cases it has on hand, put them together in any order, and bind in a hardback volume. They first separate state court decisions from federal court decisions. The state court decisions are further subdivided into regions and placed in a regional reporter appropriate for the case in question. The federal decisions are divided at the district court and appellate court level. District court decisions are further subdivided according to the subject matter of the decision be they bankruptcy, federal rules or other miscellaneous matter. This comprehensive process involves considerable planning, labor, talent, and judgment on West's part.

For its proposition that the arrangement and pagination of West's National Reporter System publications are not appropriate subject matter for copyright protection, MDC relies primarily on Banks Law Pub. Co. v. Lawyers Co-Operative Pub. Co., 169 F. 386 (2nd Cir. 1909). In *Banks*, the plaintiff was the successor-in-interest to the official reporter of the United States Supreme Court. He engaged in the business of printing, publishing, and selling the Court's decisions as compiled, edited and arranged by the official reporter. The defendant was in the business of printing, publishing and selling a competing edition of the Supreme Court's decisions. Plaintiff claimed that defendant's edition infringed its copyright since the arrangement of cases in defendant's edition, as well as the division of the decisions into volumes were the same as in plaintiff's books. Plaintiff also claimed that defendant's edition star paginated to plaintiff's official reports. The Court held that the official reporter's arrangement of cases within his volumes and the subsequent pagination of those volumes were *not* appropriate subjects of copyright protection. *Banks*, 169 F. at 390.

This Court finds that MDC, in relying upon *Banks*, has chosen a fragile bark upon which to sail the rocky shoals of copyright law. While *Banks* is offered for the proposition that "mere" pagination and arrangement do not rise to a dignity sufficient to justify the grant and protection of a copyright, this assertion bears further scrutiny. In *Banks*, the Court dealt with the rights of the assignee of the official reporter, whose statutory duty it was to report the decisions of the Supreme Court. He was required, by law, to organize them into volumes, and have them printed and published. According to the Court, it was the reporter's statutory duty to supply paging for the volumes together with an orderly arrangement of the cases. *Banks*, 169 F. at 389.

MDC claims that any distinction between the official or unofficial status of the Court's reporter is trivial. This Court disagrees. The *Banks* Court emphasized the official nature of the reporter's duties and declined to flatly deny copyright protection to pagination and arrangement. "In my estimation, no valid copyright for these elements or details *alone* can be secured to the official reporter. [A]n action for infringement does not lie if the defendant's asserted wrongdoing *simply* consisted of reprinting the decisions of the court with the paging. (Emphasis supplied)." *Banks*, 169 F. at 390, 391. The Court could easily have said, "We hold that copyright protection may not be had for printed arrangement and pagination." Why did it not do so?

The answer lies in the inherent nature of printing when one is mandated to officially record a court's decision. The raw (slip) opinions must be collated and arranged. They then must be placed with a printer whose selection of typeface and page size dictate a certain number of words or lines for each page. Each page must be numbered sequentially. When one is mandated (as an official reporter) to perform these functions, the result is not an exercise of independent judgment or discretion. The arrangement and pagination inhere in the official process and become part of the public domain. For a person who stands in this official position, no copyright protection can be granted for arrangement or pagination.

The holding in *Banks*, then, does not stand for the proposition that arrangement and pagination are not copyrightable per se. Rather, it indicates that when required to do so by law, those labors do not reflect any independent judgment or discretion and as such become part of the public domain. *Banks* does not prohibit West Publishing Company from obtaining a copyright in the pagination or arrangement of its publications. West is not the official reporter for any court in this country nor is it required by statute to arrange or page its volumes. It does these things of its own initiative expending considerable labor, talent, and judgment in the process. West's page numbers and its arrangement of cases are necessarily within the scope of copyright protection.

If this were not so, one could not collect Shakespeare's plays — themselves not subject to copyright — into a copyrighted work. See, 17 U.S.C. §103. Someone's version of the bible would be able to be duplicated by another. See, 17 U.S.C. §103. One could photoduplicate them in whole without protection. Why are these works subject to copyright? Because while the base data lies in the public sphere, the arrangement and pagination of this public material reflects the skill, discretion and effort of the person crafting the arrangement.

Lastly, the Court feels it appropriate to indicate its belief that neither the *Callaghan* Court in 1888, nor the *Banks* court in 1909, could possibly have considered the effect of the computer with its nearly infinite information-gathering capability. There now exists a cybernetic technology which will random access the entire body of decisional law in a unified database. While matching arrangement and pagination once may have made one work parallel to another, it now enables one work to be totally ingested into another. These facts beggar a simple one-to-one analogy between one printed format and another. The courts in *Callaghan* and *Banks* could not have realized that the taking of an arrangement or page numbers from a collection of cases would absolutely do away with the underlying work.

Based on the foregoing, this Court finds that *Callaghan* supports and *Banks* does not bar copyright protection for West's laboriously prepared, voluntary arrangement of cases.

Beyond analysis of caselaw, this Court finds further reason to extend copyright protection to West's arrangement and pagination of its law reports: There is an additional contribution by West Publishing Company which goes beyond the simple copyright which exists for their editorial work. The genius of this work is that it is self-indexing.[1] By assembling cases as they have been arranged in sequenced volumes, a case can be indexed by following its name with a volume number, series designation, and page number. In fact, this is the most common method of referencing cases in the field of legal research. By this device, the case of United States ex rel. Miller v. Twomey, consisting of several printed pages, and issued on May 16, 1973, by the Seventh Circuit Court of Appeals, is transformed.

---

1. The significance of this indexing function is seen by the fact that another whole enterprise, Shepard's Citations, has been established which indexes West's internal index. This is not unlike the system dealt with in New York Times Co. v. Roxbury Data Interface, Inc., 434 F. Supp. 217 (D.N.J. 1977). This has proven to be an invaluable tool for promoting legal research.

The statement of the mere existence of the case of United States ex rel. Miller v. Twomey, standing alone is useless. It is useless because that decision, as issued, cannot be accessed. Its voice is silent, and its teachings are unheeded. This is so, as long as no person, beyond the Seventh Circuit Court as author, arranges it in accessible form and indexes the case. Interestingly, both parties to the present cause have done so. It is mutually as accessible in both LEXIS and the West publications. For neither party is the decision itself susceptible to copyright, since it is the Law as expounded by the Seventh Circuit Court of Appeals. In LEXIS, the case, in full text, is available by keying in appropriate signals to a computer in the memory of which the decision is held.

Or, you can refer to it as 479 F.2d 701.

What does 479 F.2d 701 mean? It means that the decision is found on the seven-hundred-and-first page of the four-hundred-seventy-ninth volume of the second series of the Federal Reporter, *according to West Publishing Company's arrangement of cases.*

The West Publishing Company's arrangement is a significant work of skill and enterprise which is itself entitled to copyright protection. 17 U.S.C. §103. That protection has been properly perfected and is of a nature cognizable in this Court.

This set arrangement is either a virtue or a defect depending on how it is viewed. LEXIS holds as one of its strengths in the marketplace, that unlike the West Company's static arrangement, in LEXIS a case's location is variable. Where the case is forever locked in Volume 479 of West's Federal second volumes, in the LEXIS system it is computer accessible at any time. It may be random accessed in any order, preceded and followed by whatever cases the mind and skills of the legal researcher compels. Defendant's Memorandum in Opposition to Plaintiff's Preliminary Injunction Motion, at 13.

LEXIS has long noted at the beginning of each of its cases the "cite" according to the West Publishing Company's arrangement. This West acknowledges as a fair use of its copyrighted material. Plaintiff's Reply Memorandum of Law in Support of Motion for Preliminary Injunction, at 17; 17 U.S.C. §107. It should be noted, parenthetically, that this is not necessarily altruism on West's part. That cite calls a researcher to West's books — which they are in business to sell as well as create. . . .

In the present case, the text of the decisions is held in both the bound volumes of the West arrangement and the computer memory of the MDC access devices.[2] As such the body of the decisional law in our courts is equally accessible to both parties. But the Court finds that the use of the second and succeeding numbers following the initial citation to West's arrangement, the so-called "jump cite" (i.e. 479 F.2d 701, *702*), infringes on West's copyright. It does so because it goes beyond fair use. Once one has

---

2. While the parties may, at this early stage of the litigation dispute whether or not the precise words of each decision are exactly the same or vary significantly from West to MDC, for the purposes of this opinion, the texts of the decision are regarded as substantially identical.

access to the MDC data base, using the LEXIS keyboard, one has the full text of the opinion. Once one has the jump cite, one has access to the copyright-protected overall arrangement as delineated by West Publishing Company.

With immediate access to the jump cite, there is instant access to West's whole arrangement; you never again need to purchase West's books in the marketplace to get each and every aspect of West's copy-righted arrangement of cases. This is the instance when "'... a use that supplants any part of the normal market for a copyrighted work would or-dinarily be considered an infringement.' Senate Report [No. 94-473]," cited in Harper & Row Publishers v. Nation Enterprises, — U.S. — , 105 S. Ct. 2218, 2235, 85 L. Ed. 2d 588 (1985). The computer "owns" West's copy-righted arrangement.

MDC argues that West's effort to claim copyright protection for page numbers is an attempt to copyright a numbering system. This argument is a sophistry. MDC urges that the pagination of West's volumes is simply a succession of arabic numbers, in serial order commencing with "1" and continuing through a book. Of course this is so, but the statement is trivial. It is beyond cavil that one cannot copyright the arabic numbering system. 17 U.S.C. §102. But as is seen above, this is not just a series of numbers each rising by one over its predecessor, it is the basis of the West arrangement — the key to the self-index by which West's arrangement is accessed. This is, the Court finds, what is meant by the words "taken as a whole" in the copyright definition of "compilations." 17 U.S.C. §101. The sophistry is apparent when one considers that just as one cannot copyright the arabic number, so one cannot copyright the Latin alphabet or the En-glish language. If MDC's argument were to be taken seriously, West's headnotes and case synopses would be susceptible to MDC's computers, too. They are all composed of Latin letters and words in the English lan-guage.

West has made an adequate showing, for *Dataphase* purposes, that its National Reporter System publications constitute a copyrightable arrange-ment of which the numbering and pagination of its volumes are a part. Since West's claim that it has copyrighted these publications is not cur-rently disputed, West has the exclusive right to reproduce and distribute this arrangement. 17 U.S.C. §106.

MDC claims that its star pagination will not infringe West's arrange-ment because its random generated arrangement is entirely different from West's arrangement. It argues that star pagination will not bring the arrangements closer together. But for infringement purposes, MDC need not physically arrange its opinions within its computer bank in order to reproduce West's protected arrangements.[3] "[D]atabases are simply auto-mated compilations — collections of information capable of being re-trieved in various forms by an appropriate search program. . . . [I]t is often senseless to seek in them a specific fixed arrangement of data." Rand Mc-

3. In a sense, the whole concept of serial order in a computer memory is meaningless. In LEXIS, the "opinions" are actually only recorded, accessible, electronic impulses.

Nally & Co. v. Fleet Management Systems, 600 F. Supp. 933, 941 (N.D. Ill. 1984). This Court finds that MDC will reproduce West's copyrighted arrangements by systematically inserting the pagination of West's reporters into the LEXIS database. LEXIS users will have full computer access to West's copyrighted arrangement.

MDC claims that even if its star pagination would otherwise constitute infringement, it is legal fair use under 17 U.S.C. §107. This provision provides as follows:

> [T]he fair use of a copyrighted work for purposes such as criticism, comment, news reporting, teaching, . . . scholarship, or research is not an infringement of copyright. In determining whether the use made of a work in any particular case is a fair use the factors to be considered shall include —
>
> 1) the purpose and character of the use, including whether such use is of a commercial nature or is for nonprofit educational purposes;
>
> 2) the nature of the copyrighted work;
>
> 3) the amount and substantiality of the portion used;
>
> 4) the effect of the use upon the potential market for or value of the copyrighted work.

Upon consideration of the statutory factors, this Court concludes that MDC's intended star pagination does not constitute fair use.

1. Purpose and Character of the Use

MDC acknowledges that it hopes to introduce star pagination to enhance its position in the marketplace. In other words, MDC's star pagination is a commercial use intended for profit. The Supreme Court in Harper & Row Publishers v. Nation Enterprises, — U.S. —, 105 S. Ct. 2218, 2231, 85 L. Ed. 2d 588 (1985) indicated that such a use tends to weigh against a finding of fair use. "[E]very commercial use of copyrighted material is presumptively an unfair exploitation of the monopoly privilege that belongs to the owner of the copyright." Sony Corp. v. Universal City Studios, Inc., 464 U.S. 417, 451, 104 S. Ct. 774, 793, 78 L. Ed. 2d 574 (1984). Therefore, considering MDC's stated purpose of star pagination, it is difficult to find a fair use.

2. Nature of the Copyrighted Work

Original works are generally accorded a higher degree of fair use protection than that granted to compilations. Harper & Row Publishers v. Nation Enterprises, — U.S. —, 105 S. Ct. 2218, 2232, 85 L. Ed. 2d 588 (1985). While the fact that the protected work is an arrangement might otherwise mitigate in MDC's favor, fair use claims involving compilations have been rejected. See, e.g. Schroeder v. William Morrow & Co., 566 F.2d 3 (7th Cir. 1977). This is especially true when the purported fair use is commercial. Financial Information, Inc. v. Moody's Investors, 751 F.2d 501, 509 (2nd Cir. 1984). As acknowledged at argument, star pagination is being introduced to increase MDC's revenues, and enhance its market position. Under this factor, it cannot prevail on its fair use claim.

3. Amount and Substantiality of the Portion Used

MDC claims that West's page numbers constitute a miniscule portion of the total material contained in a given volume of a West reporter. While this may be true, it is not necessarily enlightening. When viewed in the light of MDC's intent and ability to expropriate each and every page number from each and every volume of West's reporters, the appropriation takes on a greater magnitude. This Court holds, above, that this "small amount" is the key to the West arrangement.

This Court is convinced that MDC's star pagination of West's arrangements is both quantitatively and qualitatively substantial. Isolated instances of minor infringements, when multiplied many times, become in the aggregate a major intrusion upon the copyrighted material and must be prevented. Harper & Row Publishers v. Nation Enterprises, — U.S. —, 105 S. Ct. 2218, 2235, 85 L. Ed. 2d 588 (1985). By taking West's page numbers, MDC is taking West's arrangement justifying the grant of a preliminary injunction.

4. Effect of the Infringing Use on the Market

The final factor to examine in determining the validity of MDC's fair use claim is the effect that star pagination will have on the market for West Reporters. The fair use doctrine has always precluded a use that supersedes the use of the original. Harper & Row Publishers v. Nation Enterprises, — U.S. —, 105 S. Ct. 2218, 2225, 2226, 85 L. Ed. 2d 588 (1985). If both plaintiff's and defendant's works are used for the same purpose and they fulfill the same function in terms of actual or potential customer demand, then a fair use cannot be found. Metro-Goldwyn-Mayer v. Showcase Atlanta Co-op Prod., 479 F. Supp. 351, 361 (N.D. Ga. 1979).

There can be little doubt that MDC's incorporation of West's page numbers into the LEXIS reports database will supersede a substantial use of West's hard bound volumes of reporters. Although each is a different medium, both MDC's computers and West's books, serve the function of providing the text of judicial opinions to the public. MDC's star pagination will supplant the need for West's National Reporter System publications; this is not a fair use.

. . . Even if the Court did not apply the presumption of irreparable harm, it is apparent that West has still made the necessary showing of harm for *Dataphase* purposes. If the defendant's use of plaintiff's copyrighted product may materially reduce the demand for West's product, a sufficient showing of irreparable injury for preliminary injunction purposes has been made. . . .

IV. Public Interest

The final factor to consider in determining whether a preliminary injunction should issue under *Dataphase* is the public interest in granting or denying the proposed injunction. The Court finds that the public interest favors preliminary injunctive relief.

The Constitution grants to Congress the power "[t]o promote the progress of . . . useful arts, by securing for limited times to authors . . . the exclusive right to their respective writings." U.S. CONST. art. I, sec. 8, cl. 8. This is a means by which an important public purpose may be achieved. It is intended to motivate creative activity by the provision of a special reward, and eventually allows the public total access to the products of their genius after the limited period of exclusive control has expired. The monopoly created by copyright thus rewards the individual author in order to benefit the public. Harper & Row Publishers v. Nation Enterprises, — U.S. — , 105 S. Ct. 2218, 2223 (1985). Without the economic incentive to create which copyright protection provides, this incentive and the advantages it creates for the society may well be lost.

MDC in its briefs and memoranda finds it both "ludicrous" and "absurd" to believe that West would abandon its currently lucrative business if copyright protection was not extended to its page numbers. Considering, however, that MDC's star pagination may do away with the need for West's reporters, this conclusion is not so hard to believe.

MDC claims that the public interest favors denying a preliminary injunction because its intended star pagination would give judges, lawyers and citizens freer access to the entire body of law. That is, the public need for access to the law, which is currently embodied in West's publications, should reduce or eliminate West's exclusive rights in its material. This Court is not persuaded. In dealing with a similar assertion, the Supreme Court in Harper & Row Publishers v. Nation Enterprises, — U.S. — , 105 S. Ct. 2218, 2230, 85 L. Ed. 2d 588 (1985) stated that:

> It is fundamentally at odds with the scheme of copyright to accord lesser rights in those works that are of greatest importance to the public. Such a notion ignores the major premise of copyright and injures author and public alike. "[T]o propose that fair use be imposed whenever the 'social value [of dissemination] . . . outweighs any detriment to the artist,' would be to propose depriving copyright owners of their right in the property precisely when they encounter those users who could afford to pay for it." . . . "If every volume that was in the public interest could be pirated away by a competing publisher, . . . the public [soon] would have nothing worth reading."

As the Supreme Court makes clear, reducing copyright protection to works of public import would create an economic disincentive to create the work which would ultimately jeopardize the creation of these very works. Therefore, the public interest mandates that MDC's star pagination be restrained.

Conclusion

Based upon the above analysis of the factors necessary for a preliminary injunction under Dataphase Systems, Inc. v. C.L. Systems, Inc., 640 F.2d 109 (8th Cir. 1981) and for the reasons set forth herein,

It is ordered that:

1. Plaintiff's motion for a preliminary injunction pursuant to Rule 65, F.R. Civ. P. is granted.

2. This preliminary injunction shall be effective upon the plaintiff's filing with the Clerk of this Court a bond pursuant to Rule 65(c), F.R. Civ. P., in the amount of $100,000.

3. Defendant's motion to dismiss plaintiff's complaint pursuant to Rule 12(b)(6) of the Federal Rules of Civil Procedure is denied.

Smollen v. Dahlmann Apartments, Ltd.
463 N.W.2d 261 (Mich. App. 1990)

Plaintiffs appeal as of right the January 11, 1989, opinion and order awarding plaintiffs $2,000 in attorney fees under the Michigan Consumer Protection Act (MCPA), M.C.L. §445.901 et. seq.; M.S.A. §19.418(1) et seq. On appeal, plaintiffs allege that the trial court erred in the amount of the award, the method of calculation and factors to be considered, the imposition of interest on the award, and the availability of discovery of defendants' attorneys' time records. We hold that the trial court erred in failing to consider plaintiffs' attorney's computer printouts of his time records and in failing to apply the factors contained in Crawley v. Schick, 48 Mich. App. 728, 211 N.W.2d 217 (1973). Thus, we reverse and remand for an evidentiary hearing.

First, plaintiffs allege that the trial court erred in refusing to consider plaintiffs' counsel's computer records indicating the amount of time spent on the case. We agree. The trial court ruled that the computer entries did not consist of original contemporaneous time records. However, our review of the record indicates that most of the information contained on the computer printout was placed directly into the computer sometime following the work performed for plaintiff. While it is true that some of the information in the computer was transferred to the computer from temporary notes indicating the amount of time spent on individual projects, we hold that this does not destroy the admissibility of the computer entries. In an analogous situation, our Supreme Court in Green v. Woods, 325 Mich. 649, 39 N.W.2d 317 (1949), held that a book of accounts, whose entries were made from slips of paper furnished by others, was admissible even though the original slips were not preserved. The *Green* Court noted that since the records were kept in the ordinary course of business, they were admissible. See also 30 Am Jur 2d, Evidence, §942, p.65. In the present case, the entries into the computer were made in the ordinary course of plaintiffs' counsel's business. Further, plaintiffs' attorney's failure to retain the various time record slips does not make the computer printout a mere compilation since the computer printout is the first permanent record of the time data. Thus, we hold that the trial court erred in refusing to consider the computer printout list as evidence of the amount of time plaintiffs' attorney spent on the present case.

In so holding, we do not express an opinion on the validity of the charges contained on the computer sheet. We only find that the trial court erred in failing to consider them. The trial court retains the discretion to assess reasonable attorney fees, not actual attorney fees. Ecclestone v. Ogne, 177 Mich. App. 74, 77, 441 N.W.2d 7 (1989). . . .

Reversed as to the amount of attorney fees awarded and remanded for an evidentiary hearing and findings of fact regarding reasonable attorney fees. We do not retain jurisdiction.

EXERCISES

1. Using Lexis, research cases involving shareholder derivative suits in your jurisdiction.
2. Using Westlaw, research cases involving shareholder derivative suits in your jurisdiction.
3. Using an electronic spreadsheet program, create a spreadsheet for your monthly expenses.
4. Discuss several methods that can be used to safeguard computer databases. What are the benefits and detriments of each system?
5. Write an analysis of the computer system with which you are most familiar. What are its strong and weak points? How could it be applied to use in a law office?
6. Discuss the impact of the *West Publishing Co.* case on law office computer technology.
7. From your own experience discuss the benefits of doing legal research on Lexis.
8. From your own experience discuss the benefits of doing legal research on Westlaw.
9. Discuss the importance of the Internet to law office technology.
10. Discuss the negative aspects of computerizing a law office.

SITUATIONAL ANALYSIS

Your office is about to update its entire computer system, and you are asked to be on the committee that will make the ultimate selection of the new system.

What are the functions and methods of retrieval that you would like to have in the new system? Which of the various programs that exist would you like to see integrated into the system? How would you acquire the pertinent data to make your recommendations?

GLOSSARY

Accounting cycle: Recording, classifying, and summarizing financial information.

Accounting equation: Assets = Liabilities + Equity.

Accounting period: Specific period of time used to summarize financial data.

Accounts payable: Money owed.

Accounts receivable: Money due.

Administrative management: The process of hiring and firing employees, financing the company, and ordering supplies.

Administrative overhead: Expenses involved in operating a business.

Advertising: All methods of marketing designed to bring the name of the office before the public's consciousness.

Age Discrimination in Employment Act of 1967: Federal law prohibiting job discrimination for workers over the age of 40.

Aged accounts receivable: Amounts billed but unpaid by the payment due date.

Americans with Disabilities Act of 1990 (ADA): Federal law prohibiting job discrimination for persons with permanent mental or physical disabilities.

Argument: The body of a persuasive memo, indicating how the law favors the writer's position.

Asset: Valuable property owned by a business.

Asset-management ratio: Method of determining whether property is being used productively.

Associate: Salaried attorney working for a law firm.

Attorney: Person licensed to practice law.

Attorney-at-law: Alternative name for a person licensed to practice law.

Attorney-client privilege: Legal right of a client to keep all information confidential that is given to an attorney or members of the attorney's office incident to providing legal representation.

Attorney hourly rate: Hourly fee set for each individual legal professional.

Authority decision: Decision made unilaterally by a person in a supervisory position.

Bachelor of Laws (LL.B.):   The law degree awarded by some schools.

Balance sheet: Written summary of the accounting equation.

Bar code: Computerized method of scanning numerical information.

Bar code reader: A bar code reader is used to scan bar codes that are used with a bar coding system.

Bar exam: State exam used to license lawyers.

Billable time: Work time actually spent on a client's problem for which the client may be billed.

Blacklining: Comparing two versions of the same document.

Blended hourly rate: Hourly fee set for each category of legal professional.

Board of directors: The group that manages a corporation.

Bond: Money posted to insure the faithful performance of specified duties.

Bookkeeping: Method of maintaining financial records.

Bottom line: Profitability of the business.

Boutique practice: Law office that specializes in a particular area of law.

Bug: A problem with a software program that can result in information being improperly stored or corrupted.

Capital: Money or property.

Capital contribution: Money or property used to purchase an interest in a business.

Card files: Storage method for index cards.

Case retainer: Nonrefundable fee paid to an attorney as an inducement to represent the client.

Cash advance retainer: Money paid to an attorney to offset future billing.

Cash-flow budget: Document used to trace inflow and outflow of cash.

Cash-flow management: Method of operating a business by keeping a tight control on income and outflow.

CD-ROM: Compact Disk Read-Only Memory. An optical disk that can only be read. Similar to music CDs, these disks require a special disk drive to be read by the computer. Many legal reference books are available on CD-ROM.

Cell: The intersection of a column and a row within an electronic spreadsheet in which data is placed.

Cell address: The address of a cell indicated by the column letter followed by the row number, such as "A1."

Certificate of incorporation: Document filed with the local secretary of state to create a corporation.

Civil Rights Act of 1964:   Federal law prohibiting discrimination based on age, race, sex, religion, or national origin.

Classification: Determining the importance of documents for the purpose of storage.

Clerk: Person who provides general administrative support for an office.

Client hourly rate: Hourly fee set for all legal work performed regardless of the person or category of professional who actually does the work.

Coaching: Management technique in which the supervisor gives frequent informal guidance to the employee.

Command driven system: Method of accessing information by using specific key words.

Commingling: Mixing client funds with office funds.

Communication barriers: Anything that hinders effective client communication, such as noise, incorrect grammar, physical distractions, and so on.

COMPARE-RIGHT: A computer program designed to compare documents.

Compensating balance: Minimum amount banks require a customer to keep in an account.

Conclusion: The last section of a legal memo, indicating the result reached in the author's analysis.

Confidentiality: Maintaining the secrecy of anything a client tells any member of a law office.

Conflict: Situation in which one person blocks progress.

Contingency fee: Fee based on a percentage of the eventual award granted to the client.

Contract attorney: Lawyer hired by a law office because of his or her special expertise for a particular project.

Controversy: Situation in which two people have a difference of opinion on how to proceed with a goal.

Copyright: The right to the exclusive use of an artistic or literary work given to the creator.

Costs: Money expended directly on behalf of a client, billable to that client.

Counselor-at-law: Attorney.

Court-awarded fee: Legal fee established by a court.

Courtesy copy: Copy of a letter sent to someone with an interest in the matters discussed in the letter.

Credit: Method of reporting outflow of assets or increase in liabilities or equity.

Cross-referencing: Method of filing information under more than one type of file to ease retrieval.

Cross-servicing: Making current clients aware of additional services the office provides.

Current assets: Assets with no more than one year of duration.

Current ratio: Equation used to measure liquidity.

Database: An organized collection of related information. Databases can be summary databases or full-text databases.

Debit: Method of reporting inflow of assets or decrease in liabilities or equity.

Depreciation: Method of allocating as an expense property with a limited useful life.

Desktop publishing: Using computer capabilities to create documents with the quality of professional printing.

Director of administration: Person in charge of administrative aspects of the office.

Director of marketing: Person in charge of finding new clients for the office.

Diskette: A magnetic disk that can be inserted and removed from disk drives at the front of the computer's system unit.

Disorganization: Work situation in which employees have no structure or policy with respect to what is expected.

Display terminal: A keyboard and monitor frequently found connected to minicomputer and mainframe computer systems.

Double billing: Billing two clients for the same work, considered unethical.

Double-entry bookkeeping: Debiting and crediting an account.

Dress code: Office rules with respect to proper attire.

Earned retainer: Fee immediately available for use by the office; not dependent on actual work performed.

Editing: Reviewing a document for correctness.

Electronic funds transfer: Transferring funds by computer.

Electronic spreadsheet: A computerized accountant's pad frequently used for accounting purposes and the analysis of alternatives.

Employee Retirement Income Security Act (ERISA):   Federal law designed to protect employee pension funds.

Employment at will: Permitting employees to hire and fire at will for any reason.

Equal Pay Act of 1963:   Federal law requiring equal pay for equal work.

Equity: Ownership interest in a business.

Equity partner: Partner in a law firm who has an ownership interest in the profits and losses of the business.

Escrow account: Trust account.

Expenses: Cost of operating a business.

Fair Labor Standards Act: Federal law establishing wage and work hours.

Family Medical Leave Act of 1993:   Federal law permitting employees to take leave for medical emergencies.

Fee splitting: Unethical practice of sharing a fee with someone who did not perform any legal work for the client.

Feedback: Response by employer to a particular task of an employee.

Fiduciary: Person held to a standard of care higher than ordinary care.

Financial director: Person in charge of the monetary aspects of operating a business.

Fiscal year: Date on which yearly books of a business are closed.

Fixed assets: Property, plant, and equipment.

Fixed fee: Set dollar amount established to perform a specific legal task regardless of the time involved.

Flat fee: Fixed fee.

Form book: Text with standardized versions of documents.

Formal communication: Written or oral information shared at set periods by members of a legal team.

Freelance attorney: Lawyer who is hired on a casual basis by law offices to handle unusually heavy workloads.

Full-text database: A database that contains the full text or image of documents or other information stored within the database.

General counsel: Head of a government or corporate law division.

General overhead: Usual expenses involved in operating a business such as rent and utilities.

Greeting: The salutation of a letter.

Gross loss: Monetary loss from the operation of a business.

Gross profit: Business profit calculated before deducting taxes due.

Group dynamics: Interactions of two or more persons working to advance a common goal.

Groupthink: Individuals acting as a unit, but in doing so sacrificing the identity and input of each member of the group.

Hardware: The physical components of the computer system.

Hierarchy: Chain of command and responsibility.

Hourly fee: Legal fee dependent on the time the work takes.

Image: Characteristic attitude and appearance presented to clients of a law office by the members of the legal team.

Imaging: The storing of a picture of a document or photograph on an optical disk.

Immediate goal: Objective that can be accomplished within a short period of time.

Impact printer: A printer that impacts the page with some part of the printer's hardware.

Income statement: Document showing all income, expenses, and taxes from operating a business during a given period.

Inflow: Money coming into a business.

Informal communication: Dialogue occurring casually.

Information systems: Term generally given to all methods of storing, maintaining, and retrieving information.

In-house counsel: Attorney employed by a corporation as a full-time employee.

Input devices: Hardware devices that allow the user to input information into the computer for processing.

Integrated pointing device: An integrated pointing device looks like the head of a pencil eraser. It is moved like a joystick to move the pointer on the screen. Buttons are then used to select the items pointed to.

Interoffice memo: Memo used for in-house purposes only.

Inventory: Business product.

Investigator: Person who provides investigative services for an office.

Issue: Question of law raised by the facts presented in an opinion memo.

Journal: Bookkeeping record of accounts prepared chronologically.

Junior partner: Partner in a law office who does not have seniority and therefore has less say in the management of the office.

Juris Doctor (J.D.):   Law degree conferred by most law schools.

Keyboard: The primary input device of a computer, it contains alphanumeric keys and keys that perform other computer functions.

Large-size firm: Generally, a law office with more than 75 attorneys.

Lateral files: Horizontally designed storage system.

Law clerk: Law student providing legal assistance to attorneys in a law office.

Law librarian: Head of the library of a law office.

Lawyer: Attorney.

Ledger: Bookkeeping record of accounts by specific account.

Legal assistant: Paralegal.

Legal clinic: Law office designed to provide low-cost or no-cost legal services.

Legal form: Standardized document used in the practice of law.

Legal team: The members of a law office working in collaboration with each other.

Letterhead: Stationery with the name and address of the office embossed on the top.

Leverage: Method of making a profit from the work of others.

Lexis: Computerized legal research program.

Liabilities: Money owed.

Limited liability company (LLC):   Unincorporated association permitted in several jurisdictions, providing limited personal liability for its members.

Liquidity ratio: Equation used to determine whether assets exceed liabilities.

Local area network (LAN):   Two or more microcomputers cabled together to share information and peripheral devices.

Long-term goal: Objective that will take more than three years to accomplish.

Lose-lose negotiation: Negotiation technique in which both sides lose.

Magnetic disk: Also called the "hard disk"; stores the programs used on the computer and any documents created on the computer.

Magnetic tape: A tape that stores data magnetically on its surface. Can be stored on reels or within cartridges.

Mainframe: The largest type of computer in terms of size, storage capacity, and speed.

Mainframe disk: Computer storage method for an entity's main computer.

Management by objectives: Management technique of setting goals.

Management committee: Group in charge of managing a large-size law firm.

Managing partner: Law partner who is in charge of the administration of the office.

Marketing: Method of generating new business by making an office's services known to the public.

Martindale-Hubbell: Directory of lawyers and law firms.

Medium-size firm: Law office consisting of between 25 and 75 attorneys.

Microcomputer: The smallest type of computer in terms of size, storage capacity, and processing speed. Sometimes referred to as a personal computer or PC.

Microcomputer disk: Computer storage method whereby every person in a law office may have his or her own computer file containing stored data.

Microfiche: Microfilm stored on sheets or cards.

Microfilm: Method of storing vast amounts of printed information on a single piece of film.

Minicomputer: The intermediate type of computer in terms of size, storage capacity, and processing speed.

Minimum billable hours: The least amount of hours an office has to bill in a given period in order to meet its expenses.

Mobile or portable files: Storage units on wheels.

Modem: A device that allows a computer to contact another computer through the telephone lines.

Monitor: A hardware device that displays data on a television-like screen.

Motivation: Method of inspiring employees to work.

Mouse: An input device that rolls on a ball located on its bottom surface.

Name recognition: Making the public aware of the office's name and image.

Negotiation: Method of compromising and resolving problems.

Net profit: Gross profit less taxes.

Network: Computers cabled together to share information and peripheral devices.

Nonbillable time: Work time that cannot be charged to any client.

Nonequity partner: Partner who does not share in the profit and losses of the office.

Nonimpact printer: A printer that prints characters without impacting the paper with the printer's hardware.

Nonverbal communication: All methods of communication other than words, such as body language, voice tone, and so on.

Occupational Safety and Health Act of 1970 (OSHA): Federal law requiring employers to maintain a safe workplace for their employees.

Of counsel: Loose term indicating a lawyer with some permanent connection with a law office, but not a partner or associate.

Office manager: Person in charge of the administrative side of a law office.

Open file: Method of storage similar to open bookshelves.

Open space concept: Design structure in which work areas are shared by persons performing similar functions rather than placing them in individual offices.

Opinion memo: Legal memo indicating the author's view of the status of the law in a given situation.

Optical character recognition: The computer's ability to recognize text from a scanned document.

Outflow: Money going out of a business.

Output device: A hardware device that stores or displays the results of a computer's processing.

Outstanding accounts: Fees billed but unpaid.

Overhead: Operating expenses of an office.

Paralegal: Person who assists an attorney in all legal matters.

Paralegal coordinator: Person in charge of hiring paralegals and assigning their workloads.

Participatory management: Management technique in which the employees provide input in setting work goals.

Partner: Lawyer who has management say and ownership rights in a law office.

Partnership: An association of two or more persons engaged in business for profit as co-owners.

Partnership agreement: Document signed by partners detailing their rights and liabilities.

Password: Letters, numbers, and characters that identify a user to the computer in order to obtain access to a computer, a disk drive, or a file.

Payables: Accounts representing monies owed.

Performance evaluation: Method of giving feedback to employees on how well they are doing.

Personal computer (PC):   Microcomputer.

Personnel director: Person in charge of hiring and firing staff.

Personnel management: Techniques for managing a staff.

Persuasive memo: Legal memo used to convince the reader of the author's legal conclusion.

Plagiarism: The unauthorized use by an author of someone else's thoughts or work.

Policies: Statement of office rules.

Policies and procedures manual: Staff manual.

Posting: Placing a number in a ledger.

Practice management: Method of accepting and distributing workloads.

Precautionary balance: Money kept to meet emergency situations.

Pregnancy Discrimination Act of 1978:   Federal law prohibiting discriminating against a woman because she is pregnant.

Prepaid legal services: Method of acquiring legal representation, similar to health insurance; a premium is paid for a set amount of legal service time.

Printer: An output device that prints data onto paper or other medium.

Pro bono: For free; charitable legal work.

Procedures: Methods of applying the office rules.

Procrastination: Putting off work until the last minute.

Professional corporation: Corporation owned exclusively by licensed professionals.

Profit margin: Percentage of profit in relation to income.

Profitability ratio: Equation used to determine the profit margin.

Proofreading: Checking a document to make sure it follows the edited draft.

Protected categories: Specific groups of persons for whom antidiscrimination laws have been enacted.

Public relations: Method of projecting an office's image to the general populace.

Punched card: Cards upon which holes are punched to represent data or instructions.

Purchase order form: Document used to order supplies, used to keep a tight control on expenses.

Pure retainer: Money paid to ensure the availability of the law office's services.

Questions presented: A section of a persuasive memo, indicating the issues involved in a legal problem.

Quick ratio: Equation used to determine a business's liquidity.

Rainmaker: Member of the office whose primary function is to develop client contacts.

Random Access Memory (RAM): Temporary memory that is utilized while the computer is operating to store data that is being processed or awaiting storage on a secondary storage device.

Ratio: Equation used to read and interpret a financial statement.

Read-Only Memory (ROM): The computer's permanent memory that can be read but not written to or altered during normal computer operations.

Realization: Moment that funds become available.

Reasonable accommodation: ADA requirement that employers take reasonable steps to aid their disabled employees.

Receivables: Account representing money owed to the business.

Receptionist: Person in charge of the front desk of an office.

Reconciliation: Monthly document sent by a bank indicating actual cash on hand and checks written.

Redlining: Editing a document for accuracy with respect to grammar, content, and so forth.

Restrictive covenant: Employment provision prohibiting an employee from competing with the company.

Retained earnings: Operational profit for a given period.

Retainer for general representation: Money paid in contemplation of ongoing representation outside of litigation.

Rotary file: Desktop storage method.

Salutation: The opening of a letter.

Scanner: A scanner is used to scan documents into a word-processing program for editing, or to capture the image of a document onto an optical disk.

Secondary memory: Place where information is stored in the computer.

Secretary: Person hired to file, word process, and take dictation.

Security personnel: Guard hired to safeguard the office and its contents.

Senior attorney: Associate who has not been asked to be a partner in the law office but who has worked for the firm for a number of years.

Senior partner: Generally a controlling partner in a law office.

Sexual harassment: Making unwelcome sexual advances, leers, touching, and so on in a work environment.

Shareholder: Attorney who has purchased an interest in a law office operating as a professional corporation.

Shortfall: Term used to indicate a lack of funds to pay presently due debt.

Short-term goal: Objective that can be accomplished within three years.

Small firm: Law office consisting of up to 25 lawyers.

Socializing: Potential time-wasting activity; engaging coworkers in non-work-related activities.

Sole practitioner: Attorney operating a law office on his or her own.

Sole proprietorship: Method of owning and managing a business by just one person who has unlimited personal liability for the obligations of the business.

Speculative balance: Money kept on hand to take advantage of unexpected business opportunities.

Spreadsheet: Columned paper used to write up a balance sheet.

Staff attorney: Lawyer employed full-time by a law office.

Staff manual: Book containing all the office's rules and procedures.

Statement of facts: Concise recitation of the factual background of a legal problem in an opinion memo.

Statement of law: Presentation of relevant cases and statutes in a legal memo.

Statute of limitations: Law designating the time limit in which a lawsuit may be instituted.

Strategic planning: Targeting the future of the office in terms of growth.

Summary database: A database that stores the summary or an abstract of data from a document or item.

System unit: The computer's main unit that houses the processing unit, circuit boards, main memory, and disk drives.

T-account: Method of documenting inflow and outflow of a particular account.

Time management: Method of organizing time efficiently.

Time to billing percentage: Percentage of time spent that can actually be charged to a client.

Timesheet: Form used to keep track of work time.

Timeslip: Timesheet.

Timeslip verification form: Document used to check accuracy of computer timesheets.

Title VII: Another name for the Civil Rights Act.

Touch screen: Touch screens are special monitors that recognize the touch of a finger or an electronic pen.

Touchpad: A pad that is sensitive to a person's touch. Moving a finger across the touchpad will move the pointer on the screen. Tapping the touchpad or pressing a button will select items.

Trackball: A device that looks like an upside-down mouse. The user moves the ball with his or her fingers and selects items with the trackball's buttons.

Traditional office design: Design structure in which each person has an individual office.

Transaction balance: Amount of deposited funds actually available for use by the customer of a bank.

Trial balance: Intermediate calculation of account totals.

Trust account: Bank account used to maintain funds belonging to a client.

Unauthorized practice of law: Giving legal advice without a license.

Unearned retainer: Money paid that is not yet available for use by the office.

Useful life: Period of time a particular item may be used before it is worn out or becomes obsolete.

Verbal communication: Method of communication by words, oral or written.

Vertical file: Storage method in which file cabinets are placed one above the other.

Vested: Having legally enforceable rights.

Virus: Software code created intentionally to damage a computer system.

War room: Design structure in which a particular space is designated for all work to be done on a specific project.

Westlaw: Computerized legal research system.

Win-lose negotiation: Negotiation technique in which one side benefits and the other side does not.

Win-win negotiation: Negotiation technique in which both sides benefit.

Word processing: The use of a computer to create a document.

Zero-based budgeting: Requiring all personnel to justify expenses.

INDEX

Accounting
    generally, 103 et seq.
    software. *See* Software
Accounts receivable, 86, 115
Administrative management, 1,
    165
Advertising, 146
Age Discrimination in Employment
    Act, 168
Alphabetical filing, 176
Americans with Disabilities Act
    (ADA), 169
Assets, 108
Associate, 28
Attorney, 26
Attorney-client privilege,
    50

Balance sheet, 107
Bar code, 255
Billing
    generally, 63 et seq.
    billable hours, 82
    blended hourly rate, 77
    case retainer, 66
    cash advance retainer, 65
    contingency fee, 67
    court-awarded fee, 79
    earned retainer, 66
    flat fee, 68
    pure retainer, 66
    retainer for general representation,
        61
    unearned retainer, 65
Blacklining, 240
Bookkeeping, 106
Boutique practice, 5
Budget, 112
Business letter, 226 et seq.

Cash flow, 115, 116
CD-ROM, 254
Chronological filing, 177
Civil Rights Act, 167
Clerks, 33
Client
    funds, 104
    representation, 51
    surveys, 144
Commingling, 105
Communication
    barriers, 47
    nonverbal, 48
    verbal, 47
Confidentiality, 50
Contract attorney, 28
Cross-referencing, 117
Cross-servicing, 144

Document preparation, 225 et seq.
Double billing, 81

Electronic funds transfer (EFT),
        115
Employee Retirement Income
        Security Act (ERISA),
        173
Employment contracts, 201
Equal Pay Act, 173
Equity, 109
Equity partner, 27
Escrow account, 105
Ethics, 13, 34, 53, 81, 121, 147, 181,
        217, 240, 267

Fair Labor Standards Act, 173
Family and Medical Leave Act, 169
Fee agreements. *See* Billing
Fee splitting, 64
Financial management, 4
Freelance attorney, 29

General counsel, 6
Group dynamics, 195, 210

Hardware, 253
Hiring and firing, 166, 196, 217

Income statement, 110
Input device, 255 et seq.
Internet, 263
Interviews, 200
Inventory control, 117

Job description, 174

Law clerks, 30
Law firm, 3
Law librarian, 32
Legal assistant, 30
Legal clinic, 66
Legal forms, 235 et seq.
Legal team, 25, 50, 208
Leveraging, 81

Lexis, 262
Liabilities, 108
Library management, 180
Limited liability company, 10
Litigation support, 265

Mainframe computer, 179, 253
Management by objectives, 212
Management committee, 4
Managing partner, 4
Marketing, 137 et seq.
Medium-size law firm, 3
Microcomputer, 179, 252
Minicomputer, 252
Modem, 256
Motivation, 207
Mouse, 255

Negotiations, 215 et seq.
Nonbillable time, 82–83
Nonequity partner, 27
Numerical filing, 177

Occupational Safety and Health Act
        (OSHA), 168
Of counsel, 29
Office manager, 31
Output device, 256
Overhead, 63, 81

Paralegal. *See* Legal assistant
Partner, 27
Partnership, 8
Performance evaluation, 211
Personnel-client relationships, 51
Personnel management, 204
Practice management, 1
Pregnancy Discrimination Act,
        168
Prepaid legal services, 79
Professional corporation, 9
Profit, 114
Public relations, 46

Rainmaker, 145
Random access memory (RAM),
        254

Ratios
  asset management, 120
  current, 119
  liquidity, 119
  profitability, 121
Read-only memory (ROM),
      254
Receptionist, 32
Redlining, 246
Retainer. *See* Billing

Secretary, 32
Security, 12, 33
Sexual harassment, 170
Shareholder, 27
Small law firm, 3
Software, 257
Sole practitioner, 2

Sole proprietorship, 7
Space management, 11
Spreadsheet, 264
Staff attorney, 28
Storage device, 178 et seq.
Strategic planning, 145

Time management, 202
Timekeeping, 82
Timesheet, 82–83
Trust account, 104

Westlaw, 263
Word processing, 258

Zero-based budgeting, 114